ALSO BY OSCAR LEWIS

SILVER KINGS

The lives and times of Mackay, Fair, Flood, and O'Brien, lords of the Nevada Comstock Lode.

THE BIG FOUR

The story of Huntington, Stanford, Hopkins, and Crocker, and of the building of the Central Pacific.

Novels:

I REMEMBER CHRISTINE

A novel about a celebrated San Francisco family and its founder, from the 1850's to the present.

THE UNCERTAIN JOURNEY

A dramatic study of a sensitive young man's infatuation for a girl who exerts a disruptive influence on his life.

By Oscar Lewis and Carroll D. Hall:

BONANZA INN

America's First Luxury Hotel

A pageant of San Francisco life in the colorful era when the Palace Hotel was the crossroads of the world.

THESE ARE BORZOI BOOKS

published in New York by ALFRED A. KNOPF

SEA ROUTES

TO THE GOLD FIELDS

SEA ROUTES

TO THE

GOLD FIELDS

THE MIGRATION
BY WATER TO CALIFORNIA
in 1849—1852

BY

OSCAR LEWIS

1949 ALFRED A. KNOPF *NEW YORK*

THIS IS A BORZOI BOOK,
PUBLISHED BY ALFRED A. KNOPF, INC.

FIRST EDITION

INTRODUCTION

THE tens of thousands who set off for California by water during the first years of the gold rush left behind an uncommonly detailed record of their journey, for theirs was one of the most articulate migrations in history. The Argonaut who failed to commit his impressions to paper was decidedly an exception. In his eagerness to be among the first to reach the diggings, he might set sail without many things necessary to his safety or comfort in the new land, but rarely was he without a notebook, a quillpen, and a bottle of ink. He provided himself with writing-materials because, to a man, he recognized that the enterprise on which he had embarked was likely to prove the most momentous happening of his life, and it was natural that he should want to preserve in black and white a record of his great adventure.

To be sure, those who made the journey by land were no less eager to put on paper a day-by-day chronicle of happenings along the way, but comparatively few were able to carry out that resolve. The westward trek over prairie and desert and mountain was a physical ordeal so grueling that not many had time or energy to keep detailed records. On the other hand, those who traveled by sea found in their journals a welcome relief from the tedium of idle weeks aboard ship. The consequence is that while overland diaries are comparatively rare, there exist today hundreds of diaries, journals, and collections of letters, all setting forth in detail every phase of life at sea on the months-long voyages from the ports of embarkation to San Francisco.

In the nature of things much of this material is of little interest to present-day readers. To the average '49er, wielding a pen was as unfamiliar a task as building a wing dam or operating a sluice box, and when he opened the virgin pages of his diary and set about describing the impact of a life completely new, he seldom accomplished more than a barren record of the length of each day's run, the state of the weather, and a catalogue of meals served, ships sighted, and fishes caught. The result is that one finds a marked similarity in these narratives. Except for the names of the ships on which they sailed, the routes followed, and the stops along the way, scores of such documents are all but indistinguishable from one another.

There were some fortunate exceptions to this rule, however. Every now and then one comes across the diary of some long-forgotten traveler who possessed—all unconsciously, one must believe—the gift of bringing to life the feel and flavor of these long coast-to-coast passages a century ago. This quality of vividly evoking the past is as difficult to define as it is rare. It bears no discoverable relation to the Argonaut's familiarity with the process of putting words on paper; the most facile diarists are often the most arid. It is not a matter of education; some of the most informative narratives were written by men not many degrees above illiteracy, and the explanation seems to be that for such as these the task of writing at all was too laborious to permit recording commonplace happenings. More than anything else, perhaps, the secret lay in the fact that when certain California-bound emigrants sat down to struggle with their diaries, they brought to bear a native shrewdness

of observation, a selective sense that discarded the familiar
and obvious and focused unerringly on what seemed to
them worthy of note because it lay beyond their former
experiences.

Thus the Maine farmer who in April 1849 found himself
on an island off the coast of Brazil had nothing to write
about his relief at regaining land after seven weeks at sea,
and little about his first contacts with an alien civilization.
These could be taken for granted. But he described in detail
an exotic tropical fruit he had never seen before: ". . . we
found benaners growing wild in the clearing & et our fill
you eat only the core first peling of the skin which is bittr &
contains little nurisshment." Again, at sea off the Horn,
while more fluent diarists filled pages with descriptions of
rough seas and strong winds (which was no news to anyone),
another, instinctively aware of the dramatic value of suggestion, wrote: "About nine last night the Captain went to
the galley and leaned over the stove to thaw the ice out of
his whiskers. . . ." Scores complained of a lack of privacy
in the overcrowded ships; few expressed this all but universal feeling so convincingly as the man who wrote: "One
of the first things I plan to do when I get home is to take
my gun and a sack of provisions and go up and camp out
on the west side of Baldy. I'll stay there a month and maybe
longer and if I don't see a single human being I won't be
disappointed. . . ."

This book attempts to picture for present-day readers
what life was like aboard the sailing ships and steamers that
plied between the two coasts a century ago; to tell something of how the emigrants passed the time in their cramped
and crowded quarters below decks, of what devices they
used to combat the tedium of idle months at sea, of how

they withstood the discomfort of extreme heat in ships badly designed for a passage of the tropics, and with what spirit they endured the privations of the bleak, weeks-long rounding of Cape Horn. It attempts, too, to tell something of the Argonauts themselves, of how, suddenly drawn from plow or shop or office stool and embarked on a hazardous adventure in a remote land, they reacted one upon another during the long voyages, of how they adjusted themselves to the excessively crowded conditions in the ships, and of their contacts with strange peoples and customs at the intermediate stops along the way.

One who hopes to throw light on this complex subject must of necessity rely mainly on the testimony of those who recorded their impressions at first hand. Extended use has therefore been made of the contemporary narratives of '49ers who made the westward journey by sea. This material exists in abundance: in diaries and journals and letters, some in print but most in manuscript, some easily accessible in research libraries or on the shelves of private collectors, much of it still in the hands of descendants of the pioneers.

Because the gold rush was a world-wide movement, drawing shiploads of emigrants from virtually every country, to give a comprehensive picture of every aspect of the migration would manifestly extend this volume to an unwieldy length. In general, therefore, the field covered has been arbitrarily limited to those vessels that sailed from Atlantic or Gulf ports of the United States between the years 1848 and 1853 (some going round the Horn, others depositing their passengers at Panama or Nicaragua), and to ships plying the west coast from the Isthmus north to San Francisco. It was over these routes that by far the majority of the sea-borne emigrants reached California during the heyday of the rush.

A list of sources consulted, and acknowledgments to individuals and institutions helpful in the preparation of this work, will be found at the end of the volume.

CONTENTS

ILLUSTRATIONS

Illustrations

SEA ROUTES

TO THE GOLD FIELDS

Chapter One : THE DEPARTURE

1

SOME gold-rush journals are lively and informative; most are limited to routine happenings, prosaically described; but whatever approach their writers took, the documents all have points in common. When the newly embarked traveler got out his notebook and, with appropriate flourishes, set down the initial entry, its dominant note was usually one of complete self-confidence. He knew little about what might lie ahead, but he did not seriously question his ability to cope with it. He was bound for California to make his fortune, and visions of the riches soon to be his profoundly altered his estimate of himself and the world. For weeks past he had been a conspicuous figure at home, one of the community's enterprising young men about to set off on the great adventure; already he had experienced the respect and deference due one of potential great wealth.

His exhilaration carried him through the turmoil of his ship's departure and persisted during the early stages of the voyage. On the pages of his diary he candidly confessed that life at sea was an unfamiliar experience and in certain definite ways uncomfortable, but he seldom had much doubt that time would take care of that. It generally did. The voyager was seldom long out of sight of land—for the first time in his life—before his journal became sprinkled with nautical terms. The state of wind and weather engaged his attention. The ship's course, her position, her daily progress, were dutifully set down. He wrote no longer of going downstairs or of visiting the kitchen or the front or back ends of the ship; these landlubber terms were quickly expunged from his vocabulary. The '49er was an adaptable fellow and there was nothing he feared so much as to be mistaken for a greenhorn.

To be sure, his metamorphosis from landsman to old salt was usually delayed in its early stages by a prolonged siege of seasickness, but once that horror had been shaken off and he had found his sea legs, his education proceeded apace. It is not unusual to find an Argonaut after only a week at sea confiding to his diary a growing doubt of the captain's seamanship. He did not always feel qualified thus early to state flatly that the skipper was incompetent, but he strongly suspected it, and of course his suspicions grew as the journey progressed. It was an unusual voyage during which somewhere along the route the passengers did not cast aside their last doubts and, constituting themselves an unofficial committee on navigation, state bluntly that the ship was being mishandled by a complete incompetent. If one accepts the evidence of the diaries, a startling new sidelight on the great migration becomes clear: nine out of ten of the ships that sailed for California were in charge of men who should not have been entrusted with the command of a rowboat.

Of course not all the Argonauts were cast in the same mold; there was no such thing as a "typical" '49er. But there were, then as always, groundswells of the national consciousness, periodical rises and falls of mass emotions that had discernible effects on how each individual regarded himself and the universe. Events of the middle and late 1840's had set in motion a mighty upsurge of patriotism, a new sense of the force and destiny of America; and the common citizen had shared to an extent the growing importance of his country. The war with Mexico, remote and unpopular while it was being waged, but glorious in its fruits; the annexation of California and, close on its heels, news of the gold discovery—all these had kindled extraordinary enthusiasm. The nation had grown in stature overnight; so had its citizens.

This new role was not altogether becoming to the average American of the period. His added responsibilities tended to make him, not humble, but blatant and boastful. He was not yet quite sure that he merited his recently acquired distinction, and to cover his doubts he inflated his chest, raised his voice, and walked with a more pronounced swagger. Foreigners did not find this new American a particularly amiable fellow. Not suspecting his inner uncertainty, they put down his arrogance to Yankee cheek, Yankee push, and Yankee boastfulness. It was not the best of all possible times for young America to crowd aboard hundreds of ships and hurry off to exploit his rich new possessions.

2

ALL over the East news of the gold discovery had caused a degree of excitement not easy to exaggerate. When James Knox Polk, prudent by nature, attached Colonel Mason's report on conditions in California to his message to Congress on December 5, 1848, he touched off the most widespread and urgent migration in history. Polk's words were the reverse of sensational: "Recent discoveries render it probable that these mines are more extensive and valuable than was anticipated." But the messenger who carried Mason's report to Washington brought also a small chest containing visible evidence of the discovery: "about $3000 worth of gold in lumps and scales." The box was put on exhibition at the War Office, where hundreds daily gathered to stare and to be convinced; then "delirium seized upon the community."

The delirium proved contagious, and there is something remarkable not only in the speed with which it spread but in the fact that it had been so slow getting under way. For Colonel Mason's message contained little new; much of what it reported was already widely known. For months tales of abundant California gold had been appearing in newspapers on the Atlantic coast, where they had been read and forgotten, arousing scarcely a ripple of interest. But Polk's message, giving official sanction to the news, plus the shining particles in the box at the War Office, had abruptly turned skepticism into certainty; they had applied a match to the fuse of the powder-keg. The resulting explosion was heard—and felt—from Maine to the Gulf, and presently at much more distant places.

Overnight the nation drastically revised its estimate of the reliability of the news seeping in from California. Overcaution gave place to extreme credulity. Any tale out of the West, however preposterous, was accepted at face value. Hard-headed Yankees were told—and believed—that over great areas of the California plains nuggets were clustered thickly about the grassroots, waiting to be garnered like berries along a roadside fence. Mountain streams were described as flowing over beds so thickly covered with flake gold that the racing water glowed with a reflected amber light. The docile savages of the land were said to follow the Americans about, eager to exchange a half-pound of the metal for a dozen glass beads—or twice that amount for a pull from the mouth of a whisky-jug. It was a fairy tale come to life, the like of which that generation, or few others, had never known. Unlimited wealth was to be had merely by scooping it into canvas sacks. Ease and security, luxury and power, were within the grasp of whoever had the enterprise to hurry out and gather his share. It was much too good to be true. And yet—there in every newspaper of the land were accounts of what men had seen with their own eyes.

The excitement overran entire communities, whole geographical areas. An urge to get to California quickly, by any means, at any cost, animated great segments of the population. Social distinctions went by the board. In a Massachusetts town a physician abandoned his office and patients and enrolled in a mining company organized and led by his own coachman. In Boston divinity students, Harvard professors, journalists, and men of science joined with clerks, mechanics, and farm boys, formed a joint-stock company, chartered and equipped a 600-ton bark, and entered the headlong race about South America. Men who held masters' and mates' licenses signed up as common seamen, unwilling to wait a few weeks until their own vessels could be readied for sea.

The entire land was soon in the grip of a prodigious mass hysteria, with normal pursuits all but forgotten. One writer observed that by the middle of 1849 New England presented the aspect of an unprepared nation about to go to war. In point of fact, the gold rush got under way in an atmosphere not much different from that of wartime. Mechanics dropped their tools, students closed their books, clerks hurried from behind counters, all intent on picking up wealth in the California creek-beds. In many communities the young men joined up en masse, leaving crops unharvested in the fields, idle machines in the factories, vacant stools in the offices.

Many, viewing this concerted exodus which threatened the economy of entire communities, became seriously alarmed. The conviction grew that the gold discovery might not prove to be an unmixed blessing, and voices of warning began to be heard. Preachers delivered sermons warning against the danger of sudden wealth and the moral hazards of life on a remote frontier, far beyond the influence of church and home. Editors viewed with concern the impending loss to their home towns of large numbers of their most enterprising young men, and urged those who had not yet taken the irrevocable step to consider well their responsibilities. Those who still hesitated were told to look about them, to observe well the men who in the security of their own communities had carved out useful careers, to weigh the advantages of slow, sure gains at home against the uncertainties of a dangerous and expensive journey to California. Economists added their voices by gravely predicting what effect a sudden, vast increase in the supply of gold would have on the world's monetary systems; some stated flatly that a new standard of currency would have to be found.

These solemn warnings did little to stem the tide; the number setting off for California grew week by week. Moreover, the arguments of many who had tried to slow down the exodus lost their force when it was learned that they themselves had abandoned their campaigns and begun preparations to join the rush. "Editors who in the columns of their papers had discouraged the movement . . . sold out, and by virtue of their character as representatives of the press, obtained extraordinary facilities for transportation and anticipated the quickest of us by at least a month. . . . Ministers . . . prophesied unutterable woes upon the country, and started on the first ship as missionaries to San Francisco. . . ." As to the theories of the economists, the Argonaut was unimpressed. His aim was to accumulate as much gold as possible as quickly as possible. If its value later declined he would still be better able to bear the hardship than those who remained at home. He left to others discussion of the effect of California's gold on the financial and moral stability of the nation and busied himself raising the cost of his passage and trying to discover how to reach the far coast ahead of his fellows.

The impact of the news rocked the country as nothing else could have done, and canceled even the prudent maxims of Poor Richard. It was a great democratic lottery, holding the promise of plenty to thousands who had never hoped for much beyond a bare living. In California, gold belonged to the man who found it, and the size of his fortune was limited only by his industry and luck. All over the nation obscure men—and their wives and families— were dazzled at the prospect of a life more varied and rewarding than any they had dared imagine: a fine house in the best part of town, new clothes and furniture, education for their children, perhaps even servants and a carriage. In January 1849 the wife of a struggling shopkeeper wrote to her parents in England: "Joseph has borrowed the money to go; but I am full of bright visions that never filled my mind before, because at the best of times I have never thought of much beyond a living, but now I feel confident of being well off."

With such enchanting daydreams to sustain them it was easy to throw off the conservatism that had once ruled their lives. The frugality of generations went out the window. Funds to finance the trip to California must be raised at any cost. Homes and farms were blithely mortgaged, thriving businesses were sacrificed for a quarter their value, and possessions of every sort were put up as security, generally at usurious interest. What matter? If all went well the profit from a week's digging on the Stanislaus would easily take care of that. It was no time to count pennies.

But to travel from the Atlantic coast to so remote a place as California involved obstacles that by no means all could overcome. Many were unable to raise the considerable cost of the journey. A number of routes were available: overland, by water, or by a combination of the two, the last involving sea trips on both oceans, with an overland crossing at Panama, at Nicaragua, or through Mexico; but whatever way was chosen, a large outlay was necessary. During the first year the fare for the all-water passage ranged from $250 to $400, and by other routes it was only slightly less. To clothe and outfit the emigrant required a large additional outlay, and it was of course desirable that he have a few dollars in his pocket when he landed. One early handbook of advice to the California-bound—a number of such works were rushed through the presses in 1849—stated that a capital of $750 was the minimum requirement for the journey. Some kept in their diaries careful records of their

10

expenses: their totals ranged from under $600 to more than twice that sum. Many saw the dollars they had been husbanding against the time they would land in California melt away on the voyage or during weeks of waiting at Panama. It was said that fully half of those who went by water reached San Francisco with empty pockets. One wrote: "I would not think of setting off on such a trip again without $1000, not counting passage money."

The United States was not a rich country in the latter 1840's, and $1,000, or even $750, was no inconsequential sum by the standards of the day. That so many succeeded in raising such amounts is proof enough that the news from California had rocked the nation to its foundations. So widespread a loosening of purse-strings was without precedent, and it was possible only because everyone visualized a fantastically large return on his investment. It was absurd to count costs when a sure fortune awaited whoever could contrive to reach the gold fields in the van of the stampede. Thus many a young man who set out none too hopefully to borrow the amount of his passage found the task surprisingly easy. Prosperous citizens who a few weeks earlier would have turned down a request for a ten-dollar loan proved strangely co-operative, often agreeing to finance the young man's journey in return for a share of his earnings. Some diaries reflect their writers' amazement at the ease with which their conservative elders were persuaded to place large sums at their disposal; the mere announcement of their decision to go to California seemed to have made them good credit risks. To those too old or too timid or too deeply involved at home to make the journey, the alternative of financing a responsible fellow townsman had many attractions. It was a gamble, to be sure; their man might fall overboard or die of fever or be ambushed by hostile Indians. But no one who survived these hazards could conceivably return empty-handed. Buoyed up by these rose-tinted hopes, stay-at-homes plunged deeply. Some financed half a dozen Argonauts, others as many as a score. There was, to be sure, a certain element of risk, but why worry about that? Wasn't it known that California's gold was inexhaustible, with plenty for all? If a man could not go himself, the only intelligent course was to send a proxy to gather in his share.

3

WHAT route to choose? The question of the comparative speed, cost, and danger of water versus land was debated around the cracker-barrels in countless stores, but over whole wide areas the arguments were never more than theoretical. By and large, the '49er chose without much question the mode of transportation with which he was most familiar. West of the Alleghenies and inland from the Gulf few wasted thought on the improbable theory that one might reach the gold fields by boarding a ship and sailing fifteen thousand miles round the tip of a triangular continent called South America. Hours given to considering such fantasies might better be spent resetting the tires of Conestoga wagons, selecting strong teams of horses or oxen, and planning the date of departure so as to reach the starting-point at Independence or St. Jo during the week of early spring when new grass on the prairies would be tall enough to sustain the animals on the long trek. This of course was a logical decision, determined by long tradition, for these regions had been settled by pioneers pushing westward with all their possessions in the beds of their wagons. For them, California was merely another and longer step in a westward movement that had begun generations earlier.

In the coastal areas the opposite was true. From Maine to New Orleans a seafaring generation had grown up in the 1830's and 1840's. Thousands of young Americans knew the ports of Europe, the whaling stations of the Pacific, and the China coast as thoroughly as they knew the streets of their own towns. New England youths who would have recoiled from the unknown dangers of a stage trip to so remote a place as Cincinnati set off with nonchalance on whaling voyages of two or three years' duration that might take them three quarters of the way around the world. To such as these the question of what route to choose was seldom raised. Go overland to California? A flight to the moon would have seemed a hardly less fantastic venture.

But even with that point settled, a variety of decisions needed to be made. So widespread was the demand for passage, and so quickly were passenger lists filled, that there was an immediate shortage of ships. By the end of January 1849 ninety vessels had cleared from Atlantic ports and the sailing dates of seventy more had been posted. To shipowners and holders of charters there was never any doubt that California meant wealth; their gold rush got promptly under way. They had but to withdraw a ship from its regular run, advertise her impending departure for San Francisco, fix passenger and freight rates as high as their consciences permitted, and await the inevitable rush. At New Bedford eleven ships sailed in the single month of

January 1849, all loaded to capacity. During the same month New York newspapers carried columns of sailing notices, and the story was soon the same at Baltimore, Philadelphia, Boston, New Orleans, and a dozen lesser ports. The pressure mounted as the year advanced. In New York, in May, the brig *Two Friends* advertised her sailing day. Within three hours after the newspapers reached the streets every passage had been sold: thirty cabin berths at $350 each; seventy below-deck bunks at $250. The charter of the *Two Friends* cost $30,000, three times the normal value of the ship. The gross revenue from passengers on this single voyage amounted to $28,000, not counting the revenue from a capacity load of freight.

As fast as ships reached their home ports, they were put on the lucrative California run. Within six months the American flag had virtually disappeared from the harbors of the world. New England's great whaling fleet was taken over almost en masse; more than seventy ships were presently part of a long procession heading down the Atlantic, their decks crowded with men impatient to dip newly bought pans into California's golden streams. Dozens of shipyards were active around the clock as ships of every kind were made ready for the new trade. Nothing drastic in the way of refitting was attempted; time was short and the Argonauts were far too eager to be on their way to inquire closely into the nature of their accommodations. With every hour their ship was detained in port they saw the wealth of the gold fields falling into other hands than theirs.

However, a certain amount of alteration could not be avoided. A 300-ton whaler with a normal crew of fifteen could hardly take on a hundred passengers and set off on a seven months' cruise without making some provision for their safety, if not their comfort. To convert the 'tween-deck area, designed for cargo space, into living- and sleeping-quarters involved some structural changes. On a voyage that would include two crossings of the equator means must be found to get light and air into this confined space. The size of the fore and aft hatches was increased and in some ships circular openings were cut in the deck and ventilators installed. Sometimes, too, draft vents, which could be closed in heavy weather, were installed on both sides of the bow. These helped make life bearable in the tropics, but they were of no use during the passage of the Horn, when for weeks on end heavy seas pounded above the closed hatches and the wretched passengers called their airless quarters the Black Hole of Calcutta and thought enviously of the wagon trains moving steadily—and on even keels— up the valley of the Platte.

With the aristocrats of the Cape Horn passage, the swift and graceful clippers, the average Argonaut had but slight acquaintance. In general his contacts with them were limited to occasional glimpses as, with a mighty spread of canvas on their tall masts, they loomed up in the distance, overhauled his own wide, blunt-bowed ship with what seemed rocket-like speed, and in a few hours disappeared over the horizon. For the clippers rarely carried passengers; their real job was the transportation of valuable merchandise between the markets of the world, and their fast runs from east-coast ports to California were usually merely a leg of a longer journey that might take them to China, India, and round the Cape of Good Hope before they returned to their home docks at New York, Boston, or Baltimore. Emigrants on the decks of the gold ships regarded

15

with admiration their handsome, sweeping lines as they streaked past, and thought with regret of how many precious weeks must elapse before their own slow-moving ships would follow them through the Golden Gate. The sighting at sea of a California-bound clipper invariably occasioned gloomy diary entries in which the Argonaut once more recorded his fears that the Sierra placers would be stripped long before their dull sailing vessels made port.

By early spring of 1849, while mile-long strings of wagons were snaking westward over the trans-Mississippi prairie, the shortage of ships in Atlantic and Gulf ports was already acute. Spurred by the certainty of huge profits, speculators set themselves up as ship brokers and ransacked every harbor and inlet for any ancient hulk able to float or capable of being made so. Dozens of long-abandoned craft were pulled off the mud, given superficial repairs, sent half around the world, and again shoved up on a mud bank, this time at San Francisco. In maritime towns sea-wise loiterers shrugged as they saw ships that had been discarded as unseaworthy a dozen years earlier warped up to the docks, loaded beyond the limits of prudence, and sent to sea on a voyage that would severely test the soundest vessel: the westward passage of the Horn.

To have attempted a word of warning would have been a waste of breath. Daily the queues lengthened before the counters of the booking agents, and the man who asked to make a personal inspection of the ship before handing over his dollars was asked to step aside and not slow up the line. It was no time to pick and choose. One took what was offered, paid what was demanded, and trundled one's belongings on board. A group from Hartford, Connecticut, pooled their resources, bought the *Henry Lee*, a little bark

THE CLIPPER SHIP "FLYING CLOUD"

Loading for San Francisco in 1851   —Wells Fargo History Room

THE BARQUE "MAZEPPA"

The Mazeppa *left New York January 27, 1849 and reached San Francisco on December 2. From a drawing by George E. Young, a passenger*   —Harold Holmes

ABOARD A CALIFORNIA-BOUND SAILING SHIP, 1849

From California; Its Past History; Its Present Position; Its Future
Prospects *(London, 1850)* —The Bancroft Library

EMIGRANTS BOUND FOR CALIFORNIA, VIA CAPE HORN, 1849

From California; Its Past History; Its Present Position; Its Future
Prospects *(London, 1850)* —The Bancroft Library

"of great antiquity, with rotten bottom, a miserable sailor," and put triumphantly to sea. In New Orleans speculators picked up a sorry-looking craft called the *Alhambra* and engaged Captain George Coffin to command her, with orders to put her in condition and take on two hundred passengers for California. "I found her completely run out of tackle . . ." wrote Coffin, "and rotten fore and aft. It was necessary to put her in dock and recopper, and it cost $10,000 to fit her for the voyage." Both ships reached San Francisco without mishap; others were not so fortunate.

4

ALL over the East, bakers and meat packers, manufacturers of firearms, shovels, clothing, and shoes, were simultaneously faced by a labor shortage and by a vastly increased demand for their products. By mid-January of 1849 a fifth of the voting population of Plymouth, Massachusetts, was already at sea and others were preparing to follow. In Boston, biscuit and small-arms factories operated around the clock. Tailors and shoemakers struggled to fill a mountain of orders, and pawnbrokers did the largest business within memory. Meantime, by train, stage, and canal boat, new recruits moved toward the towns of the coast and joined throngs already clamoring to put to sea.

Toward the end of January a writer in the *Tribune* stated that had a New Yorker returned after only a short absence he would not have recognized his city. Every second storefront displayed banners advertising miners' supplies and inviting the credulous to examine the stupendous bargains within. The word California was on every tongue; hotels and rooming-houses were jammed. Newspapers devoted half their advertising space to anouncements of ship sailings and to the cards of merchants offering supplies indispensable to the properly equipped Argonaut, and their news columns to correspondence from the new Eldorado, information regarding routes, and advice on what foods, clothing, weapons, and gold-mining machines to take along. "Never since the crusades was such a movement known; not a family but had one or more representatives gone or preparing to go." New York's sidewalks were crowded with purposeful young men in picturesque garb: "broad felt hats of reddish brown hue, loose, rough coats reaching to the knee, and high boots." The *Herald*'s account continues: "The ordinary course of business seems for a time to be changed; bakers keep their ovens hot day and night, without supplying the demand; the provision stores of all kinds are besieged with orders; manufacturers of rubber goods, rifles, pistols, bowie knives, etc., can scarcely supply the demand. . . ."

Along the East River docks and on the streets leading to them the congestion was greatest. Dozens of California ships were moored at the piersides, some at the point of sailing, with passengers and cargo on board and throngs of stay-at-homes lining the docks. Others were hurriedly loading, their hatches open and decks littered with mountains of freight. Still others were newly arrived, with their sailing rosters still to be filled, waiting, clean and shipshape, while prospective passengers came aboard to inspect the accommodations and listen while agents praised their speed and sailing qualities and named the disconcertingly large sums demanded for passage.

The Departure

The emigrant who went by sea had but a limited choice when it came to selecting his ship; in general he took whatever was offered, knowing that scores were eager to take his place should he hesitate. But in the matter of equipping himself for the voyage and for his sojourn in California he had far greater leeway. The question of what to choose was complicated by the fact that while there was no lack of advice, it was all equally uninformed. Few had any real knowledge of conditions in California, of what the country produced, of its climate, or of what sort of tools were needed to gather its treasure. The result was that hundreds set off laden with useless material that in the end had to be cast aside. Descriptions of San Francisco in the first months of the rush mention heaps of worthless equipment littering the sandy hillsides: strong-boxes designed to hold the miner's hoard of gold dust, miniature cannon to repel attacks by hostile Indians, and of course scores of gold-washing machines made by men with no knowledge of placer mining, whose acquaintance with gold was limited to the coins handed over to them in return for their useless contraptions. In the matter of how to clothe themselves the emigrants and their advisers were equally at sea. Men stepped ashore on San Francisco's raw and windy beach wearing cotton shirts and dungarees, with straw hats on their heads and nets to ward off nonexistent mosquitoes. Others carried umbrellas designed to protect them from the danger of sunstroke while they shoveled gold from the icy Sierra streams. Still others went to the opposite extreme and arrived clothed in garments more suited for a stay in the upper arctic.

The majority took too much rather than too little, a fault that could in the main be laid to the ignorance and greed of the merchants at the seaports, who set themselves up as authorities and proceeded to equip the emigrant to the limit of his purse or credulity. Catalogues of necessities, compiled by men as ill-informed as those they were advising, were widely published and as widely accepted as authoritative. One such list gives the following as the minimum amount of clothing needed for a year in the mines: three pairs of woolen pantaloons, two woolen coats, two woolen overcoats, two cotton coats, six pairs of shoes, twelve pairs of stockings, and "sufficient underclothing." The same expert advised this as a reasonable amount of food for a twelve months' stay: one barrel of salt pork, ten barrels of salt beef, one hundred pounds of ham, ten pounds of hard bread, salt, forty pounds of butter or cheese, a year's supply of tea, sugar, and spices. How one burdened with so prodigious a load of provisions was expected to reach the mines at all was not explained.

5

THE '49er has long been looked on as a man closely akin to the frontier huntsmen and trappers, those solitary trail-blazers who overran the Far West in the thirties and forties of the last century. The comparison is far from apt; the Argonaut was decidedly not a lone wolf. The hardship of which he complained most bitterly was not his isolation from his fellows but its opposite; not companionship but privacy became his heart's desire. His journals daily harp on the subject of solitude, not as something to be endured but as a condition desirable because it was seldom at-

tainable. Not only aboard ship—where crowding was unavoidable—but on the overland wagon-trains most of the
discontent, bickering, and actual physical combat sprang
from the fact that the emigrants were thrown together in
constant, close association from which there was no escape.
"At home I saw my neighbors not oftener than two or
three times a week," wrote a passenger on the *Edward
Everett*. "Now I have them about me at every hour of the
day and night. . . ."

Far less than half the Argonauts made their way to California as individuals; the majority formed themselves into
companies and traveled westward in crowds. That so many
chose to make the adventure a collective enterprise is not
surprising when one recalls how firmly Americans of the
period had embraced the principle of co-operation. Almost any local task—the building and repair of roads, the
harvesting of crops, the raising of the walls of a new house or
barn—became a community enterprise for which neighbors
gathered as a matter of course to lend a hand. Accustomed
by long habit to acting in unison, it was logical that when
they faced the far more complex problems of a journey to
California they should think in terms of joint effort.

Thus during the latter months of 1848 and later, in
scores of communities all over the east coast, and most of
all in New England, joint-stock companies were being organized. Groups of men congregated in churches or town
halls, or about the stoves in country stores, and discussed
the news coming out of the West. Inevitably some of the
more impetuous among them reached the fateful decision;
their enthusiasm fired others, and presently the nucleus of a
group had been formed. Next the date of an organization
meeting was fixed, local newspapers heralded the event,

posters were printed and pasted on walls all over town, ministers included it with other announcements before Sunday evening sermons.

The response was generally large enough to crowd the biggest hall in town. Temporary officers were elected, a committee was named to draw up a constitution and by-laws, an enrollment sheet was circulated through the hall, gathering signatures. Thereafter meetings, formal or informal, were held nightly, where every scrap of printed information about the gold fields was brought forth and read, every rumor was discussed, every decision affecting organization and procedure was thoroughly argued.

The number of such groups ran into the hundreds. One writer states that during 1849 one hundred and two joint-stock companies sailed from Massachusetts alone, the number of their members ranging from five to one hundred and eighty, the average being around fifty and their total exceeding 4,200. The titles of the companies generally included both the names of the towns of their origin and the magic word California. In them the Yankee's talent for acting in concert was admirably demonstrated. All were thoroughly democratic organizations. Each member paid an equal sum into the common treasury. Each had an equal voice in its management and stood to reap an equal share of the profits. The officers—president, vice-president, secretary, treasurer—were elected by vote, and their constitutions provided for ousting them by the vote of a simple majority. Often there was also a board of directors, chosen from among the town's leaders, older men who helped finance the expeditions but themselves remained at home. The constitutions contained numerous other clauses: rules assigning the duties and regulating the conduct of members, prohibiting gambling, drinking, and sometimes swearing, providing means by which violations of the rules could be punished: by fines or extra duties for minor offenses, by dismissal in more serious instances.

Many of these carefully thought-out regulations must have made curious reading once the emigrants had come face to face with the realities of life in California. Members of the Hartford Union Mining & Trading Company gravely adopted a rule that members must return to the ship each night, bringing in the day's harvest of gold and depositing it in the company strong-box. Another group optimistically agreed that, should the amount of gold gathered so overburden the ship as to make her dangerous to operate, part of the treasure must be left behind, under proper guard, until means of getting it safely home could be found. The greater number, however, were more realistic. One agreed that if wages in San Francisco proved as high as had been reported, members who knew trades might take jobs while their unskilled fellows tried their luck in the diggings; the income from both sources was to go into a common fund, to be divided share and share alike when the company disbanded.

A sanguine spirit pervaded all the groups during their preparations, for without bright hopes of success few would have embarked on so long and expensive a journey. But there is evidence too of a strain of healthy skepticism. With typical Yankee caution, most companies declined to put all their eggs in one basket. It might be true that the diggings would yield gold enough for everyone, but on one point there was no room for doubt: thousands were converging on California from all over the world; these would need to be fed and clothed and equipped, and it was known that few necessities were produced on the frontier. To supply these thousands with what they could not do without—at prices that would return the supplier a handsome profit—seemed to them sound business.

For the typical Yankee of the period might know less than nothing about gold mining, but few would deny that he was an extremely capable trader. The prospect, therefore, of carrying out with him a cargo of merchandise to sell at the inflated prices said to be current in California was one he regarded with pleasure and speedily put into effect. The consequence was that all but a few of the companies organized during the first year of the rush bore as part of their titles the words "mining *and trading* company," and the ships in which they sailed usually had tons of merchandise in their holds. Much was expected of these enterprises; some groups counted on the sale of their goods to cover the entire cost of the expedition and leave a profit besides. "Even if we fail to dig an ounce of gold," wrote a passenger on the schooner *Roanoke*, "the . . . supplies we are bringing out with us will return each of us a sum larger than we could have earned at home."

The trading idea was sound in principle, but here again a lack of knowledge of conditions in California and the slowness of communication between the two coasts imposed an almost insuperable obstacle. A voyage round Cape Horn might last from five to seven months; who could look that far into the future and say with certainty what goods the Argonauts would be in need of and what might be altogether unsalable? Different companies strove to meet this problem in different ways. Some took along extremely varied cargos, adopting the shotgun theory that if some articles proved to be drugs on the market others would be scarce, and the losses on the one would be offset by profits on the other. This plan was followed by those on the brig *Tigress*, from Beverly, Massachusetts: her cargo was so varied that a later writer termed her a floating department store. Her manifest listed such diverse items as smoked beef and writing-paper, lard and flower seeds, canned lobsters and Stoughton bitters, books, dried apples, shoes, honey, rifles, stockings, varnish, furniture, and Epsom salts. Others went to the opposite extreme and gambled on quantity rather than variety. Another Beverly vessel, the bark *San Francisco*, left in August 1849 heavily laden with construction materials: 63,000 feet of lumber, 10,000 bricks, and, lashed to the deck, eight prefabricated houses.

The manifests of the gold ships turn up some curious items. The *Leonore* carried, along with a lengthy list of the usual articles, a case of swords and a fireproof safe, the latter not for sale but intended to hold the company's hoard of treasure. Although San Francisco then was virtually womanless, such items as ladies' hats and dresses were hopefully included. One company gambled on a quantity of fur-lined overcoats and robes and woolen mittens, intending to dispose of them in a land where mild winters were already traditional; another carried enough woolen cloth to stock a dozen tailor shops, failing to realize that if there were any tailors in California they were likely to be much too busy hunting gold to ply their trade.

It is interesting to look ahead and see how these trading ventures fared in the extremely unstable markets of the coast. What goods might be in demand in San Francisco, Sacramento, or Stockton was altogether beyond conjecture. At a time when short-handled shovels were bringing twelve dollars each, a shipment of long-handled shovels (identical in other respects) could not be sold at any price. Tobacco was often in so little demand that boxes of fine leaf were used to fill mudholes in San Francisco streets or as foundations for houses, whereas there was an unfailing market for cheap and flashy jewelry. In the summer of 1849 the Bay State & California Trading Company (twenty-nine members), which came out in the brig *Almena*, set up a "variety store" at Sacramento and learned much of the uncertainties of merchandising on the frontier. The miners were uninterested in such staples as flannel shirts and miners' picks, but there chanced to be a shortage of flour in town, and the *Almena's* supply, "hard as granite and bad smelling," brought forty dollars a barrel. A consignment of gold watches sold quickly at a large profit, while those with silver cases (and identical movements) went begging. The company had neglected to include shoes in its stock; a customer entered, took a fancy to a pair one of the clerks was wearing, and put in his bid. The seller wrote: "The shoes I bought at Faxon's for $3.25 and wore all the passage out I sold for $14."

In San Francisco a young French journalist, Albert Benard, set himself up as an outdoor merchant on the Long Wharf. Two items only of his stock interested passers-by, but these went like hotcakes: toothpicks and watches. The former he made up in packs of twelve each: "in less than a week they were all gone at fifty cents a pack." The watches —which had cost him nine francs each—he sold at from three to six dollars, "depending on size." He discussed his merchandise with Gallic frankness. "Now I must confess that these watches were of unequal value: some ran for ten minutes, some for a quarter of an hour, others for half a day, and a few even for a whole day; but to make up for

this it cannot be denied that many would not run at all."
None the less, in his sales talk Benard stated that they had
come from "the Royal French Watch Company" and had
been carefully tested, and he unblushingly guaranteed
them to keep perfect time for five years.

Some of the companies were so fascinated by visions of
large profits from the sale of their merchandise that the
original purpose of the expeditions was pushed into the
background. This was particularly true of groups from New
England, where lucrative trading ventures in distant lands
were an old story. There was no lack of schemes to wring
dollars, not from California's mines, but her miners; few
devices that promised to pick up an easy profit were overlooked. A number of groups, having chartered a ship and
discovered that a few more could be crowded on board,
took in non-members as paying passengers and thus cut
down the cost of their own passage. Members of the Mount
Vernon Mining Association, who sailed from Mattapoisett
in April 1849 on the *Mount Vernon*, presented a further
novelty. Most of the young men of the company were
experienced whalers; they carried along harpoons and other
equipment and on the voyage down the Atlantic killed and
processed a whale, stowing away the oil for sale in California.

Whether or not the *Mount Vernon* group found a profitable
market for their sperm oil is not recorded, but few of the
trading ventures came up to their sponsors' expectations.
That so many failed was due as much to their urge for
excessive profit as to the unpredictable gyrations of the
California market. A common procedure was to gather up
at bargain prices whatever slow-moving merchandise was
cluttering the shelves of their home-town stores, in the

evident belief that the Californians would buy anything that might be offered them. Commenting on this widespread misconception, a San Francisco editor wrote late in 1850: "The merchants of the Atlantic Coast complain they have lost money on their shipments to this state. They have lost money on the useless truck they send out, things they could send nowhere else."

Often when the traders found a rising market in San Francisco the opportunity for quick profits was lost because they held out too long. The *Leonore* dropped anchor off Clark's Point in August 1849 with her hold full of tools and hardware. Her owners, the New England Mining & Trading Company, rejected bids that would have netted them a handsome profit, choosing to gamble that buyers would go still higher. But while negotiations were in progress other ships bearing similar merchandise arrived, scarcity was turned into plenty, and the market collapsed. Thus the delay cost the company's one hundred members $700 each, the amount of their individual shares of the profit dropping from $1,000 to $300. The traders on the *Leonore* made another major mistake by their refusal to sell a small steam launch they had brought out on the ship's deck. The launch had cost $1,700; the spurned offer was for $30,000. What the craft finally sold for is not of record.

Often, too, the trading companies suffered heavy losses by their inexperience in packing and stowing their goods. There was a great deal of damage and spoilage on the outward voyages: to withstand a fifteen-thousand-mile sea trip—one that included two crossings of the tropics—many commodities needed to be carefully packed, and others should not have been taken at all. Thus the chronicles of ship after ship tell a melancholy tale of barrels of salt meat turning bad and having to be cast overboard, of wine changing to vinegar, and of bottles of fruit juices fermenting and exploding in the holds with a sound like distant cannonading. Candles melted in the equatorial heat, rats gnawed at cheeses, butter and lard grew rancid, and weevils rendered flour, rice, and hard bread unsalable.

A letter from Captain Howe, master of the *Tigress*, to the ship's Massachusetts owners explains better than most why sending a miscellaneous cargo of merchandise to California was a dubious speculation. Writing from San Francisco in March 1851, he stated that the miners by then were careful buyers who knew precisely what they wanted. Only a few items of the *Tigress's* stock returned a profit. Shotgun shot brought ten dollars for a five-pound bag. Tobacco in small packages was in demand at eighty-five cents a pound, but the *Tigress's* supply, being in large containers, was not wanted at all. Cuban cigars brought sixty dollars per hundred; Howe could not sell theirs (which were of domestic make) for fifteen dollars per hundred. "If our seeds had been packed in air-tight tins they would have paid a handsome profit; as they are we cannot sell them." He added a few lines of advice, the product of costly experience: "Butter for this port should be put up in kegs not in pots and the kegs put in pickle. Stewart's Sugar House Syrup is a favorite here. Ames' steel shovels, Collins and Hunt's axes and imported regalis cigars are most used."

By 1851 the miners had become connoisseurs of quality; there is no evidence that they had ever been easy marks.

6

THE California journey was at best an expensive one, and most companies made strenuous efforts to keep the cost down. A seaworthy ship, plain food and accommodations, clothing and equipment designed for hard use rather than show—these were the common aims. A few, however, were under no obligation for rigid economy. With ample money to spend, these groups prepared to travel westward in style.

One such was the North Western Mining & Trading Company, of Boston, which bought the bark *Orb* and proceeded to refit and provision her regardless of cost. It was a small but select group, numbering only twenty-two, most of them members of leading Boston families, the best known being Charles Francis Adams, Jr. Each member contributed one thousand dollars to the common treasury, and in the comfort of her quarters, the variety and quality of her cuisine, and the completeness of her mining equipment, the *Orb* was said to surpass any other of the gold ships to clear from New England. Among other novelties, these pioneers de luxe were fitted out in uniforms, a circumstance that occasioned some wonderment—and not a little ridicule —when they stepped ashore at San Francisco. Notwithstanding her lavish equipment, the voyage of the *Orb* was neither fast nor comfortable. The amount of supplies considered necessary for the voyage so overloaded the 230-ton craft that she shipped water badly in heavy weather; moreover, her cargo had been inexpertly stowed. The consequence was that she was so badly battered during the first weeks of the passage that she had to put into Rio for repairs. There part of her cargo was removed and sold; the remainder was restowed, and the *Orb*, seven inches higher in the water, continued southward toward the Horn. The company reached San Francisco in September 1849, after a voyage of nearly seven months.

Only slightly less luxurious than the *Orb* group were those who belonged to the Boston and California Joint Mining & Trading Company. This, the first organized contingent to leave Boston, sailed on January 13, 1849, in the speedy 700-ton *Edward Everett*. The company—it numbered one hundred and fifty men—was a mixed one, its roster including no less than eight sea captains, four doctors, a clergyman, a mineralogist, a geologist, merchants, manufacturers, farmers, artisans, and a sprinkling of medical and divinity students.

The *Edward Everett* expedition was as well organized and equipped as money and careful planning could make it. The ship was comparatively new, having been launched only six years earlier; by the standards of the day she was fast and commodious. Her equipment included such seldom encountered devices as lightning rods and—for protection in possible encounters with pirates—two small brass cannon. The 'tween-deck space was converted into a spacious dormitory and social hall, with triple rows of berths around the sides. Provisions sufficient for two years were carried. In addition, the hold was jammed with a varied cargo for the use of the company in California and for trading purposes. This included wagons, spades, picks, and wheelbarrows, a supply of bricks, a steam-operated launch, four steam engines, and the material for two houses.

One of the houses, called Hanover House in honor of the Boston hotel where the organization meetings had been held, was to be erected in San Francisco and used as the company's headquarters. As a further reminder of home, the corridors between the bunks below deck were named after Boston localities: Ann Street, Beacon Street, Riggers Row, North End, Dock Square.

To combat the boredom of the voyage, a great deal of organized activity was planned on the *Edward Everett*. Musicians formed a band and prepared to serenade their companions nightly; a weekly newspaper was projected to circulate the ship's news and, for those inclined toward literature, to print "original contributions in prose and verse." The clergymen on board undertook to deliver a sermon each Sunday, and there would be midweek prayer meetings. Once a week professional men of the company were to deliver lectures on scientific subjects; in addition a well-stocked library was provided for the free use of members. Other eventualities were prepared for by this far-seeing group. A police force was appointed to preserve order, and a brig provided for the incarceration of recalcitrants. The four physician members constituted a board of health, with a room below fitted up as a dispensary, well supplied with drugs, including twenty-five gallons of whisky, "for medicinal purposes only."

The cost of membership varied widely with the different companies. The Bunker Hill Company (one of two of that name), which sailed from Boston in January 1849, had a paid-up capital of fifteen thousand dollars, despite the fact that the group was small and made up mostly of mechanics and others of moderate means. The *Almena*, another Boston ship, carried a company of twenty-nine, each of whom paid six hundred dollars for a round-trip passage and a pro-rata share in the anticipated profits from mining and trading. On the other hand, the sixty members of the Cochituate Company, who sailed late in 1849 on the schooner *Civilian*, made one of the least expensive voyages on record: each man put up only two hundred dollars.

Sometimes, as in the case of the *Henry Lee*, which carried the Hartford Union Mining & Trading Company, the desire to hold down expenses led to difficulties, for the cost of outfitting exceeded calculations and an assessment had to be levied. The original plan was to limit the roll to one hundred and to capitalize the company for thirty thousand dollars—three hundred dollars for each member. Later the capitalization was increased to $37,025—what the odd twenty-five dollars was for was not stated. An unusual feature of this voyage was that a printer member of the *Henry Lee's* company took along the implements of his trade: a small hand press and a supply of type and paper. He set up his equipment below decks and printed, four pages at a time, a day-by-day narrative of the trip. The result, an eighty-eight-page book, entirely written and printed on shipboard, was completed while the ship lay in San Francisco Bay; today book-collectors regard it as one of the prime rarities of Californiana.

Perhaps the greatest bargain in transportation to California was on the bark *Canton*, which left New York in March 1849. One of her passengers, Charles Kendall, wrote: "The sum for the whole voyage there and back, with share of the vessel, provisions for two years, equal share in company, possessing all the apparatus for mining and making you one in the interests of the company is

$250." Kendall's account of this voyage, however, is such as to make a charge of $250 seem excessive. And, of course, the return voyage never materialized; like every other organized company to set out for California, this one disbanded soon after landing at San Francisco, leaving the members to get home as best they could.

More than five hundred vessels left Atlantic and Gulf ports during 1849. The best ships were speedily pressed into service, and those who were late in joining the rush had of necessity to take what was left. They took, as a matter of fact, practically anything that would float: ancient traders and obsolete whalers, small coastwise schooners (among them the 28-ton *Toccao*) antiquated hulks so outmoded they had long since been withdrawn from service.

Throughout 1849, shipyards from Maine to New Orleans were congested with vessels being readied for California, all working night and day, urged on by impatient miners awaiting passage. Frequently company members themselves did most of the refitting, enlarging galleys and deckhouses and converting the cargo space into sleeping-quarters by installing tiers of narrow bunks, enlarging the hatches, and building companionways to provide access from the decks to these dim, airless, 'tween-deck caverns. Usually no provision could be made for an open space below; the entire area was occupied by tiers or bunks. When heavy weather drove passengers from the deck, they had no choice but to retire to the narrow shelves on which they slept.

7

MOST ships that left during the first months carried men only, and this permitted an informality of sleeping-arrangements and general deportment that would not have been seemly had women been present. Companies originating in the United States were, without exception, limited to males, but this was not invariably so with groups from other countries. This accounts for the fact that the first females to reach the coast in 1849 were nearly all of foreign birth, mainly of French or Spanish extraction, the latter mostly from South American countries. By no means all were of unblemished respectability. Many, in fact, were brought in specifically to set up brothels in San Francisco, Sacramento, Stockton, and other towns. But of course, even during the earliest phases of the rush, not all the women emigrants were prostitutes. Some vessels leaving east-coast ports carried, not organized companies, but general passenger lists, and among these there was sometimes a sprinkling of women. These were usually quartered in staterooms on deck and so afforded a degree of privacy.

But the voyage by sailing ship, either round the Horn or via Panama, was so severe an ordeal that few women had the hardihood to undertake it. Only after the initial rush was over and some of the hardships of the passage had been eliminated did the traffic lose its preponderantly male character. By the beginning of 1850 the passenger lists of vessels reaching San Francisco had begun to reveal a growing number of women and children. By then conditions had grown more stabilized on the coast. Certain of the pioneers, having prospered moderately and having decided to link their fortunes with the new land, sent for their wives and families. Others, who had hesitated to join the rush because they were unwilling to break family ties— and having learned that loneliness and lack of domestic comforts were major causes of discontent in the gold camps —had delayed their departure until it became feasible to take their wives and children with them. Yet other causes contributed to the increase of female passengers as the year 1850 advanced. Steamers were then operating on regular schedules on both coasts, with reasonably comfortable land crossings at Panama and Nicaragua, and the trip could be made in a month or less and with comparative ease.

But the most potent reason of all for the increased number of women passengers from 1850 onward lay in the fact that the gold rush had deprived most Eastern communities of many of their more industrious and ambitious young men. The result was that women of marriageable age, finding competition for the eligible bachelors increasingly keen at home, began casting speculative eyes toward the booming— and virtually womanless—towns and camps of the far coast. Thus it was not long until the slow and circuitous mail routes between the two shores came to be laden with friendly letters from home-town girls to acquaintances suffering exile in the gold fields. It was a kindly act for these young women to fill a few pages with local news and gossip, and perhaps to drop a hint that they were finding life a shade dull at home. When such a letter reached its recipient in some raw camp in the California foothills, it is easy to imagine that it brought into sharp relief the shortcomings of his drab bachelor life. The chances are that he answered at once, delighted at the chance to pour into sympathetic ears the story of his adventures, with perhaps some incidental references to the loneliness of mining-camp life.

Many of these long-distance romances flowered rapidly. Often the second or third letter from California contained a proposal, and if the return post (only three months later) brought the hoped-for assent, the bridegroom-to-be marshaled his resources and dispatched funds to pay his fiancée's transportation, accompanying this with careful instructions about routes and ships and advice on how best to assure her safety and comfort on the voyage. Not many weeks later—but how long it must have seemed to the lonely miner!—the looked-for ship sailed safely into San Francisco Bay. From her rail and from the dock itself our young couple—and sometimes a score of others like them—strained their eyes until the loved ones had been identified. No sooner was the gangplank down than the young men swarmed aboard, claimed their brides, and hurried ashore to find a preacher.

There were of course instances when these romances ended less happily. Sometimes one or another of the pair failed to keep the dockside rendezvous. Life was uncertain in California and deaths from violence or disease were frequent. The long sea voyages likewise held hazards, including the danger of cholera or yellow fever at the Isthmus. Not much less tragic were those instances when during the tropic nights the bride-to-be lost her heart to some fellow passenger and reached port facing the hard necessity of informing the waiting miner that she was already the wife of

37

another. Such occurrences were frequent enough to provide the theme for a doleful ballad that was sung with lachrymose effect in the theaters of the coast.

Not all the women who reached California came as a result of their own individual enterprise; at least one attempt was made to bring out marriageable females in quantity. The promoter of this venture was an energetic New Yorker named Eliza Woodson Burhans Farnham, formerly a matron in the female wing at Sing Sing, who was headed for California to oversee the settlement of her husband's estate. Because she wished, in her own words, "to accomplish some greater good by my journey thither than to give the necessary attention to my private affairs," she dispatched a letter to the *New York Tribune* pointing out that of the many "deteriorating influences" of life on the far coast the absence of women was the greatest. "It would exceed the limits of this circular," she added, "to hint at the benefits that would flow to the growing population of that wonderful region, from the introduction among them of intelligent, virtuous, and efficient women." Mrs. Farnham went on to state her conviction that "there are hundreds, if not thousands, of such females in our country who are not bound by any tie that would hold them here, who might, by going thither, have the satisfaction of employing themselves greatly to the benefit of those who are there, and at the same time of serving their own interest more effectually than by following any employment that offers to them here."

Having sketched the auguries favoring the success of her plan, the lady proceeded to outline its practical details. She had tentatively engaged the comfortable packet ship *Angelique*, and fixed April 15, 1850 as the date of departure.

Meantime she was engaged in enrolling one hundred and thirty females, each of whom would be required to put up $250 "to defray the expenses of the voyage and make suitable provision for their accommodation after reaching San Francisco." Moreover, she was careful to point out that applicants would be subjected to a variety of tests to determine their fitness to take part in so lofty a mission. Young ladies who had not yet reached their twenty-fifth birthdays were automatically excluded. (There was seemingly no maximum age limit, although all were expected to be in robust health.) Applicants would be required to furnish "from their clergymen, or some authority of the town where they reside, satisfactory testimonials of education, character, capacity, etc." In return Mrs. Farnham guaranteed that everything necessary to their comfort and safety would be provided both during the voyage and after landing. As a further safeguard, chaperonage during the trip would be the personal responsibility of Mrs. Farnham, assisted by "six or eight respectable married men and their families."

So worthy and well-planned an enterprise won the instant support of the *Tribune* and the endorsement of a long list of notables, including Horace Greeley, William Cullen Bryant, and Henry Ward Beecher. Meantime Mrs. Farnham shuttled between cities of the Atlantic coast addressing meetings, examining applicants, and giving interviews to the press. By early April, despite a siege of illness that had incapacitated her for several weeks, she was able to announce that more than two hundred young women had signified a desire to join up. Success seemed assured. On April 12 the *Tribune* printed a parting salute to the indomitable promoter and "her company of migrating ladies who, having no husbands to engage their attention here, are desirous of going on an errand of mercy to the golden land." After complimenting Mrs. Farnham on her organizing ability and courage, the *Tribune* concluded: "Her reward will be found in the blessings which her countrymen will invoke for her when the vessel in which the association is to sail shall have arrived in California with her precious cargo. May favoring gales attend the good ship *Angelique*."

Meanwhile news of what was afoot had reached the west coast. The result was little less than sensational. One San Francisco paper reported that for days after word of their impending good fortune arrived smiles of anticipation wreathed the countenance of every bachelor in town. But California's joy was short-lived, for later mails brought progressively less encouraging reports. Mrs. Farnham was having trouble completing her association's roster, and the sailing of the *Angelique* had been postponed. Some thought the $250 fee was proving an insuperable obstacle; others blamed Mrs. Farnham's high cultural and moral standards for keeping the enrollment down. In any event, it presently grew clear that this worthy plan for importing marriageable young ladies in wholesale lots was doomed to fail. On June 28, 1850 the *Alta California* reprinted from the *Baltimore Sun* a brief paragraph stating that the *Angelique* had sailed from New York a week earlier with Mrs. Farnham on board. It added this melancholy note: "This enterprising lady, after all her efforts . . . has had to leave for California with a very small number of ladies accompanying her." The *Angelique's* passenger list, as a matter of fact, included—not counting fifteen gentlemen—only the following: Miss Simpson, Mrs. Barker, Mrs. Griswold, Mrs. Farnham, her two children, and a servant. California swallowed its disappointment, and the *Alta* commented philosophically: "The will is always taken for the deed, and bachelors will unquestionably cherish the liveliest feelings of regard for the lady who so warmly exerted herself to bring a few spareribs to this market . . ."

Six years later, after she had acquired an extensive first-hand knowledge of California, Mrs. Farnham was to write feelingly: "I may say that since I have experienced the moral and social poverty of the country, I have felt grateful that my endeavors failed. It would be a painful responsibility, which I could never throw off, if I had to reflect that there were persons here through my instrumentality who were less happy or good than they might have been by remaining at home. . . ."

And on this plaintive note Eliza Farnham and her idealistic plan to bring a bevy of grade-A spareribs to the Argonauts fades from view.

8

THERE is no record that any special ceremony marked the *Angelique's* departure from the New York pier, but the sailings of most California-bound ships were the occasion for extended celebrations.

The leave-taking of the *Henry Lee* on February 17, 1849 is described in detail by John Linville Hall. He mentions the bustle and confusion, the final parting of families and friends, the voyagers hurrying to and from the ship making final purchases at near-by shops or from peddlers on the pier, "getting the morning papers . . . and whatever men commencing a long voyage may be supposed to be busy with." Roll-call was held on deck and two members were found to be missing; then, just as the command to cast off was given, the absent ones appeared and scrambled on board. The ship swung out into the stream, to the accompaniment of "loud cheering of the throng-crowded Pier 4 of East River—a throng hemmed on one side by segar-boys, orange women, and venders of pain-killer, upon the other by ladies and gentlemen. Amid huzzas and music the distance widens, and we now, for the first time, feel gladly conscious that the hour of leaving has really come. . . ."

Less detailed is this account of the sailing of the *General Worth*, which left Newburyport on November 28, 1849: "After bidding our friends a hearty good-by, which was responded to with ringing cheers, and moistened eyes by those left behind, the brig spread its wings, and flew down the harbor before a strong northwest breeze." The *Anna Reynolds's* sailing from New Haven on March 12, with the California & New Haven Joint Stock Company on board, is thus reported by Nelson Kingsley: "Pleasant, prepareing in the morning the dock crowded to overflowing had services on board, hymn One Hundred and address by Rev Mr Smyth, after which the vessell was cleared and searched to prevent smuggling Men called on by roll call, and not allowed to go ashore a song sung and we cast off haveing no wind, was towed out of the harbor by the steamboat *New York*. . . ."

Sermons and hymn-singing attended most departures, although usually the ceremonies were conducted, not on shipboard, but at one of the churches. In New England it was the custom, on the Sunday before sailing, for the entire

company, passengers and crew alike, to assemble in church
and listen to a sermon of "admonition and warning."

Concern for the spiritual welfare of the adventurers
sometimes manifested itself in so many ways that the men
rebelled against so much wholesome advice. In a vein of
mild irony a member of the *Edward Everett* company, William Thomes—who later won renown as an author of
adventure novels—wrote:

"The Rev. Mr. Kirk of the Ashburton Place Orthodox
Church delivered one Sunday evening a special discourse
before the Company or such as chose to attend. He said
we were going to a far country where all were in ignorance
and sin and we should take our Bibles in one hand and our
good New England civilization in the other and conquer
all the wickedness that stood in our path. We promised to
follow his advice. Mr. Abbe, who then resided on Boylston
Street and whose two sons were members of the Company,
gave to each of us a Bible. He told us when the good books
were presented that we were going to a strange, immoral
country and that we must take our Bibles in one hand and
our New England civilization in the other and implant our
principles on the soil. The Hon. Edward Everett, then
President of Harvard College, made us a present of 100
volumes as a library and in his letter conveying the gift
said, 'You are going to a strange country. Take the Bible
in one hand and your New England civilization in the
other and make your mark on the people and the country.'
The reader will hardly believe it but it is nevertheless true
that only a few remembered the excellent advice of the
good men, while some of our most promising students of

divinity swore like pirates when they lost at monte and had hard luck at the mines; that one day at Sacramento I saw on the counter of a grogshop one of the Bibles which had been presented to us with so much thoughtful care for the welfare of our souls. One of our civilizers had sold his holy book for a drink."

The departure of the 650-ton ship *Sweden*, which cleared from Boston in March 1849 with not one but three companies on board, was attended even more elaborate ceremonies. On the Sunday before sailing the entire group gathered at the Seamen's Bethel, listened to an hour-long sermon, sang a hymn, then looked on while a citizen of Brookline presented the commander with "a banner of white satin, fringed with gold." It bore the word "Excelsior," above a representation of the *Sweden* lying off California, with miners leaving the ship and ascending a golden hill. "Take this banner, with the noble inscription it bears," admonished the donor. "Unfurl it as you leave your native shore and bear it over the broad ocean as a passport to a distant land. Let it be to you a cloud by day and a pillar of fire by night." The presentation of five Bibles followed, each with a speech: one to the expedition's commander, "in order to protect the banner," one to Captain Cutter, one for the forward cabin, and two for the 'tween-deck quarters. After this, one of the *Sweden's* owners delivered a lengthy address outlining the history of the vessel and describing the organization and purposes of the expedition. Then, after a final prayer, the meeting broke up.

Most diaries present detailed accounts of the departure, sometimes extending for many pages. On the other hand, a few—as anxious as their readers for them to get to sea—

dismissed the preliminaries in a terse sentence or two, re-
serving their pages for recording the novelty of life at sea.
In the latter class was Mrs. D. B. Bates, who stated simply:
"On the 27th of July, 1850, I sailed from Baltimore in the
ship *Nonantum*, of Boston, bound for San Francisco."
Equally terse was T. Robinson Warren's adieu to dry land.
"After maturing all our plans," he wrote, "we set
sail. . . ."

Chapter Two : THE VOYAGE

1

TRAVELERS round the Horn had, for the most part, to look to their own little world for means of keeping themselves occupied over long periods of time. Their ship was a self-contained unit, their universe bounded by an unlimited expanse of sea and sky. They were bound on one of the longest and most varied of all sea voyages; the great lonely void of the ocean was an ever present companion, and few failed to discover that, for all its apparent sameness, it was full of interest and variety.

"In her moods and caprices," wrote one, "the sea would put the most spoiled and pampered beauty in the shade" —and went on to describe her benign charms when, "mild and gentle as a lamb, with friendly, helpful hands she wafts you on your way. . . . Her eager eyes dance in the sunlight and you tell yourself you have never met anyone so gentle and fair. . . ." A few days pass, or perhaps only a few hours, "but what in the meantime has happened to your friendly and radiant beauty? She has become a vixen and a shrew. . . ." The sunny face has become "a dark and forbidding countenance, her icy glances chill you to the marrow and you flee in dismay from the torrents of her abuse. . . ." Then she is presently her old self again and you rejoin the circle of her admirers—"but not with your old confidence, for you have begun to learn something about your lady's moods. . . ."

Those who sailed from North Atlantic ports often made their first acquaintance with this capricious lady under distinctly unfavorable circumstances. Heavy seas and strong winds were usually their lot during the first days at sea, with results that filled countless landsmen with bitter regret that they had not chosen to travel the overland trails.

During these first days the Argonaut's morale was frequently at its lowest ebb of the entire voyage. Some journals pass over the ordeal in complete and eloquent silence. Those whose owners were able to write at all confined their entries to brief and heartfelt comments on the horrors of the seafaring life. "Descriptions of a 'life on the ocean wave,' " wrote Samuel C. Upham from the brig *Osceola*, ten days out from Philadelphia, "read very prettily on shore, but the *reality* of a sea voyage speedily dispells the romance." Wet and slippery decks, leaky cabins, the pounding of seas against the hull, and the howling of wind through the rigging—these were almost invariably part of the picture, but only a part. In the dim recesses below decks conditions were about as bad as could be imagined. With all but a few incapacitated, little attempt was made to clean up the litter, to care for the sick, or even to secure and lash down the passengers' belongings, which in the haste of departure had been piled in disorderly heaps both above and below decks. The victims lay clinging weakly to their slanting bunks while trunks, boxes, valises, and anything else movable slid from side to side with each roll of the ship, and the prostrate ones wondered, without really caring, if their straining vessel would survive the next shuddering lunge into the oncoming seas.

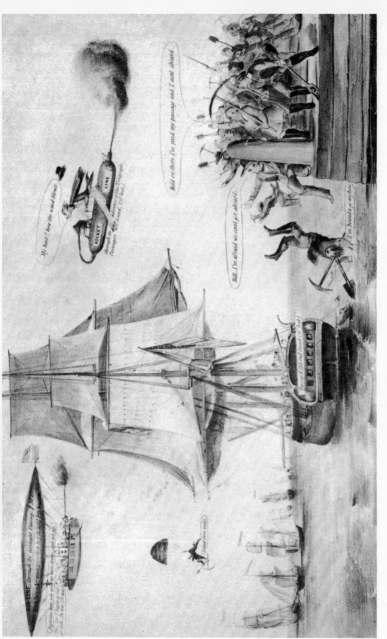

THE WAY THEY GO TO CALIFORNIA

The widespread demand for fast passage to California is humorously treated in this lithograph published in 1849 by N. Currier.

—California Historical Society

To my affectionate and beloved Wife
Philomela Johnston Adams
is this Work, now dedicated
And may be entitled
A Journal of a Voyage
to Calafornia,
In the Barque
Mazeppa
John Girdler
Commander
Which sailed from New York January 27th 1849
Arrived at Riodejaneiro. March 15th & 24th April 9 20 mn to 2 P.M.
Struck with lightening April 22d 11½ oclock at Midnight. Our Bow
Sprit was carried away & bows much injured. Put back to Rio for repairs
25th & arrived May 16th This volume closes June 8/49, while vessel is repairing
Written at her particular request. and will Contain
a hasty Sketch of the prominent Motives which
induced Me to undertake the voyage, My thoughts
and feelings with the incidents that may occure
and whatever I may meet with to interest and profit. on the
way   By her husband Samuel Adams

THE OPENING PAGE OF SAMUEL ADAMS'S JOURNAL OF A VOYAGE
TO CALIFORNIA ON THE BARQUE "MAZEPPA"

—Harold Holmes

In February 1849 one newly embarked adventurer filled two pages with a description of a storm off Cape Hatteras, when all but a few of the sixty-five men on board were prone in their bunks or lining the rail "casting up accounts." His description ended on this wistful note: "Commenced reading today a work entitled *What I Saw In California*, by Edwin Bryant. . . . Mr. Bryant traveled the overland route to California, via Independence, Missouri; and I regret very much that I did not take the same route."

Fortunately, the misery of seasickness seldom lasted more than a few days. The weather abated as the ship beat its way into more temperate latitudes, the seas grew less mountainous, and one by one the sufferers began to take a renewed interest in their surroundings. Their spirits and appetites returned and they began to get their sea legs. All hands set to work cleaning up their quarters, putting their possessions in order and—the galley being now in operation—organizing messes and accustoming themselves to the novelty of eating on shipboard—"a feat requiring a high degree of muscular coordination, if your plate and cup are to remain right side up and your well-laden spoon successfully make the perilous trip from dish to mouth."

It was during this period, too, that the passengers settled into the routine of their strange new life. This last was a problem that taxed the ingenuity of every emigrant. Nearly all were men active by habit and temperament, and of course the days and weeks just prior to their departure had been crowded with incident. The transition from extreme activity to complete idleness was one of the most difficult adjustments the Argonauts were called on to make. The historian of the *Henry Lee* gives this picture of how members of that company conducted themselves during the early stages of their interminable voyage. The time was five o'clock in the afternoon of a pleasant day:

"There are on the hurricane deck, at this moment, twenty-five persons, four of whom are playing backgammon; two chess; four, checkers; one reading the 'Outlaw's Bride,' one on his side sleeping soundly; two are on their backs, and three on their faces, musing; one is whittling; two are a little separate, engaged in conversation; three are overlooking the plays; two are sitting cross-legged looking at me while writing this note. Just on a level with the deck and seated on some spars . . . are the minister and lawyer engaged in conversation, apparently on Shakespeare which one holds in his hands; a third is lying close by, reading 'Morrell's Travels'; at one side in the longboat two are stretched at length reading, one a 'Waverley Novel,' the other a 'New Englander'; two are in the same boat bothering each other by pulling legs &c; sitting on the rail, between the deck and the boat, are three persons, one reading an old newspaper, one telling yarns and the other listening. . . . On the potato bins, each side of the wheel, are six persons; on one side guessing ages; on the other, one is reading a novel; a little back on the stern a man is polishing a dirk knife, while three are superintending the job. Casting our eyes aloft there can be seen six persons in the mizzen top, one-half engaged in playing cards, the other half 'helping Saul'; immediately forward of the wheel a game of checkers is on the tapis, while twelve others, including the mate, are watching with intense interest. . . . Seated on the rail each side of the quarterdeck are seven more, looking over the side or aloft, or at the passers-by. . . ."

The picture is one of extreme boredom, of men crowded

beyond the possibility of comfort enduring as best they can the monotony of endless hours of idleness. They resorted to all manner of expedients to kill time, each according to his tastes and temperament. The lazy or stolid or unimaginative fared best. These, the wonder and envy of their fellows, would compose themselves in some sheltered spot on deck or, when the weather was bad, stretch out on their bunks and there remain from sunrise to dusk, arousing themselves only when the mess bell rang or when some unusual incident—a school of flying fish, a distant sail, or a fight on deck—provided a welcome diversion.

The majority, however, were unable to sink into this desirable condition of sustained lethargy, and these resorted to all manner of expedients to combat the prevailing ennui. "Today," wrote one, "I opened my big box and spread all its contents out on my bunk, examining each article carefully and then stowing it away again. One man came below and seeing me thus engaged, proceeded to unpack *his* trunk. We both agreed that it was a pointless proceeding, yet the time passed pleasantly. . . ." A passenger on the brig *Leonore* attracted the attention of his fellows by devoting hours each day to cleaning and polishing his arsenal of weapons: rifle, two pistols, and a variety of vicious-looking knives. Another spent many days practicing feats of juggling, and yet another devoted most of the trip to the construction of the mechanism of a clock, all but a few parts of which were whittled from wood. Dozens found solace in their diaries, while others wrote interminable letters home, planning to mail them at one or another of the stops en route or to transfer them to some homeward-bound ship encountered along the way.

2

THE boredom of the long trips sharpened the Yankee's natural liking for practical jokes, and few narratives fail to describe one or more such exploits. A group on the schooner *Dolphin*, which left New York in January 1849, had a particular liking for this diversion. The ship made a stop at Rio, where most passengers laid in a supply of the strong native wine, hoping thus to fortify themselves against the cold and stormy passage of Cape Horn. Weeks later, after most of the jugs had been emptied, one passenger, a Mr. Gay (who still retained a supply), was accused of a minor infraction of the ship's rules. An impromptu court was convened; he was tried, found guilty, and sentenced to provide claret punch for the company. The victim demurred, protesting that this would make too heavy a drain on his stores. Thereupon an attachment was issued and the wine for a pailful of punch was forcibly seized. Dr. J. D. B. Stillman, one of the *Dolphin's* passengers, details what followed: "Some of us thought it was rather hard on Gay, and a physician on board obtained a dose of tarter emetic for forty men, and a friend of Gay's, watching his opportunity, slipped it into the punch." Thereupon Gay and his friends "looked down through the after hatch upon the assembled court administering justice. The punch was good, evidently, for it was drunk to the last drop. The marshall proclaimed the demands of justice satisfied, and the court adjourned."

A quarter hour passed and the observers above saw

hilarity give way to pensiveness; then one by one the celebrants made their way on deck. With each new arrival at the ship's rail, "an awful suspicion" took shape. " 'Have you been putting ipecac in the punch?' one of them demanded fiercely of Gay. 'Gentlemen,' said he, 'it is not my wine that disagrees with you, but it is justice. . . . You are not accustomed to it; you will do better by longer practice.' "

Many of the jokes were mere horseplay, a natural outlet for the pent-up energy of young men too long and too closely confined. One such prank, practiced on nearly all the gold ships, consisted in suspending a bucket above a doorway, so arranged that the first to pass beneath it would trip over a line on the deck and release five gallons of sea water on his head. On the *Henry Lee* this entertainment abruptly ended when, not the intended victim, but the captain himself emerged from the doorway. Another stunt was to lure one of the fishermen (of whom there were some on every ship) away from his line and so prepare a surprise for him when he returned. One of the *Dolphin's* anglers was a man named Marvin, a native of Brooklyn; with the patience of his kind, he daily spent hours at the after rail watching a line that trailed in the ship's wake. "The fact that he caught no fish disturbed him little; he was convinced that the next hour, or at most the next day or two would properly reward his perseverance." And so it proved. One day conspirators raised a commotion in another part of the ship; Marvin rushed off to investigate and was called back again by shouts that he had made a catch. "There was a rush by all hands to the quarterdeck, and Marvin, his face flushed with excitement, made all haste to pull in his line. 'I've got him! I've got a dolphin!' he shouted." Cheered on by his fellows, the fisherman struggled with his catch, "the resisting prize now sheering to the right, now to the left, but every instant nearing the ship. . . . At length the line was hove short. Marvin paused . . . looked over his shoulder at the laughter-convulsed crowd, with an expression of mingled disappointment and chagrin." Well he might. For by then it had grown clear that his catch was a porcelain chamberpot. "That utensil," adds Dr. Stillman, "will hereafter be known among us as 'the dolphin.' "

One of the favorite time-killing devices was "running the gantlet," a schoolyard game, during which the participants lined up on deck and, armed with paddles, "put through" whatever unlucky companions hove in sight. Sometimes the diversions took a more serious turn. On the *Charlotte* a passenger asleep on the afterdeck was violently awakened when companions tied a line about his leg, fastened the other end to a canvas bucket, and tossed the bucket over the side. The sudden pull on the line jerked the victim into the scuppers and might have dragged him overboard had not bystanders rushed to his aid. The man escaped with severe bruises, the pranksters were fined, and the captain issued orders forbidding further mischief of that sort.

Not all these stunts were initiated by the passengers; frequently the ship's officers took a hand. One such prank, which might also have had a serious outcome, took place on the *Washington Irving*. This vessel left New York on December 8, 1850, in command of a Captain Plumer and with an uncommonly picturesque assortment of passengers. One of the latter was an elderly Bostonian named Whippet, who earned the ill will of the captain by his constant complaints. When Christmas was permitted to pass without any celebration, Whippet demanded to know if Captain Plumer planned any observance of the holidays. The captain took this under advisement and then announced that a ceremony called "King" would be conducted that afternoon. When the entire ship's company gathered on deck, it was found that the captain had caused a canvas-covered throne to be set up, with two sailors, designated pages, seated beside it. Passengers were polled to determine whom they wished to choose as king, and the score-keeper—the mate—announced that the honor had fallen to Mr. Whippet. Four sailors, constituting a color guard, escorted the Bostonian to the throne, speeches were made, a green paper crown was placed on the kingly head, and he was instructed to be seated. He sat down and immediately sank up to his neck in sea water, for the canvas concealed a large tub. The joke had a less humorous aftermath. The victim's health had been bad, his ducking in the icy water brought on a chill, and the chill developed into pneumonia. For a week his life was in danger; he eventually recovered, but his feud with the captain continued.

Then as now a crossing of the equator was a time for entertainment at the expense of credulous landlubbers. On most ships the exercises were conducted with decorum, but on others the horseplay got completely out of hand. Just how welcome a diversion Father Neptune's visit was becomes clear from a reading of the Argonauts' diaries. Most writers devote pages to a description of the ceremonies: the arrival of the Sea King over the side, clothed in flowing robes, with wig and beard fashioned from Manila rope; his deferential welcome by the captain, who turned over to him the command of the vessel and escorted him to an improvised throne, where he proceeded to hold court.

There, following the immemorial custom, all who had not previously crossed the equator were brought forward and shaved by Neptune with a razor fashioned from a barrel-hoop, the victim first having his face thoroughly lathered with a paintbrush dipped in a pot of grease. This ceremony was subject to considerable variation. On the *Alhambra*, Captain Coffin prepared in advance for the visitation by having a barrel of water hoisted to the foretop and stationing two sailors beside it. When Neptune climbed over the bow, he was escorted to the windlass, where the ship's officers and crew had gathered about, offering "profound obeisance" to his majesty. Naturally, the passengers crowded forward for a close view. "Just as they came under the foretop," wrote Coffin, "Neptune was saying: 'I rule on the sea, I cause the winds, and when I order it, it rains.' —and the sailors on the top capsized the barrel and down came a cataract. . . ."

Except on company-owned ships where intoxicants were prohibited, it was customary for those anxious to avoid the ordeal of initiation to purchase immunity by presenting Neptune with a bottle of rum. Woe to the passenger who refused either to submit or to pay the bribe. Captain Coffin relates what happened to one recalcitrant, a young man named Hall:

"So by the command of the Sovereign of the Seas, the seamen blindfolded Hall and seated him on a board laid loosely across a deep tub, half full of pure seawater. One of the tars acted as barber, while Neptune questioned the candidate as to his former life, cautioning him to make true answers on pain of his future displeasure. 'Where were you born?' but the moment poor Hall opened his mouth to reply, the barber lathered his lips with a paint brush and afterward scraped off the lather with his iron hoop. Then at a signal from his majesty, the board slipped out, and Hall slipped into the deep tub and the sailors scrubbed and scrubbed until their sovereign master told them to stop. Neptune then bestowed his blessing upon the novice, with a free permit to traverse any part of his dominion in the future. . . ."

Rather than submit to such treatment, most candidates chose to yield up a bottle of spirits. The resulting celebrations were usually both enthusiastic and prolonged. Joseph Kendall pictures the aftermath of Neptune's visit to the bark *Canton:* "When all was over, the drinking began, which was kept up until many were . . . lying about in every direction on deck, cabins, etc. The sailors and the rest of the passengers collected, I guess, from thirty to forty bottles . . . and the heads of some by tomorrow will be aching badly indeed."

By comparison with the above, crossing the line on the bark *James W. Paige*, bound from Bangor to San Francisco, was mild indeed. J. Lamson describes the arrival of Neptune and his "queenly mate," the latter a sailor inadequately disguised in canvas gown and straw bonnet. "They amused us with a dance to the music of a fiddle, and in return were treated with some brandy, of which they partook with great gusto. Neptune enquired into the affairs of the ship, cautioned the stewards and cooks to do their duty, gave some wholesome advice to the officers, cracked a good many jokes upon the passengers, and disappeared. The frolic went off with great good humor. . . ."

Some particularly elaborate hoaxes were engineered by

the bored passengers on this craft. One day a ship was sighted to the windward, proceeding on the same general course as the *James W. Paige*. Someone remarked that the stranger looked like a pirate ship, and it was observed that one credulous passenger showed signs of concern. This was enough for the jokesters. That night rumors were circulated that the strange craft was closing in with the evident intention of plundering their ship. Later there were shouts that she was alongside, and this was followed by a concerted rush for weapons with which to repel the attack. "Several barrels were thrown overboard to represent the piratical boat, and those were fired on as they floated by the ship. Then came a man rolling about with terrible groans, pretending to be wounded. . . . The poor fellow for whose benefit all this hubbub was gotten up . . . responded with the cry—'They *are* boarding us, they *are* boarding us! Where's a handspike?' and he ran and unshipped a pump handle and hastened to the spot where the supposed attack was made, determined to make a desperate defense. . . ."

Practical jokes on the *James W. Paige* were "as thick as weevils in the ship's bread." Most of them sprang from the fertile brain of a passenger named John Dolliff. Dolliff's voice bore a marked resemblance to that of the ship's captain, a circumstance that gave him ample opportunity for mischief. "He sometimes orders the stewards to trim the lamp in the binnacle, calls out to the man at the wheel to tell him how the ship heads, and gives a variety of orders." One night after the skipper had gone to bed Dolliff put on the latter's coat and cap and, approaching the mate, inquired the state of the wind and weather. Receiving respectful answers, the impostor proceeded to direct that the topsails be reefed. "This order, absurd enough under the

58

circumstances, was not given in nautical style, and while the perplexed mate hesitated, someone who was in the secret laughed, and betrayed the joke." Another of Dolliff's whimseys was directed against the *Paige's* cook. When the cook produced a batch of biscuits "as hard as rocks" he affixed two to the heels of his boots, asserting that they made admirable substitutes for shoe leather.

Even on the cruise of the *Edward Everett,* most of whose hand-picked passengers were professional men or college students, there was no lack of persons gullible enough to be taken in by practical jokers. When the *Edward Everett* was nearing the Horn the captain let it be known that those who wished to do so might escape that part of the voyage by debarking at Patagonia, marching overland to Valparaiso, and rejoining the ship there. About twenty promptly volunteered for the expedition. The captain then warned them that Patagonia was an uncivilized land and that they must be prepared for encounters with cannibals and ferocious wild beasts. This sobered the group but failed to deter them. Accordingly, daily drills were instituted, designed to put them in proper physical shape and to instil the discipline necessary on so hazardous an undertaking. In the ship's crew was an able seaman who had served a hitch in the army, and he was prevailed on to oversee their training. "Presently a sailor, dressed in an old uniform with a sword at his side, came up from the steerage and drilled them for an hour before they saw the joke."

The necessarily monotonous meals served during the long voyages sharpened the appetites of the travelers, and passengers fortunate enough to have a supply of sweets learned the wisdom of guarding it well. Any cache of preserved fruit or horehound candy, or a bottle of peach brandy—the last excellent for making palatable the brackish water—was considered fair game. Hours of patient spying were spent ferreting out the hiding-places of such treasures, and elaborate schemes were devised to lure their owners to remote parts of the ship while confederates went about the business of looting. Dozens of unfortunates, after half an hour at the rail straining their eyes to catch sight of an imaginary ship or headland or the spout of a nonexistent whale, returned to their bunks to find their supply of delicacies mysteriously missing.

Pilfering from the galley was another favorite sport. On one ship this form of larceny came to a permanent halt when the cook, having had a newly baked mince pie stolen, prepared another, which he seasoned liberally with jalap, a particularly effective purgative. He placed it temptingly outside the galley door and awaited results. These must have been all he expected, for one of the ship's diarists wrote of the victims: "I warrant they will not go a second time to the pantry." Somewhat similar is an episode recorded in the journal of the *Canton:* "The Doctor stole a piece of pie and put it in his room; having locked the door and thinking all safe, he went to his daily game of backgammon. Thereupon, while two or three of the company watched him, another tied a fork to a long stick and putting it into the window hooked the pie."

Even such naïve stunts as this one on the *Cantero* was a manifestation of the comic spirit and provided a welcome half-hour of fun. The ship had stopped briefly at Valparaiso; soon after she put to sea again, two of the passengers busied themselves making a stand designed to hold a grindstone. Early next morning there was a commotion on deck, and those who hurried up through the hatches found that some wag had converted the stand into a life-like representation of one of the tiny, heavily burdened donkeys familiar on Valparaiso streets, "with the hen coop hung onto him and a basket of onions and a keg of veno." Beside the "animal" stood one of the ship's humorists, plying a whip industriously and, imitating a street huckster, crying out his wares in bad Spanish. "It was quite amusing for a while," commented Benjamin Dore.

Far less amusing were the exploits of those unimaginative jokesters whose idea of entertainment never rose above such tricks as stealing up behind a fellow passenger who was reading or playing cards, tying a rope to his chair, and jerking it from beneath him. On some ships horseplay of that sort went on constantly, to the vast annoyance of the majority, who were able to end the mischief only by joining forces and taking drastic countermeasures. One passenger relates that he had to climb into the rigging whenever he wished to make a drawing in his sketchbook. "It was the best place I could find . . . the boys are so rogueish they will not let anyone have any peace."

3

In its early stages the migration by sea was limited almost entirely to men, as said, but by the middle of 1850 the conditions that had deterred women from attempting the trip had largely disappeared. The initial rush had then passed its crest; the pressure for passage—for any sort of passage on any sort of craft—was easing off, and ship-owners and agents were soliciting family groups and providing accommodations designed to assure some degree of privacy and comfort. Moreover, the crossings at Panama and Nicaragua, while they were still a severe test of strength and endurance, were far less hazardous than they had been during the disorganized early months. Transportation by small boat and pack train had been provided between the two coasts, and facilities for meals and shelter had been made available along the way.

With passage no longer the ordeal it had been during the first months, the number of women passengers began a slow but steady increase. Many Argonauts, having decided to cast their lot permanently with the new land, sent for their wives and children; brides-to-be embarked to join their impatient swains, and family groups, following in the wake of the first rush, braved the rigors of the trip.

From that time on, practically every ship to sail for California had at least a few women on board, with consequences that were frequently diverting and sometimes explosive. One of many examples of what might happen to mixed groups on the months-long voyages is to be found in the recollections of the young Frenchman Albert Benard, who made the passage from Havre to San Francisco in 1850–1. His ship, the *Joseph*, bore an odd cargo: Parisian shopkeepers, journalists, artisans, clerks, a theatrical troupe, "slightly decayed women and petty, disintegrated men planning new starts in life, all the disappointed ones who fondly believed that geographical change would improve their condition." With shrewdness and malice Benard set down the day-by-day happenings while the *Joseph* crossed the South Atlantic, rounded the Horn, and, after a stop at Valparaiso, beat northward toward the promised land.

The pairing off of one ill-assorted couple after another engaged the young man's attention, and all found their way into his journal. Before the ship had been many weeks at sea he was reporting that small, tubercular M. Mayer, a former curio dealer in Paris, and his buxom blonde companion were not the respectably married couple they pretended to be, that Mlle Fanny's violin-playing swain was not really her cousin but her lover; that the *Joseph's* captain, a crude and violent man of thirty-two, had persuaded Mme Chalas to share his cabin, to the disapproval of the passengers, who felt that one in his position should have more regard for the conventions. But these were only the preliminaries. On the final leg of the voyage a virtual epidemic of romance spread over the ship, and Benard was kept busy reporting its consequences: "that M. Des Marais was pre-occupied with Mme Sapin, that M. Leboucher had supplanted the musician in the favors of Mlle Fanny, that Mme Lucienne, a member of the theatrical troupe, was on good terms with the second officer, and Mme Mayer with the steward. Mme Falco, with her dishevelled gray hair and red face round as a moon, found a comrade in young M. Oitou, ex-student, ex-hussard, ex-wit, who was now vulgar beyond words and a drunkard to boot; and she offered a bad example to her daughter for whom she planned to find a rich husband in California. . . ."

By and large, American ships did not witness so extended a carnival of love as brightened the voyage of the *Joseph*, or it may be merely that the Yankee diary-writers lacked young Benard's zest for chronicling each successive flowering of romance. But this does not mean that every vessel leaving east-coast ports with a contingent of ladies was able to avoid serious breaches of decorum. The voyage of the *James W. Paige* is a case in point. The historian of the *Paige* was an observant young man named J. Lamson, whose pen remained busy during the five months' voyage and whose eye missed little of the human comedy played out by more than one hundred persons whom fate had brought together in the tiny, overcrowded craft. Lamson prudently refrained from publishing his journal until many years later, but the frankness of certain of its passages got him into hot water while the ship was still at sea. The voyage was far from tranquil. There was, as usual, constant bickering among the passengers, and before long a great deal of gossip. Much of this centered on a lady whom Lamson identifies only as Mrs. L—t, who, with her young daughter, was on her way to join her husband in San Francisco. Having set down a candid account of Mrs. L—t's irregular romance with the skipper of the *Paige*, Captain Jackson (who had a wife and family in Maine), Lamson made the mistake of sharing his journal with others, and of course it was not long before word of what it contained reached the ears of those most concerned. Lamson describes what happened next:

"Captain J. and Mrs. L—t, have volunteered some very disinterested advice on the subject of my journal, and have enlightened me on the difficult question, what is proper, or rather, what is not proper, to record in it. Mrs. L—t thinks that all the little squabbles and disputes that have been rife among us, and all the scandal, would be improper subjects to record, and would prove uninteresting to the reader. She was desirous of knowing if my journal was intended for publication, and spoke very earnestly on the impropriety of giving the names of persons."

To this the young man replied that, while his journal was written for his own amusement, he thought it likely that some portions of it might find their way into the newspapers. As to what was proper to put in a journal, that was a matter that every man must decide for himself. He went on to point out that "many events of an unpleasant nature were to be found in most books of travel, and they very often proved interesting to the general reader."

Mrs. L—t having made no progress, Captain Jackson hunted up the diarist. Lamson's report of this interview is brief: "he didn't care what was said about him, he was independent; but he didn't want the slanders that were going on about the ship to get home to his wife, though he was not afraid but that he could satisfy her about them when he got home. He hoped I would not say anything about them, and ended with a general threat intended to intimidate me. I made no reply to him, except that I had said nothing of him or Mrs. L—t in my journal which it would be necessary to expunge or alter."

Before a week had passed, *l'affaire* L—t had thrown the entire ship into turmoil. Among the passengers was the Reverend John Johnson, himself a source of considerable comment because of his unclerical temper, he having once, "in the heat of an argument over a Biblical subject," slapped a female passenger. Johnson was friendly with both the Captain and Mrs. L—t; presently he began to seek out Lamson and to make himself agreeable. Lamson was persuaded to allow the preacher to read portions of his by then notorious manuscript, but not until he had promised to reveal nothing of what it contained. That evening the clergyman returned the document and announced that, "considering all the circumstances of the case, he felt it his duty, notwithstanding his promise, to repeat these obnoxious passages to the captain." The diarist, naturally enough, vigorously objected to this procedure, but without avail, and he closed his account of the episode on this note: "So he left me to perform his duty and quiet his conscience by breaking his word and violating his promise, and making a revelation, which could answer no other purpose than to make mischief, to create personal animosity, which was already bitter enough, to prolong a quarrel which it should have been his duty . . . to allay, and stir up strife when he should have endeavored to promote conciliation. 'Blessed are the peace-makers!' "

Interest in the matter increased as the journey neared its end. Pro-Lamson passengers urged him to publish his journal when they reached port, and when he agreed to do so, "a subscription was immediately got up, and one hundred and twenty copies subscribed." The effect of this was of course further to alarm Captain Jackson, Mrs. L—t, and their clerical ally. The Reverend Mr. Johnson busied himself trying to defeat the plan. First he urged the passengers not to subscribe for the proposed book, and when this failed he demanded a public reading of the work before the entire ship's company, "not that he had any personal interest in it . . . but he thought that in justice to Captain Jackson . . . and the passengers, who knew not what they were subscribing for," the author should be required to read it publicly.

This suggestion was vetoed by the now hard-pressed Lamson, whose account continues:

"Hints had been repeatedly given me that the captain intended to seize the obnoxious document. Consultations had been held upon the subject, and it was stated—and I have no doubt of the fact—that Mr. Johnson had expressed the opinion, that the captain was fully authorized by law to break open my trunk and seize it. Uncertain as to what the ignorant madman might be tempted to do, I deposited my journal with a friend in the main cabin, where it remained until I left the ship."

There was one final skirmish before the battle of the diary ended. The *Paige* dropped anchor at San Francisco on September 7, and Lamson went ashore. When he returned the next day to gather up his belongings, he saw, laid out on a table in the after cabin, a testimonial letter, in the Reverend Mr. Johnson's handwriting, warmly praising the captain's gentlemanly conduct during the voyage. The names of a few passengers were appended. Unwilling to leave without one parting shot, Lamson drew up a statement of his own, charging that the captain's conduct had been "arbitrary, ungentlemanly, insulting and abusive, and that even female passengers have, in many instances, been subjected to the grossest abuse from him." He added: "I obtained twenty-five signatures to my paper in a few minutes, and then, gathering up my baggage, I bade a final adieu to the *James W. Paige* with a regret which I think was remarkable only for its minuteness."

In the end the fears of Captain Jackson and the shadowy Mrs. L—t and their supporters proved groundless. In California Lamson found the struggle to support himself too severe to allow him to expend either the time or the money necessary to put in print his controversial story of the voyage. Not for many years did the document reach the public; by then time had softened old animosities, and when Lamson prepared his journal for the printer (it was published at Bangor, Maine, in 1878) he appended this note:

"Many incidents of an unpleasant nature . . . have been omitted, and the omissions have somewhat shortened the book. . . ."

4

THE feud on the *James W. Paige* was by no means unique; often as few as half a dozen women passengers would throw an entire ship's company into an uproar and keep it so for weeks on end. Among the accounts of such matters that have come down to us, one of the most dramatic is that recorded in the journal of Garrett W. Low, who sailed from New York in November 1850 on board the packet *Washington Irving*. Low was an up-state New Yorker, the possessor of a very pretty wit, and evidently not averse to pointing up his narrative with details drawn from his lively imagination. By his engaging and almost certainly romanticized account, the *Washington Irving's* voyage was unusual both in the number of eccentric characters on board and in the variety of difficulties in which they got embroiled. Source of most of the trouble was two young ladies, Fay and Lilly Barkley, aged twenty and eighteen respectively, who were bound for San Francisco to join their father. The handsome Barkley sisters were closely seconded, however, by Mrs. Whippet, a pretty but lamentably scatterbrained young woman whose elderly husband had embarked in the hope that the voyage would improve his health.

Before the *Washington Irving* had been a month at sea, passengers and crew were coping with a situation as fan-

tastic as any ever presented in the melodramas of the day.
The ship had on board a device designed to distill sea water
scooped up from the adequate supply overside. On New
Year's Day this machine broke down, and the captain,
who had a collection of spare parts in his cabin, refused
to make these available so repairs could be made. For several days, while the ship plowed through tropic waters,
with the heat so intense that tar oozed from the rigging,
the suffering of the passengers was intense. Still the captain
remained adamant; he would neither permit the distilling
apparatus to be repaired nor give any reason for his behavior. Finally, by questioning the third mate, the passengers got a hint of what was afoot: one person, he stated
mysteriously, had the power to end the impasse and relieve
the suffering of the entire company. He made a further
disclosure: this person was Fay, the elder of the Barkley
sisters. Gradually details of the plot became known: Captain Plumer would end the drought only on condition that
Miss Barkley agree to share his cabin—a demand with
which that young woman showed a strong disinclination
to comply. For another full day the issue remained unde-
cided while the group discussed this delicate ethical problem: would Miss Barkley be morally justified in sacrificing
her virtue in order to rescue her companions from their
desperate situation?

Diarist Low, fascinated by the dramatic possibilities of
this dilemma, had a field day reporting the passengers'
reactions. Professor Dodd, who prided himself on his cyn-
icism, took a realistic view of the situation. Captain Plumer,
he pointed out, had all the firearms on board under lock
and key and it would therefore be useless to try to overcome
him. Under the circumstances did he believe the young

woman should be sacrificed? Dodd could see no other solution. The Reverend Mr. Thorne was of course consulted; the issues involved clearly came within his professional province. He declared emphatically that he could find no moral or ethical justification for encouraging such a sacrifice, and proceeded to fortify his position by quoting Scripture. Hadn't the Lord severely punished the wanton daughters of Moab? Didn't Moses instruct the judges of Israel to slay the men joined unto Baalpeor? To this Professor Dodd replied by pointing out that Moses was unfortunately not a passenger on the *Washington Irving*, and that their problem was not one of Biblical morality but of a ruthless and determined man bent on gaining the favors of an extremely comely young woman.

The discussion continued, getting nowhere until a bystander had a happy thought: why not first unite Captain Plumer and Fay Barkley in marriage? The Reverend Mr. Thorne hurried off to the cabin of the Barkley sisters to lay this plan before them; he returned promptly, reporting defeat. Fay had flatly refused to consider marriage to Captain Plumer, whom she pronounced an obnoxious, hateful, and repulsive brute. She showed no inclination to make herself a sacrificial offering, even though her refusal might cause the entire ship's company to perish of thirst. At the end of their resources, the group went to bed, dry-mouthed and despondent.

Low's next diary entry reported that on coming up from below the following morning the passengers discovered a cask of fresh water on the deck, and beside it the parts needed to put the distilling machine in operation.

Half a day of sleuthing passed before the mystified passengers learned the reason for their deliverance. Fay Barkley

appeared as usual on deck and took her morning constitutional, but her manner was so reserved that no one dared
question her. Not until late afternoon did it occur to the
group that Fay's sister, Lilly, had not been seen all day.
Little by little the truth got about: it was not to Fay Barkley
but to her sister that the group owed their deliverance.
Lilly had gone to share the captain's cabin.

The aftermath of this episode was hardly more credible
than the event itself. For a few days passengers discussed
schemes for rescuing the young woman from the monster
who was holding her prisoner, and laid plans to deliver him
over to authorities at the first port of call. But within a week
Lilly was back in her sister's stateroom, seemingly holding
no rancor against her captor, and before the voyage ended
she had formed a romantic attachment for the Reverend
Mr. Thorne and the happy pair had announced their engagement!

Clearly life on board the *Washington Irving* was one long
succession of surprises. Or could it be that diarist Low found
the real events lamentably prosaic and so amused himself
by giving rein to an uncommonly fertile imagination?

5

WITH so much time on his hands, the seagoing miner had
opportunity to develop whatever latent talents he might
possess. The result was the emergence, often from unlikely
sources, of amateur artists, poets, actors, and musicians, to
say nothing of ornithologists, wood-carvers, and specialists
in numerous other fields, including meteorology, medicine,
and navigation.

The reason for this widespread flowering of new interests is not obscure: to the great majority these months at sea provided for the first time in their adult lives an extended period of leisure. Enforced idleness bred first restlessness, then discontent, and it was not long before they were driven to turn their minds and hands to whatever activity seemed to offer the surest escape from the prevailing boredom.

The keeping of diaries or journals was a favorite time-consuming device for many, and one of the unplanned results was that the migration by sea was described in great detail and from many viewpoints. But not all the Argonauts kept written records of their voyages, and even those who did were not constantly occupied with them. Those with a knack for drawing set about illustrating their journals with a variety of sketches. Many such amateurs found, probably to their surprise, that they were looked on as "artists" by their fellows, and so were kept busy during the remainder of the voyage turning out drawings of their ship, of birds or fishes, or portraits of other passengers. It was a rare ship that did not soon find itself with an official artist; often there was more than one, and they were among the busiest men on board.

Not drawing, however, but music contributed most to relieving the monotony of the voyages. The ship that did not have on board a fiddle, a flute, or a banjo and a man reasonably proficient at playing it was counted unfortunate, for music—almost any sort of music—provided an ever welcome diversion. One diarist expressed a feeling that must have been common to all when he wrote: "The squeak of the fiddle and the sound of many voices pouring forth the familiar words of songs we have known since childhood, is wonderfully sweet on the deck at night, with the restless sea all about and a tropical moon in the sky."

The music was as various as the ships themselves. Both talent and musical equipment were scarce on many vessels, but in their determination to have a "band" certain groups were able to overcome even the handicap of having no instruments at all. "This afternoon," wrote Richard Hale, one of the company on the *General Worth*, ". . . came the exhibition of the 'California Tin and Wood Band.' The leader, Mr. Varney, was all right, but . . . the instruments of his band include anything that is hollow or on which anyone can make a noise. Tin pans, barrels, tubs, buckets, hand-spikes, whatever makes racket or discord. . . . It is said music sounds sweetest coming over the water . . . but the only thing that could have made this band sound sweet was to hear it going *under* water. . . ."

Few groups had to resort to such drastic measures to supply their craving for music. At the opposite extreme was the excellent orchestra on that model of gold-rush vessels, the *Edward Everett*. As part of their observance of July 4, 1849, the pampered passengers were entertained with a medley of patriotic airs expertly rendered by "four violins, an octave flute, three other flutes, and several guitars." The *San Francisco*, Captain Baker, was hardly less fortunate; its "San Francisco Melodeon Band" consisted of bass drum, kettledrum, cymbals, accordion, tambourine, and bells. Those on the *Leonore*, another New England ship, did not lack the solace music is said to bring travelers far from home. One of this group wrote: "We have formed a company of Sacramento Minstrels, banjo, tambourine, and fiddle, and we sing all the popular songs. We have a dance

nearly every night until eight bells . . . then we have fun
below, songs, stories, and games. . . ."

"The twilight hour is the most pleasant of the day,"
wrote a farm boy from Pennsylvania from the deck of a
bark inching southward through the central Atlantic. "A
cool wind off our bow revives the spirits of all. Soon the
entire company is on deck, some sprawled at full length,
some leaning against the rail, and others finding perches
aloft. There is a great deal of skylarking, of laughing and
shouting back and forth, then someone strikes up a song."
On the *San Francisco* the summons to this social evening
hour was more formal: "Suddenly the rub-a-dub-dub of
the kettle drum, calling the roll, may be heard and the
various instruments of music appear from various parts of
the ship as if by magic. . . . Yankee Doodle, Soldier's
Joy, Fisher's Hornpipe, Farmer's Boy, Auld Lang Syne . . .
are sung until eight bells are heard, then the din stops and
all is quiet." Many other diaries describe similar scenes;
here is the picture on the *Henry Lee:* "After tea a few stars
shone forth—several singers of the company gathered and
gladdened the crowd . . . around the quarterdeck; never,
we thought, was music more pleasing. Around us . . . we
felt the waste of waters, the time was fitted to turn the mind
back to the friends behind us; in the soothing influences of
Flow Gently, Sweet Afton . . . we again, we thought,
heard the tones of home, and looked upon friendly faces."

Most popular by far of the songs sung at these evening
gatherings was *Oh! Susanna;* inevitably it was the favorite of
every ship's company to sail from American ports during
the first years of the rush. The ballad, with its lilting air and
humorous words, expressed something fundamental in the
national consciousness: the spirit, half irony, half bragga-

74

docio, in which the nation's young men set off on the great gamble; it was destined from the beginning to become the theme melody of the gold rush. "The song," wrote John S. Hittell, ". . . gave the California fever to thousands, who without its stimulus would have remained in their native towns. . . . It was sung everywhere and by everybody, at concerts in the theatres, and even when poorly rendered, was received with . . . fervor by the multitude. . . . The song bears to California a relation similar to that borne to the United States by the music of Yankee Doodle." Of course there were numerous parodies; many groups composed their own versions, filling them with topical references to their voyage and prospects. The company on the *San Francisco* celebrated themselves in a dozen mildly satirical verses, of which this is an example:

> *We've forty men in Company,*
> *A cook and steward too,*
> *We've twenty pigs, a dog and cat,*
> *And what is that to you?*

But the diaries make clear that music could be a trial as well as a pleasure; even so fetching a ballad as *Oh! Susanna* lost its charm from too much repetition or when it was sung at unseasonable hours. The most common complaint was that the singers were prone to prolong the concerts long after the rest of the company had had their fill. The latter, having retired to their bunks and composed themselves for sleep, were unlikely to listen with pleasure to the strains drifting down the open hatches. On most vessels protests against these too prolonged deck concerts eventually made themselves heard and resulted in the adoption of rules prohibiting unnecessary noise after eight bells. But such regulations were far from universal, and even when they existed they were seldom strictly enforced. "The peace of the ship is nightly violated by a group of ruffians with neither manners nor consciences," one sleepless Argonaut confided to his diary, and went on to state that only on shipboard would such outrages be tolerated. Another wrote: "There is now a disagreeable noise—two flutes being played—different tunes! Also, Barricklo blowing his confounded flageolet on purpose to disturb someone. My head aches very much. . . ."

6

WHATEVER else might be said of the round-the-Horn voyage, all who experienced it agreed that it offered an unrivaled opportunity to observe the sea in all its countless moods. Those who left from North Atlantic ports frequently encountered heavy weather during the first few days; but the ship soon passed into more temperate regions and the next week or two were likely to be the most pleasant of the entire voyage. There were balmy days and brisk trade winds that sent the ship scudding rapidly on its way. It was during this period that the travelers settled by degrees into the routine of their new life, organized the messes, put their personal effects in order, and, having found their sea legs, began to enjoy the pleasures of life afloat.

But the tropics lay ahead, and by barely perceptible degrees the passage entered a new phase. The northern trades faltered, then slowly died away. There followed a season of light, erratic winds that might come from any quarter; then, as like as not, these too vanished and for days the ship lay becalmed, rolling in the long oily swells of the tropics. Men who not many days earlier had bundled themselves in their heaviest clothing to withstand the sharp northern winds shed their garments to the irreducible minimum and spent their days and nights in futile efforts to find a cool spot. On few of the ships had any provision been made for the comfort of passengers during the heat-ridden equatorial passage. The areas below decks were usually quite without ventilation save for such air as might be coaxed through the open hatches; these areas became virtually uninhabitable once the full heat of the tropics was encountered. One wrote that to descend into these steaming caverns "was like stepping into a furnace. . . . You shrink from your first contact with the heavy, stale air; if it is necessary for you to remain below more than a few minutes you discover when you again reach the deck that your clothing sticks to your skin and rivers of sweat run down your forehead and into your eyes."

Entire companies lived and ate and slept on deck. Pieces of sail were rigged on the afterdeck and groups gathered beneath them for protection from the searing rays of midday. "We are lying on deck like so many drunken or disabled men," wrote Joseph Kendall, "scarcely able to walk about or stir for anything, so great is the heat. . . . When shall we ever get out of this hot and melting climate?" Others made reference to the exposed metal parts of the ship growing so hot that one shrank from making contact with them, to air currents visibly radiating upward from the decks, to liquefied tar oozing from the rigging and from between the planks underfoot.

The discomfort of the ordeal was increased by the fact that by the time hot weather was encountered the ships had been several weeks at sea and supplies of fresh meat, fruit, and vegetables had long since been consumed. Often too the supply of fresh water had been so depleted that rationing had to be inaugurated. This was the time when bitter complaints about the quality and quantity of food and drink began to loom large on the pages of the diaries. Dried or smoked fish, beans, salt meats—the last frequently on the borderline of spoiling and sometimes well over it—these were the staples, and few considered them an ideal hot-weather diet. Some conducted revolts against such fare, refusing to eat at all until driven to it by hunger. The source of the bitterest complaints, however, was the meager allotment of water. A passenger on the *Canton* wrote:

"We receive half a pint of the stinking, rusty, brackish fluid twice a day and each man disposes of it as he sees fit. . . . The thoughtless gulp it down at once and a few hours later they are to be seen with parched tongues and dry lips cursing the ship, the captain and the day they left their comfortable homes. The prudent husband their supply like misers, now and then permitting themselves a tiny sip and smacking their lips with satisfaction. They guard their remaining supply of the warm, obnoxious liquid with the utmost care, and woe be to anyone who thoughtlessly approaches so close as to run the risk of upsetting their precious cups of nectar. . . . The fastidious adds to his portion a dram of brandy, or, if he cannot obtain that, he mixes in a spoonful of molasses and a few drops of vinegar. This makes the concoction drinkable, I will not go so far as to call it palatable. . . ."

During periods when their ships were becalmed the more adventurous found relief by diving overside, while those who remained on deck drenched one another with buckets of sea water. Nightfall brought but little relief from the oppressive heat, yet few were insensible to the chromatic splendor of the sunsets or the novelty of black skies powdered with stars in strange constellations that appeared so near "one could almost believe that by climbing aloft it would be possible to touch the nearest of them." Sleeping on deck had drawbacks as well as advantages, for the limited space was badly overcrowded and few rose refreshed from a night spent on the unyielding planks. Some were convinced that sleeping beneath the open sky held still other hazards. One passenger, Joseph Kendall, reported: "It is very dangerous, the Captain says, to sleep with the moon shining on one. . . . He says it is as bad as being sun-struck." This prudent skipper's warning seems to have been widely disregarded, however, for a day or two later the same writer observed: "I woke this morning after a good night's sleep on deck; Mr. Allen, another man, and myself in the middle. I lay cool and comfortable. I had my flannel shirt and drawers on, which is my daily dress. I took a first-rate wash in salt water, then shaved in warm, fresh water, which is a treat to get hold of, but I manage to get on the right side of the steward and cook, and being a very early riser can get a little comfort ere the Yankees arise. . . ."

7

NEARLY all ships on the round-the-Horn route made an intermediate stop at a South Atlantic port, usually at Rio or the island of St. Catherine's. At sea again and beating toward the Cape, the days grew shorter, the heat less oppressive. Presently passengers were seeking the warm sunlight instead of shunning it; the canvas came down from the afterdeck and the custom of sleeping in possibly dangerous exposure to the moon was abandoned. Crew members busied themselves overhauling the sails, strengthening the rigging, and otherwise preparing for the stresses ahead, while passengers broke out their sea chests and drew forth their warmest clothing. Interest focused on the high point of the voyage, the rounding of the frigid and stormy tip of the continent.

"The change from summer to winter [wrote John Linville Hall from the *Henry Lee*] has been so sudden and great that few of us passengers are at all ready for it. Only about ten days since, the soft, summer zephyr fanned our temples. . . . Men moved about in their light clothing, and straw hat and bare feet; or, perhaps, stretched themselves flat on the hurricane deck and basked at eventide in the genial warmth. But now let a man appear above without overcoat, and gloves . . . and you will see him shivering with cold fingers and blue lips, or making his way between-decks again, where the air is a little more mild, although less pure."

The violent storms off the Cape impressed all who were experiencing them for the first time. "We thought our ship had struggled with maddening waves," wrote one, "indeed our passion for the sublime and terrible had already been sufficiently gratified." But as the ship neared Cape Stiff their previous standards had to be revised. "The gales such as we have met in the last dozen hours, are not mere gusts or squalls . . . but long, loud, fierce blasts, bearing down on the sea and ship for hours and hours together. . . . Their effect . . . is to produce long, huge swells, over which the ship mounts with a roll, then plunges into the abyss again as if never to rise."

In such conditions life below decks became a continued struggle, with sleep impossible save when induced by complete exhaustion. "Too fiercely are we jerked from side to side to get anything in the shape of rest. When a heavy lurch shakes us we have to hold on with all our might . . . then lie in terrible suspense lest the next wave bring the ship herself to her beam-ends." Those who ventured from the comparative safety of their bunks had to be both agile and alert, choosing the instant when the ship was on an even keel to leap from support to support, then holding on while the bow tilted downward for the dizzy descent that ended in a shuddering crash as it met the next wave head-on.

The time consumed rounding the Cape varied with wind and weather, with the ship's sailing qualities and the skill and daring of her skipper. A lucky few completed the passage in less than a week; others, battling contrary winds and lashed by unremitting storms, were more than a month before they emerged into the Pacific. In order to shorten this period of hardship and strain the temptation was strong to take one of two alternate routes, both shorter (although more dangerous) than the wide southerly sweep. One was via the Strait of Le Maire, a fifteen-mile-long and comparatively wide channel between Staten Island and Tierra del Fuego. This was fairly easy to negotiate when winds and visibility were favorable, and many ships made use of it, usually at a substantial saving of time. The other route, through the formidable Strait of Magellan, was quite another matter. Although it cut hundreds of miles from the far southerly route, this narrow, storm-lashed passage held so many hazards that prudent captains commonly gave it a wide berth. None the less, the eagerness of many to reach the gold fields at the earliest possible date, and in some cases the element of danger involved, appealed to the reckless spirit of the Argonauts, and a considerable number made the gamble. They sometimes had cause to regret their rashness. From end to end the strait was nearly three hundred miles long; the prevailing winds were unfavorable to the east-west passage, the currents were swift and treacherous, and the channel—seldom more than a dozen miles wide and sometimes narrowing to less than two—made navigation extremely hazardous for sailing ships.

The one safe anchorage in the strait was at Port Famine, a wind-swept outpost maintained by the Chilean government as a penal colony, which stood at approximately the halfway point. Its surroundings were wild and desolate in the extreme. The diarist of the *Sea Eagle* reported that it took their ship thirty-six days to cover the hundred and fifty miles from the eastern gateway to Port Famine. This company spent July 4, 1849 there, their thoughts dwelling on the summer heat of home. "As I looked on the snow and ice I assure you old South Reading looked good. . . ." The bark *Valasco* reached Port Famine in thirty-five days. Those on board pronounced that ill-favored spot singularly well named—"the most horrible, gloomy place you can imagine." This writer's account continues: "The weather was bad and five miles was a good day's run. The days were short, light at 8:30 A.M., dark at 4 P.M. Rain or snow the whole time. We lay for two weeks at a place called Berja

Bay and during that time never saw sun, moon or stars. We had two hundred fathom of cable out and three anchors. . . ." One afternoon while the *Valasco* was making anchorage at a frozen inlet called Elizabeth's Bay, a sudden squall hit the ship with such violence that the anchor dragged and she went ashore. By great effort she was floated, but only in the nick of time, for a terrific gale followed that would surely have pounded her to pieces had it come an hour earlier. The *Valasco* was seventy days picking her way through the bleak and hazardous strait, and when she emerged into the safer waters of the Pacific one passenger commented: "Magellan is all right for steamers but square rigged vessels had better keep away."

The majority followed that advice, prudently choosing the longer route south of the Cape. By so doing they escaped most of the dangers of the passage but few of its discomforts or delays. Winds that blew with maddening consistency from the wrong direction, almost continuous storms, sub-zero temperatures, and nights sixteen hours long combined to depress the spirits even of confirmed optimists. "Making westing" was an inconceivably tedious process. "For every mile of forward progress," wrote Nathaniel Taylor, "we travel ten to twenty times that distance. If this continues, who can tell how many weeks it will be before we leave these lonely and inhospitable waters?" Heavy gales out of the west often nullified all the painfully hoarded gains, blasting the ships back in a few hours to points where they had been days, sometimes weeks before. After three such setbacks one Massachusetts company abandoned hope of ever completing the passage and petitioned the captain to turn about and head for California by way of the Cape of Good Hope. "But our Captain would not listen to such a proposal for a moment. Finally it was agreed that he was the proper umpire in the case and here the matter ended."

There was of course frequent reference in diaries and journals to the very real hardships of this period, but most of it was good-humored; in general the Argonauts endured their privations with fortitude. John Linville Hall, the able historian of the *Henry Lee*, made this philosophical comment: "The fact that man has wonderful power of adapting himself to circumstances, is exemplified, we think, in our own case—inasmuch as we are fast getting acclimated to winter weather without the accompaniment of artificial heat. . . . Still, though we may soon yield when no other course is left us, and bring ourselves with tolerable grace to bear what we cannot shun, we must nevertheless say, that a snug room well warmed with anthracite, and a few friends we might name, are not wholly disassociated from our ideas of comfort."

With the temperature constantly hovering around, or below, the freezing-point, and with a clammy dampness permeating clothing, bedding, and everything used or touched, life in the unheated below-deck quarters was an ordeal few would willingly have repeated. For days at a time the hatches were closed and the groups huddled in their dim, icy quarters, living "like moles in a swamp," and venturing onto the sleet-swept deck only when, as sometimes happened, volunteers were asked to lend a hand to the overworked crews. Yet life somehow went on, following a fixed routine. "Many suffer from chilblains and swollen hands, yet we do not know of the hands of any that have refused duty at mealtimes. . . . We . . . keep the lamps going from the time of rising to the hour of rest, by which we sit or lie and read, and cogitate, and think of home, and eat peanuts, and do any little needlework . . . that may be required."

Because the migration got fully under way in the spring of 1849, scores of ships rounded the Cape during the height of the antarctic winter, and those on board were often conscious that their friends at home were enjoying a quite different sort of weather. "I put on the Gernsey shirt over the two flannel ones," Joseph Kendall wrote to his wife in mid-June, "yet I feel cold. . . . Every degree we make to the south brings colder and colder weather, while with you, my dearest, the heat must be very delightful and cheering. I guess you have strawberries and all kinds of vegetables by this time. . . ." A writer on the *Francis* harps on the same theme: "We can hardly realize that friends at home are now enjoying the lovely season of Summer . . . it is difficult to realize a condition exactly the reverse of our own."

On the *Canton* heavy shutters were lashed above the cabin skylight, for the seas constantly broke over the deck, "and might break in . . . and fill the cabin." In darkness save for dim whale-oil lamps, the groups occupied themselves as best they might. "I am sitting on the side of my berth, as if glued, being wedged in on all sides by stools to prevent the breakage of my limbs. . . . I now make up my bed, then in with stockings, drawers and three flannel shirts. Yet with all these, and sleeping between blankets, I am still not warm. . . ."

Under such conditions meals were events at which anything might happen, and usually did. J. Lamson gives this picture of a Cape Horn breakfast on the *James W. Paige:*

"The gale became furious last night, and seemed increasing in force this morning. We had no little difficulty in eating. . . . A pan of fried pork and boiled beef, another pan of hardbread, and a pot of coffee, were set on the table, but how to keep them there required a greater degree of skill than we possessed. We could not sit, and we were in danger every moment of being pitched over the table, and across the cabin. To avoid such a catastrophe, we were obliged to hold by the berths with both hands. We made an effort, however, to eat, but had hardly made a beginning when a violent lurch of the ship sent our pork, bread, coffee, and all, in an instant upon the floor and into a neighboring berth. The scene was rather ludicrous, and we managed to extract a laugh from it as we picked up the fragments. . . ."

Such melees were far from uncommon, with diners and food frequently ending in a confused mass at one end of the cabin, and the breakage of crockery was so heavy that one remarked: "I think before we reach our destination we shall not have a plate or cup of any kind left for us to use." Such trials were universal, but on many vessels there were added moments of real and imminent peril. Not all the gold ships that attempted the passage round the Horn emerged safely into the Pacific. Some, inexpertly handled or too ancient to withstand the violent stresses of the Cape, had masts and gear carried away, and, their attempts to repair the damage defeated, drifted helplessly until they were engulfed and foundered or were battered to pieces by the seas. Others, off their course in darkness or blinding snowstorms, were caught by contrary winds and currents and tossed on the desolate coast of Tierra del Fuego, with the loss of all hands.

How frequent were these tragedies is indicated by the fact that for years afterward the relatives of missing men wrote to the editors of California newspapers asking information about ships last reported on the Atlantic heading toward the Horn, but from which no further word was ever heard. It is evident too from the frequency with which the diarists reported having sighted pieces of floating wreckage in the troubled waters. Sometimes, indeed, the shattered hull of some craft recently come to grief was sighted at the base of one of the lonely headlands—"a sight so moving and terrible as to fill the breast of the beholder with reverent awe."

The ever present threat of disaster, driven home by such melancholy relics, kept the more imaginative Argonauts under a constant strain during the entire stay in antarctic waters. "I go to bed with a kind of horror," wrote one, "knowing we are so near the Cape." The *James W. Paige* one afternoon passed within a few rods of a broken yard, "with several ropes still attached to it." The break was new, sure evidence that the ship to which it had belonged had recently met serious trouble. This chance encounter sobered the entire company, filling them with apprehension. In his diary that night J. Lamson permitted his imagination to run riot:

"What a history of suffering and disaster may there be connected with that spar! Perhaps it belonged to our acquaintance at Rio, the *North America*. She may have been wrecked on this coast, and her five hundred souls have been sunk in the waves and dashed on the rocks. In their efforts to save themselves, may not some of them have been lashed to this very yard? Perhaps, as the vessel went to pieces, and one after another was swallowed up, the lives of a few may have been prolonged beyond that of their fellow sufferers. And Oh! what an hour of horror must that have been to them! What thoughts of deep and bitter anguish did they send to the homes they had seen for the last time, and to the wives, daughters, mothers, sisters and friends, to whom they had bidden farewell forever. . . . How near may we have been to sharing the same fate with them? And may we not, even now . . . be reserved for the same or a worse doom?"

8

BUT grim as the ordeal was, the rounding of Cape Stiff was but an incident in the passage, and to compensate for its trials and anxieties there were periods when tensions relaxed and entire ships' companies contemplated the novelty of their lives and took stock of its good and bad points.

The latter were clearly in the majority, and if the evidence of the diaries is to be accepted the deprivation the voyagers found hardest to bear was a comprehensive lack of variety: in food, in amusements, in occupation for hand and eye and mind. One passenger, in a letter written after his ship, the *Oriole*, had reached San Francisco, remarked that the thing he had missed most throughout the trip had been reading-matter. The few books and newspapers on board had been read to tatters before the voyage had well begun, and he reported the disappointment of the group when they were unable to replenish their supply of books in English at either Rio or Valparaiso. "If you can find room in your trunk," he added, "for half a dozen good, thick, books you will discover . . . that you have become one of the most sought-after men on board."

Some ships were well supplied with reading-matter, libraries of one sort or another having been furnished either by the emigrants themselves or by friends at home. Others had to overcome the lack by their own ingenuity. An essay might be written on gold-rush journalism as it was practiced on the high seas during the outward voyages. Reference has been made to John Linville Hall's journal, written and printed on the *Henry Lee*. That was unique only to the extent that it was a running history of the voyage put into type and printed from day to day during the journey itself. Other ventures lacked the formality of print but more nearly approached conventional journalism. Probably the earliest of the gold-ship "newspapers" was the *Barometer*, a four-page hand-written sheet issued every Saturday during the voyage of the *Edward Everett*. A board of five editors was responsible for the journal, the columns of which were filled with daily happenings on the ship, together with a record of her position and speed, and a leavening of lighter fare in the form of "original prose and poetical matter."

Another weekly, the *Shark*, was issued on the *Duxbury* throughout the spring of 1849, but a more readable sheet was "published" on the *Alhambra*, outward bound from New Orleans in the fall of that year. The paper, "two sheets of foolscap, closely written out in full, by Mr. Moss," was christened the *Emigrant*, and the plan (not fulfilled) was to issue it weekly during the whole period of the cruise. The *Emigrant* lasted only four numbers. That it did not perish even sooner seems to have been due mainly to the *Alhambra's* master, Captain Coffin, an industrious and facile rhymester whose verses filled well over half of each issue. The captain (perhaps a prejudiced witness) reported that the *Emigrant's* first number—which contained his ten-stanza poem entitled "Simon Spriggins' Trip to California"—was received with so much enthusiasm that when the second was ready, measures had to be taken to preserve order. "So great was the desire to get hold of it that it was voted that one of the passengers should read it aloud to the rest." The man picked to do the reading was a Dr. Clark, a recent medical-school graduate, who, in Captain Coffin's opinion, was too lacking in force to make his way in that profession. This conclusion may have been influenced by the fact that the doctor failed to put proper fire and feeling into his rendering of Captain Coffin's second poem, "Simon Spriggins' Letter to his Wife." The final stanza of this work—there were seven more—read as follows:

> *Now Nancy dear, dry up that tear,*
> *Remember you're my precious diamond,*
> *And I'll prove true to none but you,*
> *I am your faithful, loving Simon.*

The *Emigrant's* third issue (featured article: "Simon Spriggins' Soliloquy") appeared September 5, and contained, along with other matter, this "advertisement":

WANTED: *A few degrees of south latitude. Any person being able to furnish them shall be installed an honorary member of the Committee on Navigation. Apply at the Surgeon's office.*

The Committee on Navigation was the title ironically given a group of the *Alhambra's* passengers who were in the habit of offering the ship's officers unsolicited advice on how to improve the operation of the vessel.

The *Alhambra's* newspaper struggled through one more issue, then peacefully died. Captain Coffin thus salutes its passing: "From this time *The Emigrant* languished for want

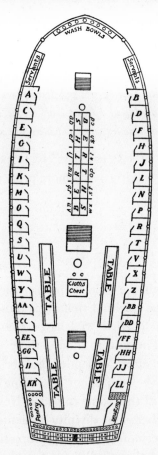

PLAN OF THE BERTH DECK OF THE SHIP "ALHAMBRA," WHICH
SAILED FROM NEW ORLEANS, APRIL 12, 1849.

*Refitted for the California trade at a cost of $10,000, the Alhambra
was far better equipped than most gold ships.*
(From Coffin's A Pioneer Voyage)

of sustanance; it did not appear the next Saturday. It made one more effort on Saturday, September 20th, and then gave up the ghost. The editorial valedictory had some reference to 'casting pearls before swine. . . .' " Simon Spriggins bowed himself out with a final poem, the inspirational character of which may be gathered from this stanza:

> *Your saddle bags shall yet be filled*
> *With Sacramento's glittering ore.*
> *Your doubts and fears shall all be still'd*
> *And troubles come not near you more.*

The *Alhambra* at last came safely to port—perhaps an indication that her skipper was more proficient with sextant than pen.

9

ON VIRTUALLY all the gold ships provisions of some sort were made for the spiritual welfare of those on board, and often these were carried to lengths that the passengers found irksome. There were indeed those who complained that part of the effort expended bolstering their morals might better have been spent providing a few material comforts. It is said that some ships left New England ports with more preachers and divinity students on board than able seamen. A sermon on Sunday—sometimes two—and a prayer meeting in the middle of the week were the rule on many such vessels, although it was observed that congregations tended to dwindle as the voyage progressed and that services were suspended entirely during the passage of the Horn. Once the Pacific side was reached, however, the praying—which had been on a strictly individual basis on the gale-swept antarctic waters—again achieved organized status. But by and large the diarists devote much less space to preaching during the final weeks of the journey than in its early stages, and the conclusion is unescapable that the Argonaut's religious fervor declined as the distance lengthened between him and his home parish.

It had been keen enough while the companies were being organized and made ready to depart. The evangelical ardor of the time was such that some expeditions might have been mistaken for nineteenth-century crusades designed to convert the California heathen; the true purpose—that of digging gold or of accumulating it by profitable trading deals—was all but forgotten. The devout atmosphere that surrounded the farewells, heightened by the emotional stresses of parting from family and friends and facing an uncertain future, did not immediately evaporate once the adventurers were at sea. If the schedule of the *Duxbury*, a Boston ship that sailed in February 1849, carrying the Old Harvard Company, may be accepted as typical, one passenger's observation that there was "too much praying on board" was not entirely unjustified. Each morning the *Duxbury's* preacher, the Reverend Mr. Brierly, read a chapter from the Bible, offered a prayer, and delivered a brief sermon. On Wednesdays he presided over a prayer meeting; on Sundays he preached "a full length sermon" and followed this with a class discussion group; on Tuesdays and Fridays he conducted a lyceum. This was during the early stages of the voyage; later this comprehensive program collapsed—as it did on so many other ships—and during the final weeks the *Duxbury's* company seems to have been without religious instruction of any kind.

Sermons and prayer meetings were but one of the steps taken by the organized companies to bolster the morale and morals of their members. Rules governing their conduct during the voyage and in the gold fields had been carefully drawn up, and few of the documents failed to include clauses prohibiting strong drink, gambling, and profanity. Some charters bristled with such restrictive regulations. The Hartford Mining & Trading Company forbade smoking below decks. The *Aurora*, Captain Swain, left Nantucket "without a drop of intoxicating liquid on board." The *Edward Everett's* well-stocked hold contained twenty-five gallons of whisky, but this was exclusively for medicinal purposes and could be doled out only on orders of one of the physicians on board. The consumption of alcohol by members was universally prohibited, although few saw any inconsistency in taking out barrels of whisky or West Indian rum to sell to the other '49ers.

In their zeal to curb the excesses of the few those who drafted the company regulations sometimes set their standards impossibly high. Members of the Bunker Hill Mining & Trading Company, which sailed on the *Pauline*, solemnly pledged "to abstain from all the vices and temptations incident to the expedition." On many ships not only gambling but card-playing of any sort was prohibited, as was also profanity, although on one vessel this last rule was modified, stating merely that a fine would be assessed against any member heard swearing on Sunday.

That measures designed to regulate the conduct of certain members, and so promote the well-being of the majority, were both wise and necessary there can be little doubt, for all the ships were badly overcrowded and a few undisciplined souls, if unrestrained, could make life miserable for all. But here as elsewhere events proved that it was easier to lay down rules than to enforce them. In most cases the company charters set forth in detail methods of coping with offenders. Usually these followed regular courtroom procedure, with judge and jury, prosecutor and defendant, all in the best democratic tradition. Punishment of those found guilty usually took the form of fines paid into the company's treasury, or of sentencing the culprit to work in the galley or to clean up the 'tween-deck quarters.

But admirable as this system was in theory, in nearly every case it seems to have worked out badly. With scores of men confined in small space over long periods, differences inevitably arose, opposing factions formed, and those in charge found their authority challenged. Often this cleavage resulted in the calling of new elections, at which the original officers were ousted and new ones installed. Moreover, rules adopted while the organizations were still on dry land proved unworkable in actual practice, and in the end the more drastic restrictions went into the discard.

One of the rules most widely broken was that forbidding the possession or consumption of intoxicants. The charter of every company contained this prohibition, yet the voyages were rarely bone-dry. There were always a few who smuggled aboard a bottle or two of rum or brandy for use in possible future emergencies, or perhaps merely as a means of combating boredom. These were presently brought forth and passed surreptitiously from hand to hand, although later drinking went on more or less openly. One of the strictest of the temperance ships was the *Henry Lee*. The group on board celebrated July 4, 1849 by a banquet, followed by no less than thirty toasts, "all pledged in bumpers of cold water and interspersed with appropriate music." But usually the first of the stops en route—at St. Catherine's or Rio—ended the drought and passengers returned on board fortified against the rigors of the Horn with a supply of brandy or strong Brazilian wine.

These hoarded bottles were brought forth to add zest to numerous special celebrations. Christmas, Washington's Birthday, Thanksgiving, and—most of all—the Fourth of July were looked on by loyal Americans as occasions when liquor-produced hilarity was not only permissible but a positive obligation. Captain Coffin tells of the *Alhambra's* company getting "gloriously and patriotically drunk" while celebrating Independence Day somewhere in the South Atlantic:

"*July 4th.*—I was aroused at 3 A.M. by what I supposed was a row on deck. On going out to see what was to pay, I found it but the beginning of the celebration. A parcel of wild ones had got on deck, with their liquor and their revolvers, and seemed determined to make a day of it. . . . I convinced them of the impropriety of having their firearms about, and persuaded them to give them all up. . . ."

Deprived of their armament, the *Alhambra's* passengers turned to oratory. An attorney from Alabama was chosen speaker of the day; willing hands hoisted him to the top a capstan, where, swaying dangerously, he delivered this address:

" 'Fellow citizens, by God: This, by God, is the greatest day, by God, that ever dawned, by God, since the creation. We, by God, are the greatest American people, by God . . .' and so on, the listeners expressing their approval by frequent shouts of 'Good, by God!' "

The celebration continued all day, in what Captain Coffin described as "an uproarious manifestation of patriotism," and it was not until late that night that the last of the patriots were one by one assisted to their bunks. "July fifth found a subdued and chastened spirit on board the *Alhambra*."

Somewhat similar was the aftermath of a celebration on the *Canton:*

"When all was over [wrote Joseph Kendall] the drinking began, which was kept up until many were tipsy and lying about in every direction on deck, cabins, etc. The sailors and the rest of the passengers collected, I guess, from thirty to forty bottles of brandy, red wine, etc., and the heads of some by tomorrow will be aching badly indeed."

These, however, were extreme instances; in general those who went out as organized groups conducted themselves with moderation. Their leaders were usually men of consequence in their home communities, and those who applied for membership were obliged to meet certain rigid requirements before they were permitted to enroll. The majority were young men of ambition, good sense, and serious purpose. Most groups, to be sure, included a few black sheep whose families had bundled them off to get rid of them or in the hope—usually futile—that a season in the mines would "make men of them." These, however, were so much in the minority that in general they caused little trouble during the voyage. What happened after they reached San Francisco, where there was no lack of companions with like inclinations, need not concern us here.

10

OF COURSE not all the gold ships carried organized groups. Nearly half the men who sailed in 1849—the proportion grew larger as time passed—were on their own, traveling as simple passengers on vessels hurriedly put on the profitable California run. The general level of behavior on these ships was usually below that on regulated vessels. Here no inquiry was made into the morals or qualifications of prospective passengers; whoever could pay the cost of passage was accepted without question.

On many such ships discipline was strict, the officers and crews competent, and the passengers as well treated as the vessels' limited size and facilities permitted. But this was not universally so; most really severe hardships and deprivations were on such independently operated ships. With the demand for passage everywhere exceeding the supply, unscrupulous owners did not hesitate to practice outrageous frauds. Ancient hulks ready for the marine junkyards were advertised as swift modern ships of superior comfort and safety. Prospective passengers going on board were shown neat deck cabins, and paid handsome bonuses to secure them, only to discover after they were at sea that the same cabins had been sold a dozen times over. As many as two hundred tickets were sold on ships that had accommodations for less than half that many. Some owners kept the galley in operation while the ships lay at the pier and the passenger lists were filling; hesitating visitors were invited to partake of a "sample meal"—a bountiful repast, well cooked and tastefully served. Once at sea, these delicacies disappeared permanently from the ships' menus. There were sometimes more serious matters to contend with: drunken captains, abusive and arrogant; incompetent officers and mutinous crews, leaky, unseaworthy ships, tainted meat and wormy biscuits, inadequate supplies of brackish water. The term "hell ship" was not inappropriately applied to some vessels on which unsuspecting travelers paid exorbitant sums for passage and, once embarked, had little choice but to endure the hardships and dangers to the end of the voyage.

The passengers, however, were never entirely defenseless, for when the greed of the owners or the arrogance of the ship's officers went too far, their long-suffering victims took drastic countermeasures. One of these periodical passenger revolts took place on the *Capitol*, a 700-ton ship that sailed from Boston in January 1849 with close to two hundred and fifty on board. Although the *Capitol's* owners had held forth the lure of excellent food and comfortable quarters, the cruise had hardly begun before passengers were dispatching delegations to the captain demanding more and better food. The skipper met these complaints—as did others—by professing to be helpless: the owners had specified what food must be served and how much, and he had no power to alter his instructions. This so incensed the passengers that a new meeting was called at which plans were laid to seize control of the ship, imprison officers in their quarters, and sail her into the nearest port. These threats, and the obvious determination of the men making them, proved sufficient. The skipper overcame his reluctance to increase the food ration and, once that was done, tempers cooled and the threat of mutiny evaporated.

Another ship on which much bad feeling developed between officers and passengers was the *Duxbury*, and here again the chief complaint was against the quality of the food and the manner of its serving. The *Duxbury*, an ancient three-masted craft, so hard to maneuver that she was said to require all of Massachusetts Bay in which to turn, left Boston in February 1849. Of course she was loaded to capacity, so much so that her tiny galley proved wholly inadequate. After a week of subsisting on two sparse meals a day, the passengers met and made known their grievances. For a long time their protests were disregarded. "Petition after petition was sent in to the captain without producing any other effect than the reply, 'If it is not enough, go without.' " The group continued on short rations—"we were allowed one-half pint of weak tea a day and three pounds of sugar a month"—until the *Duxbury* reached Rio. There a committee of passengers related their troubles to the United States consul. The result was that the capacity of the galley was ordered enlarged and the passengers thereafter fared rather better.

Threats to carry their grievances to the consulates at whatever South American ports the vessels touched were a favorite theme of disgruntled groups on ship after ship. The Argonauts' diaries make it clear that all during 1849 and '50 the office of United States consul at Rio, or Valparaiso, or half a dozen other ports, was no sinecure. The men who held these posts were called on to hear an endless variety of charges and countercharges, to conduct hearings, and, when it was clear that the nation's maritime laws had been violated, to mete out whatever punishment the statutes required. Thus the consuls had authority when the evidence warranted it to remove incompetent captains from their commands, to levy fines against owners, to order mutinous sailors sent home in irons, and to force skippers to provide supplies and services necessary to the health or safety of their passengers.

The power of the consuls was such that as certain ships neared port the skippers were likely to become uncommonly solicitous of the welfare and comfort of their charges. Unexpected delicacies appeared at mealtime, the water ration was increased, unpopular rules were relaxed, and a spirit of amiability was fostered, designed to dissipate the memory of past differences. Sometimes this beguiling friendliness had the hoped-for effect. Convinced that an era of goodwill had descended on the ship, the passengers forgot their grievances and prepared to enjoy comfort and harmony to the end of the voyage—only often to find that all the old abuses returned once they had put to sea again.

Of course, a great deal of the grumbling that found its way into the Argonauts' journals was not a result of deliberate mistreatment on the part of owners or captains; often it was the unavoidable consequence of so many being confined in small space over long periods, with little to occupy their time and a complete lack of the privacy and freedom to which they were accustomed. The majority were reasonable men who recognized that a fifteen-thousand-mile voyage, involving two crossings of the tropics and the rounding of Cape Horn, could not under any conditions be regarded as a pleasure jaunt. Space was precious on the little ships and crowding inevitable, supplies of fresh water had to be husbanded on weeks-long passages from port to port, and the meals were necessarily lacking in variety because perishable foodstuffs could not be kept indefinitely. Most Argonauts resigned themselves philosophically to the

101

discomforts they knew could not be avoided, accepted the inconvenience of being constantly surrounded by their fellows, and made the best of a diet composed of a succession of salt meat, dried fish, and hardtack. Only when the quality of this fare fell below what they considered the minimum standard, when the meat was putrid, the ship's bread full of weevils, and the drinking water dirty and evil-smelling, did their complaints grow violent.

Indeed, the diaries make clear that the trials their writers found hardest to bear often stemmed, not from their ships' officers and crew, but from their fellow passengers. This too was to be expected; when scores of men, coming from all walks of life, with varied interests and backgrounds, were thrown into close association for many weeks, clashes were inevitable. It is interesting to trace through the yellowed pages of a typical journal the complex record of its writer's relationship with his fellows. Often at the beginning of the voyage he made the acquaintance of someone of like interests and enthusiasms. For a time the daily entries record the growth of their friendship; they shared neighboring bunks, joined the same mess, and spent hours leaning on the rail in critical discussion of their fellow passengers or laying plans for their joint assault on California's golden creek-beds. This might go on for days or weeks; then by degrees the friendship cooled, the names of new intimates appeared, and the first vanished from view. This process was likely to continue throughout the voyage, with friendships being made, dissolved, and remade with monotonous regularity.

That such shipboard friendships were unstable is not hard to explain; they were formed because strangers were thrown together in close association, and dissolved when further acquaintance revealed the incompatibility of their backgrounds and temperaments. In the end the process completed itself; those of like interests joined together, forming self-contained and mutually exclusive groups. Thus, on every ship there were those who played cards, gambled, and used profanity, and others who deplored this worldliness, avoided associating with those who shared it, and recorded their disapproval in frequent journal entries. The card-players, in fact, were a favorite target of the diarists, one of whom commented that their devotion to the game—often they played from daylight to dark, stopping only for meals—gave them the bearing and appearance of men under the influence of a powerful drug, their motions those of automatons, their eyes and ears oblivious of all except the business at hand. Another was impressed, not by the behavior of the players, but by the condition of the cards, which were put to such continuous use that soon each card became tattered, the markings on its face all but obliterated.

Profanity, like card-playing, flourished on the outward trips and proved an annoyance to many, who regarded the rapid spread of the vice as evidence that a long sea voyage brought on a weakening of the moral fiber. One writer went further; he foresaw that the blasphemy of so many of his fellows might imperil the safety of the ship. "I hope that we may all be preserved," he wrote as the vessel entered the rough waters off the Horn, "but when I hear such cursing and swearing from many it seems to me almost a miracle if we are!" A few days later, when they were in the midst of their first storm, he braced himself in his violently pitching bunk and composed this prayer: "O Lord, have mercy on us, and extend Thy arms and save such wicked sinners as we are! We do not even deserve the least protection, when such wickedness and profanity are daily exercised in this frail bark; but Thou canst in Thy goodness forgive and save us."

Along with profanity and liquor, gambling was sternly legislated against in many of the miniature sea-borne communities—and proved as difficult to suppress. The degree to which the rules were disregarded varied from ship to ship. An extreme case was recorded by T. R. Warren, who wrote: "Drinking and gambling became the order of the day, and from early morning until late at night, nothing was heard but the fierce oaths of the gambler. . . ." On most ships gambling was far less open, but the prevailing boredom drove many to cards, and by a natural progression it was not long before small wagers were being placed on the outcome. In some instances these mild social games developed into outright gambling sessions, with the stakes mounting from day to day. The gambling spirit, once aroused, was hard to put down, and sometimes it reached the proportions of an epidemic. Wagers were made on the length of the day's run, the day and hour of reaching the next port or of sighting another ship, even on the identity of the next man to emerge from a companionway. The stakes were as various as the bets themselves: ready cash (which grew scarcer as the voyages progressed), clothing, jackknives, shoes, pistols, possessions of all sorts. But the law of averages remained operative here as elsewhere, and although a great deal of property changed hands before the game palled, the player usually ended with about as much as he had had at the start. "He owned as many things as before, but not the same things."

Gambling was even more prevalent on the ships on which the Argonauts returned home. For during their stay in California they had been exposed to the hazards of the gaming table, and not a few had become addicted to the vice. Thus, many homeward-bound ships not only carried a high percentage of miners who had acquired the habit, but provided convenient facilities to permit him to indulge it. Professional gamblers regularly made the run on steamers plying between San Francisco and Panama and openly operated roulette wheels and faro games, sometimes setting up their apparatus on the tables in the dining-salon. This gentry had working agreements with the ship's officers, to whom they paid over a share of their profits in return for exclusive gaming rights.

This was far less frequent on the sailing ships, although it was not unknown. On the brig *Hector*, plying Pacific waters, the skipper himself claimed the sole privilege of fleecing passengers. The captain, whose name was E. Kemp, and who was described by a French miner named Ernest de Massey as "the lowest type of pure-blooded Yankee," seemed to de Massey to be far more interested in mulcting his charges than of delivering them safely to their destination. "His one aim is to relieve them of all their money before drowning them, wrecking them on the coast, or forcing them off the ship." Captain Kemp's method of leading on his victims was the classic one of the card-sharper. "This evening," de Massey continues, "the Captain got up a game of monte—a Spanish card game—and lost several hundred dollars; the Captain is an expert gambler and many will soon find their purses empty. . . . Plain common sense warns me to keep away . . . sly player that he is, he has done this to entice the foolish to join his gambling table. . . ." This prophecy was amply fulfilled by subsequent developments.

11

"DURING all the discomfort and misery of the passage [through the Strait of Le Maire] our appetites remained as keen as ever." This was the observation of a passenger on the brig *Christiana*. Historians of other voyages observed a like phenomenon, for the most welcome break in each day's routine occurred at mealtime. The average Argonaut's preoccupation with thoughts of food is abundantly clear from the records he left behind; it is a rare diary that fails to return to the subject every page or two. Very little of this comment was written in terms of approval, yet there were instances when the diarist, having partaken of an elaborate meal on some special occasion, set about with gusto composing a catalogue of the delicacies spread before the company: pickles, jam, fresh-baked bread, cheese, even "plum pudding with brandy," the last an unimagined luxury. At Christmas, Thanksgiving, or the Fourth of July the cooks dipped deep into their food reserves, and the repasts they produced assumed the proportions of a banquet. One such Lucullan feast was served on the *Henry Lee* on July 4 of 1849, and young Hall devoted much diary space to descriptions of beef and pork "handsomely sliced," of fresh-baked cake and "excellent pickles," topped off with "a large, *whole* pie for each man."

Much of the enthusiasm for such spreads sprang, of

course, from the fact that they differed so much from those usually served. Wordy revolts against the sort of meals provided were common on nearly all the gold ships, the passengers complaining that the food was monotonous and unpalatable or, if its quality passed muster, protesting against the manner of its preparation and serving. Some groups had just cause for complaint, but much of the abuse heaped on captains and cooks was undeserved. In the days before refrigeration it was manifestly impossible to provide varied or particularly appetizing menus on ships that were at sea for months at a time. Passengers might—and usually did—complain of a steady diet of salt meat or fish, potatoes, beans, hardtack, and tea, but the food was nourishing and usually sufficient in quantity, and at least once a day the monotony was broken by the addition of a sweet. The last was of two sorts: dandy funk, a heavy pudding made of seabiscuit broken up and boiled in molasses, sometimes with cinnamon and raisins added; and fruit grunt—dried apples or peaches or plums baked in bread dough.

The gastronomical *pièce de résistance* on all the California ships, the dish that most frequently issued from the galleys, was lobscouse, a hash of potatoes, salt beef or pork, and hard bread. This was nutritious and filling, but after having it served them twice a day for weeks on end, few Argonauts found it a positive delight to the palate. "It is very greasy," wrote a passenger on the *Canton*, "but we eat it." Passengers on other ships had to contend with more than grease. A writer on the *Falcon* tells of beans that contained "two bugs for every bean," and accounts of weevil-infested flour, tainted meat, wormy cereals, and adulterated tea are frequent in Cape Horn literature.

Typical of those voyages on which passengers suffered

real privations was that of the *Cachalot*, a French-owned brig that sailed from Panama in June 1850. At the agency where the travelers had bought their tickets—paying extremely high prices for them—they were shown what purported to be a schedule of the meals to be served on the *Cachalot* during a typical week: Sunday: beef, potatoes, and pudding; Monday: pork, beans, and potatoes; Tuesday: pork, beans, rice, and molasses; Wednesday: ham, pork and beans, and potatoes; Thursday: beef, rice, and molasses; Friday: pork, beans, and potatoes; Saturday: beef, rice, and molasses. One ticket-holder commented: "This, with coffee in the morning, tea in the evening, and plenty of good bread, which the agent assured us we should have, presented a tolerable bill of fare for the voyage." But the actuality fell far short of expectations. The *Cachalot* had just weathered a difficult passage of the Horn; the regular cook had decamped at the first stop on the Pacific side and been replaced by a native Peruvian. The latter speedily proved himself not only lazy and incompetent, "but of all things filthy, the filthiest." His method of serving meals was even less appetizing than the food itself. "There was no such thing as a table, in lieu of which he used the deck, where with one hand he held a chunk of meat down and with the other cut off pieces as each called for it. The potatoes were scattered about him, and in the rush, noise and confusion were pretty well mashed and richly seasoned with dirt. The bread was hard and old, tho' rich, as we soon found upon breaking it, there appearing any quantity of nice looking worms and bugs." Supper consisted of the promised tea, "made on the Homeopathic principle, one leaf of the herb to a pint of water, and some of the pork we ought to have eaten at dinner." Breakfast next morning was succinctly described: "Coffee bad, sugar dirty and bread wormy." The second dinner was like the first, with the addition of "Isthmus-made molasses, with dirt, gravel and sticks in it, besides some curious looking things, which I did not exactly understand."

A few days of this was enough to goad the *Cachalot's* passengers into open revolt. The usual petitions to the captain having proved futile, on the third evening out one miner hurled his cup at the passing captain and followed with a threat to throw him overboard unless there was an immediate change for the better in the ship's galley. "The scene was a rich one, passengers hungry and infuriated, brandishing cups, plates, knives, spoons, etc., while the Captain, not understanding a word of our language, thought that every moment would be his last." An interpreter was found and a parley held, with the result that the Peruvian cook was deposed and the passengers themselves took over the galley. They adopted the usual system of dividing their number into messes, each with a leader. One group chose a Tennessee clergyman for the post, on the theory that "Methodist preachers always live on the best, provided they can get it." Subsequent meals were an improvement over what had gone before, although not much could be done about the quality of the food itself. "Our breakfast under the management of the new cooks was some better, tho' yet worse than any person not a savage would give his servants."

Food remained a major concern on the *Cachalot* to the end of the voyage. A week after the cook had been banished passengers were boasting ironically that theirs was the only vessel on the California run that served fresh meat three times a day. "This was the fresh meat contained in the bread, for that we got at every meal." A new source of trouble presently developed on this uncommonly contentious voyage. Rivalry sprang up between the different messes, each group on the alert to see that it got its rightful share. "For dinner we had what was called bean soup, and for dessert . . . a fight between one of our mess and W—, of S— County, Tennessee. Vinegar was said to be the cause of the fracas. No damage was done, but there was a large amount of talking and some tall swearing. . . ."

Conditions on such ships as the *Cachalot* were deplorable enough. In view of the real privations their passengers suffered, the complaints of those on better-managed vessels seem trivial. Thus the group on the *Capitol*, after only a week at sea, was demanding rations "equal to those furnished on ships of the United States Navy" and listing among their grievances the fact that there were not enough spoons and forks. On both the *Crescent City* and the *Canton* indignation meetings were held because their plum duff was boiled in salt water, and on the *Euphrasia* an unnamed poet composed a twenty-verse poem detailing the shortcomings of that vessel's cuisine. When the author read this work to the assembled company, a listener commented: "If our meals were half as bad as F—'s verse then there would be few appetites on board." The *Canton's* company was treated to a novelty when the skipper joined passengers in revolt against the galley. "Our steward has grown very consequential, and the Captain has threatened to flog him if he does not cook and see to things better in the future. . . ." But it developed that what the captain—a Maine Yankee—wanted were more frequent servings of salt fish, whereas most of the passengers, who hailed from upper New York State, had other ideas. One commented: "While

110

writing this the Steward has just passed me with a tubful of this filthy and rotten codfish, which some of these beauties prefer and call a treat!''

Dissatisfaction with the commissary always grew in volume during the latter stages of the voyages. As the number of days at sea multiplied, perishable foodstuffs disappeared from the table one by one until nothing remained but salt or dried meat and fish, beans, rice, and hard bread. Richard L. Hale, writing from the brig *General Worth* in the fall of 1849, observed plaintively:

"It is impossible to appreciate the value of fresh food on shipboard. The usual fare is hard baked biscuit, called by the sailors 'hard-tack,' baked very hard to prevent moulding, and beef as salt as salt itself, to keep it from spoiling, named in sea language 'salt junk,' and 'salt horse,' with 'duff,' or boiled pudding, served once a week, and hash when they are fortunate enough to have potatoes, while an occasional dish of beans, together with tea and coffee, constitute the sea-going bill of fare."

By 1849 the cause of scurvy was well understood and few ships set out for California without a supply of fresh fruit and vegetables, and this was replenished at the intermediate stops en route. But there were always long periods between ports when passengers were reduced to the Spartan "salt-and-horse-and-hardtack" diet. It was during these intervals that the far-sighted Argonaut who had provided himself with a few jars of preserved fruit or pickles had reason to applaud his foresight, and if he chanced also to be a shrewd trader he could dispose of his treasures on very favorable terms indeed. There is record of one Yankee who offered a jar of spiced plums at public auction, realizing upwards of a dollar apiece for them. But those who wished to reserve such dainties for their own use had to consume them in private, never an easy feat in their badly over-crowded quarters. "I often take a spoonful or two of the preserved quinces on the sly," wrote Joseph Kendall from the *Canton*. "I have a bottom berth, and I have to get down on my hands and knees, and, lying nearly flat, open my little box and take the quinces. I have to watch some time before I can get this opportunity."

Not only a lack of fresh food but a scarcity of water added to the hardships of the cruises. "Weevily bread and tainted meat are not always to be avoided," stated one writer, "but a bad or insufficient supply of water was a thing they would not stand." Although there is little record of actual suffering from thirst, it often happened that calms or contrary winds kept the vessels at sea far longer than expected, and the reserves of fresh water sank to the danger point. In such cases the skipper took the precaution of rationing the supply—a procedure that had the psychological effect of enormously increasing the thirst of every man aboard. After one ship had lain for a week in a tropical calm with the daily allotment reduced to one pint, a passenger wrote feelingly: "Oh, for a glass of cool, fresh water to cool my parched tongue! It would be better than all the liquors and wine. . . ." Such periods of drought were usually relieved by equatorial storms, during which receptacles of every sort were brought on deck to catch the downpour and pas-sengers reveled in the luxury of fresh-water baths.

Not the limited supply of water but its inferior quality was the chief hardship. Standing for many weeks in wooden casks, the lukewarm fluid became stale and stagnant, cloudy in appearance, and giving off an odor offensive even to strong stomachs. One writer thought it smelled like "bad lamp-oil"; another likened it to bilge-water, adding: "the scent of it twice a day while being pumped up is truly sickening." Still another commented: "A pitcher of water, when brought to the table, will have one-third of filthy sediment at the bottom. . . . The way I take it when needed is by holding my nose." Efforts to make the beverage less obnoxious by disguising its taste and smell taxed the ingenuity of many. Some found that it could be made drinkable, if not palatable, by adding a small amount o brandy or fruit cordial. But these ingredients were rare and the most common device was to add a mixture of molasses and vinegar; the resulting concoction was known as "switchel."

12

THE eagerness with which all hands looked forward to the stops nearly all the Cape Horn vessels made at South American ports was due, not to the opportunity these offered for first-hand acquaintance with an alien civilization, or even to the promise of a break in the monotony of a voyage that had grown more tedious day by day. What they chiefly wanted was a change of diet—a longing that had been built up during weeks of subsisting on salt meat and fish and brackish water. The pioneers' diaries abound with descriptions of the gastronomic delights of these first days ashore, of making acquaintance with such exotic fruits as bananas and pineapples, of enjoying the unimagined luxury of fresh milk and iced drinks, of stupendous dinners ashore, with green vegetables, roast fowl, and rich, aromatic Brazilian coffee. Benjamin Dore, a passenger on the *Cantero*, wrote from St. Catherine's: "All hands bought a lot of green stuff to take with us such as melons pineapples oranges wine, &c, of the natives . . . the first and last breakfast I ate in port was milk which was very good. . . ." When the *Leonora* put in at Talcahuano, Chile, the travel-weary group found the climate bland and the fruit abundant and delicious—also the wines. "We have bought a lot of the wine of the country for twenty-five cents a gallon and the best cordials for fifty cents a gallon." This writer was sure that thus fortified the last leg of the cruise would pass pleasantly. Equally attractive was Juan Fernández, an island off the coast of Chile, known to every young American from his reading of Defoe's classic. Few Argonauts who came on this tiny haven after the hard passage of Cape Horn could understand why Crusoe had willingly abandoned it. "I should like to prolong my stay here for weeks," wrote Richard Hale, whose ship, the *General Worth*, anchored in the palm-fringed inlet in March 1850. "It is certainly a lovely spot!" A party from the *General Worth*, Hale among them, spent a day exploring the island's interior. "With bags and baskets we started for the fertile little valleys, through the nearest pass in the hills. Here we found fruit in abundance, growing wild and free to be gathered. I never saw more delicious peaches. We climbed into the trees, shaking down those we could not reach, and filling baskets and bags to overflowing." The ship left port with fifty bushels of peaches, quinces, and other fruits stored on deck—most of which spoiled in the heat as the vessel pressed northward toward the equator.

But the Argonauts did not have to depend entirely on

these interludes ashore for fresh food to vary their wearisome salt diet. Nearly all ships carried a few chickens, a pig
or two, and sometimes a cow, all housed in temporary quarters in some sheltered angle of the deck. These animals,
subsisting in part on refuse from the galley, seem to have
adapted themselves readily enough to their unfamiliar
environment; certainly they were an unfailing source of
interest to their human companions. But as the journey
progressed, a new interest came to possess those who gathered about the livestock pens. Week by week the congestion
within grew less and the journals recorded in eloquent passages the delights of chicken stew or fresh roast pork at Sunday night suppers.

Occasionally the animals came to other than their intended ends. Some sickened and died, finding the seafaring
life insupportable; others were washed overboard during
storms or, their shelters having been inadequately pro-
tected against the elements, were frozen to death while the
ships were still in northern waters. Sometimes sheer mischief was responsible. The bark *San Francisco,* which left
Boston in August 1849, carried twenty pigs, housed in a
stout pen on the afterdeck. A month later one of the ship's
diarists wrote:

"Pig No. 1 was accidentally murdered last week under
circumstances of extreme pain to him. . . . One of our
after guards, having nothing else to do, and the fear of the
devil not being before his eyes, did wantonly and mali-
ciously draw his knife and cut off the creature's tail, just
for a lark, and the poor animal bled to death. No. 2 died
as a pig should die, being stuck in a scientific manner, and
therefore a good sea pie is expected."

Balancing this callous exploit is another drawn from the annals of the *LaGrange*. Ten days out from Salem, three hens escaped from their coop and flew over the rail. The ship hove to, a boat was lowered, and the runaway fowls were brought safely back on board. This act of mercy paid off, with interest, after the ship reached California, for the survivors and descendants of the original flock were said to have been sold in San Francisco for *twenty-five dollars each*. Another New England ship, the *Metropolis*, had a similar experience with the fantastic California prices. One member of this Beverly, Massachusetts, company wrote from San Francisco: "We sold one old and five little pigs for one hundred dollars, I think they would have brought fifteen dollars in Beverly." In some instances the ships' livestock escaped their intended fate because passengers and crew made pets of them and could not bring themselves to lead them to slaughter. A passenger on the *Canton*, writing in October 1849, presents this amiable picture: "It is a curious thing, but . . . all kinds of animals seem to take a liking to me. The unwieldy terrapin [picked up off the South American coast], as much as I can lift, is at this moment creeping around my feet. The pet pig follows me like a dog, and the two dogs are always about. . . ."

But it was to the sea itself that the voyagers looked most frequently for means of varying their diet. Except when bad weather kept the passengers below decks a few fishermen could be seen on every ship, attending their lines hour after hour with the patient optimism common to their kind the world over. Their success was usually small; few succeeded in drawing fish in quantity from the uncooperative depths. The sea journals abound in such entries as this: "Caught a red snapper which weighed ten pounds.

116

You bet it tasted good but it was only a taste for forty hungry men." Occasionally, however, good fishing was encountered, and when this happened the excitement was high. Benjamin Dore of the *Cantero* tells of sailing through an area so full of bonitas (which Dore called "bone eaters") that "the water was black with them as far as the eye could see." But the fish refused to take the bait offered, and attempts to spear them were hardly more successful; after hours of effort only two, both small, had been hauled aboard.

Larger than the "bone eaters" but not less elusive were the dolphins, schools of which were encountered on virtually every voyage. Fast and graceful, they were the source of endless interest. "When caught and lying in the sun," wrote one observer, "the colors of its skin are changeable violett green, yellow, blue, orange, and red; it is the marine chameleon." But the dolphin was as wary as it was beautiful, The one way to capture it was by using an instrumen. having barbed iron prongs set into the end of a pole, not unlike a whaler's harpoon. But the dolphin's fleetness made it a difficult target even for men skilled in the use of the spears. Porpoises were hunted by the same method, and usually with more success. "Saturday evening a porpoise was speared," wrote John Linville Hall, "and was served up for breakfast the next morning; the flavor and appearance were very much like venison." Later, after a second porpoise breakfast, Hall decided that its taste more closely resembled beefsteak. A related variety of fish was described by Richard Hale on the *General Worth:* "This afternoon passed through large schools of cowfish, a warm-blooded, air-breathing animal, much resembling a porpoise, but considerably larger. The ocean seemed alive with them.

Thousands, perhaps tens of thousands, sported as we passed, apparently wholly unconscious of the enemy in their midst." The ship's captain, an ex-whaler, took up a position in the bobstay and succeeded in harpooning "a huge fellow, eight feet six inches long, weighing at least four hundred pounds." During the next few days the *General Worth's* company enjoyed a welcome change from their regular diet.

Even shark meat was not disdained; the secret, it was explained, was to catch young ones, not over three feet long; the larger ones were tough and oily. Captain Coffin contended that half-grown sharks were a delicacy, tender, juicy, and sweet, and when a passenger exclaimed with distaste: "What! Eat a shark!" the captain retorted: "And why not? If I should fall overboard, they would not hesitate to eat me." The shark is a born scavenger, and in certain latitudes most ships were attended by one or more of the creatures, which circled endlessly about, hungrily consuming whatever was tossed overboard. Such was the boredom on the *General Worth* that Captain Coffin, observing a large and voracious specimen following the ship, prepared an unwelcome surprise for him:

"I had a shin bone of beef boiled as hot as fire could make it, and watching a chance when he was close under the stern, let it down by a rope-yarn. The shark saw it coming, and swallowed it without stopping to consider whether it was good to digest. He found it a bit more than he bargained for. . . . He leaped his whole length, fifteen feet, out of the water and started off with the speed of a locomotive, and the last we saw of him, he was leaping . . . in a direct line for the coast of Africa."

Not only water but sky was scanned in the Argonauts'

search for whatever might lend variety to their daily fare. As the ships entered the waters off the Horn, nearly all encountered the fabled albatross, and since this clumsy bird could easily be captured by baiting a hook and throwing it overboard, there were few vessels that did not haul a few specimens over the side. The creatures aroused great interest, particularly because of their size—many measured more than a dozen feet from wing tip to wing tip—but all attempts to eat them ended in defeat; no amount of boiling and seasoning could make the tough, rank flesh palatable. Quite different was another species of bird encountered in the same latitudes. This was the Cape pigeon, a plump, flavorsome bird that sometimes circled about in immense flocks and could be caught, like the albatross, with hook and line, baited with a piece of pork. The capture of a bag of Cape pigeons was sufficient to inspire even the dullest diarist to flights of epicurean eloquence. Pigeon pie, properly cooked, was pronounced "better than chicken"; but there was a trick to preparing it, and not every sea-cook knew the secret. Thus one Argonaut who had heard much of its pleasures was keenly disappointed when the looked-for treat was set before him. He complained bitterly that the careless cook had "failed to neutralize the abominable rankness of the flesh."

There was, in fact, a special culinary technique in the preparation of such fish-eating animals and fowls, and fortunate was the ship that had in its galley one versed in its mysteries. The *Samson*, a 500-ton schooner that sailed from Philadelphia in October 1849, was one of the fortunate ships. The historian of the voyage, E. I. Barra, described with a gourmet's relish various treats provided by the *Samson's* accomplished cook; moreover, Barra was care-

ful to explain exactly how each delicacy had been prepared. Toward the end of November the skipper harpooned
a four-hundred-pound porpoise. As soon as it had been
hoisted on deck the captain ordered a special treat for the
vessel's eight women passengers. "The monster was immediately opened and its liver taken out. . . . The cook
cut the liver into slices and washed it in salt and water,
after which he wiped it dry, dredged it with dry flour and
fried it with slices of bacon." The odor of frying liver and
bacon that issued from the galley permeated the ship,
stimulating the salivary glands of everyone on board, and
the fortunate lady diners pronounced it "the most delicious
morsel they had eaten in many a day."

Barra continues:

"Then the body of the porpoise was stripped of the
blubber, which was tried out for oil for the forecastle lamps,
and the meat was cut in strips, parboiled in salt and water
and wiped dry. After this it was mixed with a small portion
of salt pork and chopped fine. It was then seasoned with
dried sage and summer savory, pepper and salt, and rolled
into small balls, covered with dry flour, and then fried in a
pan of hot fat, and served piping hot. It must be said that
to us it tasted as palatable as a dish of Fulton market
sausage meat ever tasted to us in New York. . . . The
French passengers were so well pleased that one of them
sent a bottle of brandy . . . to Amaziah as a reward for
his prowess."

Several weeks later the *Samson's* captain succeeded in
landing a five-foot dolphin. This time, however, the passengers' hopes of another gastronomic treat went un-
realized.

"The captain ordered the cook to fry it. He handed him a silver half dollar piece and told him to let it remain in the frying-pan while the fish was cooking. . . . After the fish was fried the cook returned the half dollar to the captain, and it had become as black as a piece of coal. The captain became convinced that the fish was poisonous, and ordered it to be thrown overboard. . . ."

Captain Blanchard, the *Samson's* all-knowing skipper, explained that the bottom of the ocean over which they were passing contained a great deal of copper, and that the seaweed on which the dolphin fed had become impregnated with verdigris given off by the copper ore, thus rendering the flesh poisonous. Whether or not this theory had any scientific basis the *Samson's* passengers had no means of knowing.

Lobscouse, a sort of generic term for stew, was a mainstay on all the gold ships, being served at least once a day. But its quality varied widely, depending on the skill of the cook and the number and condition of the ingredients on hand. Here is Barra's version of the proper way to prepare it:

". . . one onion cut and put into a gallon of water, a dozen potatoes peeled and cut into quarters, four cakes of navy bread soaked and broken up. Boil for half an hour. Cut up salt pork into small square pieces equal to one third of the whole mass, and boil all again for half an hour. Then add pepper to taste, and add, when it is about to be taken up, a half cupful of thickening."

This writer adds that in the cold weather of the southern latitudes this was a dish "fit for the Gods."

There were other Barra recipes; one was for sea pie:

"A sea pie consists of onions fried brown, lean pork cut in small pieces, potatoes cut in quarters, and then all simmered together; then make dough enough to cover the sides of the baking pan . . . and put in the filling of stew, season with tomato ketchup and pepper, sprinkle in a little flour to thicken it, and cover the pan with a thick crust and put it in the oven for two hours."

The proper course to follow lobscouse or sea pie, writes this authority, is a sweet, either plum duff or dandyfunk. He tells how to prepare both:

"Dandyfunk is a dish composed of navy biscuit soaked in water, mashed with a pestle, mixed with fat taken from the coppers in which the meat is boiled, sweetened with molasses and flavored with allspice, then put into a pan and baked in the oven. It isn't a very high-toned dish, but in the absence of something better is very palatable to a sailor."

Plum duff, a more elaborate confection, was made thus on board the *Samson:*

"The duff is composed of flour, lard, raisins and saleratus, with eggs mixed in when they can be had. When well mixed it is put into a canvas bag, wide at the top and very narrow at the bottom, boiled for two hours and then turned out into a platter and served with wine sauce when it can be had, or else with vinegar, butter, sugar and water boiled well together and thickened with flour and flavored with nutmeg."

Still another dessert highly regarded on the gold ships was mince turnover, made with salt beef, dried apples, allspice, and molasses, wrapped in dough, boiled in a pan of fat until brown, and served steaming hot.

Having negotiated the Horn, the long trip up the west coast was sometimes broken by a stop at one or another of the remote offshore islands, and when this happened the passengers made the most of another gastronomic treat: tortoises. The *Canton* stopped at Chatham Island, one of the Galapagos group, and it was not long before the deck of the bark was crowded with the great creatures—"we have about sixty on board, many of them all that two men can lift." The sea turtles were easily caught, for about midday they came up on the beaches to sleep. One had but to turn them over on their backs, where they lay helpless until their captors were ready to carry them on board. Terrapin, known to the Argonauts as land turtles, were more difficult to procure, for this species was to be found only several miles inland (it being their breeding season during the visit of the *Canton*), and their great weight made carrying them to the ship a wearisome task. Their tender and delicately flavored meat, however, was pronounced worth almost any effort. But even terrapin lost its allure when it was served too often. "Unhappily, nothing now is put on the table but turtle for breakfast and dinner every day," wrote Joseph Kendall. "The fact is that I am not very partial to it as it is served. If I could get good catsup and port wine I could make a glorious dish, fit for anyone. . . ."

Considering the length of the round-the-Horn voyage and the overcrowded condition of the ships, the Argonauts in general fared reasonably well. There were occasional cases of genuine hardship, and rather more where a shortage of food or water put the companies on short rations for periods that varied from a few days to several weeks. Inconvenience rather than actual want was the lot of most, and this was usually unavoidable. The cooks, laboring in tiny cramped galleys that were stiflingly hot during the passage of the tropics, or struggling to keep their wood or coal fires burning during the icy storms of the antarctic, somehow managed to allay the voracious appetites of all on board, and if their offerings were not invariably appetizing, at least they served to sustain life, and few records exist of gold-hunters perishing of malnutrition. Unquestionably the food was often lacking in variety and sometimes in quantity, but the passengers led inactive lives and a slender diet was probably more healthful than an over-bountiful one. Few of the miners bore out the promise the *Samson's* Captain Blanchard made a prospective passenger on the dock at Philadelphia: "Why, sir, by the time that we arrive in California, in place of being as lean as a dolphin, as you are now, you'll be as fat as a porpoise." On the other hand, most emigrants landed in San Francisco in good health and spirits and in better physical condition than when they had embarked. After four months at sea a member of the *Cantero's* company wrote: "I think we are the helthyest crew I have seen since we left Bangor, all hearty and rugged. I have gained 9 pounds . . . seven from St. Catherine's. My weight is now the heavyest I ever have bin & several have gained much more than I have. . . ." Another took the philosophic view that the austerities of the voyage would stand them in good stead by preparing them for the privations of life in the gold fields. "I believe after we land we shall be able to eat and drink anything."

Chapter Three: STOPS ASHORE

1

THE voyage from east-coast ports to San Francisco via Cape Horn was so long that all but a few of the ships had to make at least two intermediate stops to replenish supplies of food and water and to make needed repairs. The favorite ports of call were Rio de Janeiro, just below the great bulge of Brazil, and Valparaiso, about midway on the long coastline of Chile. These, however, were by no means the only stopping-places. Some ships put in at Havana, but this was mainly to take on cargoes of sugar, molasses, or rum that the owners, or the trading companies that had the crafts under charter, hoped to sell profitably in California.

Most Argonauts made their first contact with foreign soil in Brazil, either at Rio or on the island of St. Catherine's. Many skippers preferred St. Catherine's, which had long been a stopping-place for American whalers and which had a good harbor, excellent water, and ample supplies of wood and fruit. Moreover, it was more nearly on their course than Rio and promised less delay than they were likely to encounter in that crowded harbor. Finally, and perhaps most important, government regulations were laxly enforced on the island and it was often possible for a foreign ship, by offering proper inducements to the port officials, to pay far less in harbor fees than would have been collected at Rio.

After five or six weeks at sea the northerners commonly found their first sight of this tropical island picturesque in the extreme. "St. Catherine's," wrote Richard Hale, "presents a very lovely picture . . . its high peaked rocks, its tree covered mountains, make a beautiful picture from the deck of the brig. . . . The surrounding views of scattered isles dotting the blue waters, with villages of shining white houses on the crescent shaped shores . . . presented a scene long to be remembered—a paradisian hiding place."

Closer acquaintance, however, usually tempered the enthusiasm of the newcomers. The town was small, with little to offer in the way of amusements. Houses that had appeared picturesque when viewed across an expanse of blue water proved to be ramshackle adobes, overcrowded, evil-smelling, and squalid. "The streets," wrote one disillusioned visitor, "are dirty, crooked and do not speak highly of the sanitary officers' attention." The inhabitants— Spaniards, Portuguese, Negroes, or a mixture of all three— seemed to the brisk northerners a deplorably unenterprising lot. They were not long in discovering, however, that these unprepossessing natives were crafty traders. The appearance of a ship off the roadstead was a signal for a numerous crew of peddlers, "swarthy, fierce-looking men in huge straw hats and not much else," to put off from the beach in small boats, converging on the newcomer like a fleet of pirates. Their frail crafts were loaded with oranges, bananas, limes, plantains, guavas, and other exotic fruits, which they proceeded to offer at extremely high prices. Later, the first keen edge taken off their appetites, the bargaining instincts of the Yankees came to the fore, and this, aided by competition between rival peddlers, sent prices tumbling. One New Englander, having delayed making his purchases during the first ten minutes of trading, ended by buying a basket containing a hundred large oranges for the equivalent of ten cents. His more impetuous fellows had paid a like sum for a mere half dozen.

During the height of the California rush St. Catherine's was overrun with Yankees. When the *Cantero* dropped anchor there in December 1849, there were eleven other vessels in the harbor, all flying the American flag and all but two bound for the gold fields. Numerous small boats shuttled between the ships and the beach, loaded with young men who after weeks of confinement were full of high spirits and avid for excitement. Naïve and curious, they engulfed the town, crowded the stores and restaurants, and took long tramps into the countryside, where they marveled at rank tropical growth, so different from the austere hills of home. Of course they found little of which they approved. Having observed the inhabitants at their work and play and compared their primitive, easygoing ways with the energy and bustle of the home folks, with characteristic Yankee brashness they concluded that this indolent race could teach them nothing. The narrow streets were in bad repair and littered with rubbish. In the country, roads were deplorable, little more than trails, full of ruts and mudholes. There were few wagons and fewer carriages; some rode horseback, but the majority walked, and most goods were carried by slaves. The northerners were fascinated by the enormous loads these stalwart blacks supported as they swung along the rough trails of the back country, and by the Negro women who moved with unconcern through the crowded streets with heavily laden trays, three feet wide, balanced on their heads. The houses had no glass in their windows, a gate served as a door, and few of the rooms had wooden floors.

But if the natives were lax and unenterprising, nature herself was prodigal. Benjamin Dore, fresh from the stony, uncooperative fields of his native Maine, reported:

"Everything grows spontaniously such as pineapples oranges lemons figs grapes peaches bananers water melons onions sweet potatoes rice coffee corn cucmbers potatoes &c. with but little cultivation they live very easy but a very little intelligence or enterprize about them a man that is worth four or five thousand dollars is thought to be very rich. the most of the rich ones have slaves to work for them all most one half of the people is black. . . ."

In general the visitors were well behaved, but their delight at finding themselves on land, in a country foreign to anything they had experienced, was such that their exuberance sometimes got out of hand. Some were reluctant to go back to their ships at all the first night ashore. Dore, who had returned to the *Cantero* at ten and "retired to rest." complained in his journal: "I was waked in the night by singing and holering of the yankees for there was a great many of them in the city. . . ." The next night, however, Dore himself was among the noise-makers: "in the evening 2 boat loads of us went ashore with musick called at an englishmans house and stopped a few moments from there we marched about 1 mile down the shore to a place called the widows where found several boat crews dancing and running around on the beach . . . it was a place for refreshments and mareners home. . . ."

Not all the noise was due to simple high spirits. The shops purveyed a cheap and potent aguardiente, "two drinks of which sufficed to paralyze the unwary," and drunkenness among the visitors was reported by most diarists. When there were clashes between Yankees and local authorities, alcohol was usually to blame. Another source of friction was the Americans' ignorance of the customs of the country and their habit of regarding as reprehensible whatever differed from the usages at home. Much was written about the Latin American's habit of naming an exorbitant price for whatever he had to sell in the expectation that the buyer would make his offering price correspondingly low, the deal being consummated after a prolonged and mutually enjoyable period of haggling. Unacquainted with this tradition, the northerner either paid the asking price or stalked angrily out of the shop; in either case he left with the conviction that all South American merchants were rascals.

One group of Americans were so incensed at a bill tendered them in a St. Catherine's restaurant that they not only refused to pay but set to and wrecked the place. The owner complained to the authorities, who placed an armed guard on the ship and refused to allow her to sail until the damage had been paid for. More serious fracases happened while the *General Worth* was in port. One of the town's few attractions was an ancient fort guarding the harbor's entrance. One day a group of young men from the ship and from the schooner *Frances*, anchored near by, set off in a whaleboat to explore the spot. Their exploit taught them something of the delicacy of Latin sensibilities. As they drew near the fort a sentry sternly ordered them to halt. "At the same time he commanded us not to land, with his musket levelled at our crew, while a cannon was quickly wheeled to rake us if so ordered." The sightseers hastily withdrew, "but we gave them, while retreating, a lively serenade of tunes . . . Yankee Doodle, Hail, Columbia, etc. . . ."

The sightseers were unprepared for the result of their frolic. The *General Worth's* captain lined them up on deck and read them a stern lecture, liberally mixed with profanity. "Trying to visit a foreign fort without the permit of its government, were you?—playing foreign national airs to aggravate the officers for honestly doing their duty, were you?—which, by God, they have neglected by sparing you." Convinced by now that they had committed a serious breach of international etiquette, the group was further alarmed when an hour later a boatload of soldiers bore down on the *General Worth* and the captain of the port climbed aboard. He was a "nervous, irritable old hombre, quite small in stature, almost hidden in lace and epaulets, with a big, shaggy white mustache covering his mouth that seemed to keep time to the constant twitching of his dark, angry face and fierce, glittering eyes." While the culprits looked on uneasily, the *Worth's* skipper greeted this dignitary with deference and agreed that the offense to the dignity of Brazil had been enormous and unpardonable and that the perpetrators must be suitably punished. After ten minutes of apologies, interspersed with flattery, the official condescended to forgive the transgression. "He seized the captain's hand, shaking it warmly and . . . with a glance at us that would have destroyed us if it had been a dagger, took his departure."

For all his magnificence, the little commandante of the port was not St. Catherine's most picturesque figure; that honor belonged to a huge ex-sailor, a native of Maryland, who had appeared at the island years before and by a combination of energy, bluster, and push had made himself a figure of consequence. The journals of nearly every gold ship that touched at St. Catherine's make at least a passing reference to him, and in time he became a legendary figure to the '49ers. T. Robinson Warren, whose ship put into the harbor late in 1849, thus describes his first sight of this Yankee adventurer: "Shooting down under the shore of the mainland came a six oared whale boat, pulled by Negroes. In a moment she was alongside, and from the sternsheets a burly, sailor looking man jumped aboard, noisily announcing himself in a breath as a pilot and as our countryman." It was said that he first appeared at St. Catherine's in the late 1820's as master of a whaler, that he became enamored of the beauties of the place, "but more particularly of one of its dark-eyed daughters," and, having decided to stay, sold the vessel and with the proceeds— which he neglected to transmit to the owners—bought the plantation on which he lived. Whether or not this version of his coming to the island is accurate, his subsequent history was known to all. "By his Yankee energy and knowledge of the world," continues Warren, "he has gained a great ascendancy over the simple people among whom he lives, and in matters nautical is the oracle of the province. . . . He holds the responsible position of pilot, and at the same time is agent for the American consul . . . a glorious representative of the first maritime nation in the world."

2

Not St. Catherine's but Rio was the first port of call for most of the gold ships. That renowned harbor vastly impressed the northerners, and the writers of scores of diaries marshaled their adjectives to describe its beauties. "Our attention was drawn first to the high, fantastic and abrupt peaks of Gavia, Corcovado and the Sugar Loaf on the left," wrote John Linville Hall. "On the right, is the bold prominence of Santa Cruz—a fortress whose massive foundation was laid by the hand of nature, which it challenges the world to overthrow. . . ." As the ships passed close under the guns of Santa Cruz the harbor itself came into view. "Before us lies the city of Rio Janeiro," continued the *Henry Lee's* scribe, "and the towns of San Gomingo and Preia Grande opposite; the beautiful expanse of water, decked here and there with islands . . . create an enchanting picture." Some were struck by the difference between this magnificent port and the battered little ships that had carried them so far. E. I. Barra, having "cast my eyes toward the beautiful harbor before us," was aware of a vast contrast "as I looked around upon our leaky ship, short of provisions, short of water. . . ."

Landing at Rio was attended by more formality than at St. Catherine's. No one was allowed to board the incoming ship or leave her until she had passed inspection by two groups of Brazilian officials, representing the board of health and the customs service. But once these formalities were over, the bars were let down and a whole fleet of small boats drew alongside. Soon the deck was crowded with visitors, all on urgent business: reporters for Rio newspapers, seeking details of the voyage and news of the outer world, agents for local business firms, many of them American-owned, soliciting trade and offering advice—which was not always disinterested—on what shops, hotels, and restaurants to patronize.

Passengers were not permitted to disembark the first night in port; instead they lined the rails for hours, drinking in sounds and sights that had grown curiously unreal after the vast emptiness of the sea, listening to the city's multitudinous church bells, watching the lights outlining the crescent-shaped shoreline; and presently growing aware of the descent of quiet as the city composed itself for sleep and the medley of sounds were hushed—"excepting the hailing of some recreant boat from the guard-ship naught disturbed the silence which wrapt all things near and far."

A large city even in gold-rush times, Rio was not overrun with Yankees as were the smaller South American ports. But the gold-hunters were numerous enough, and noisy enough, to make their presence felt. In the first three months of 1849 eighty-six California-bound ships put into the harbor; sometimes a dozen arrived in a single day, bearing as many as a thousand passengers. "A large number, you think," commented John Linville Hall, "to pour into the streets of a town in a single day. But the number were nothing in so populous a city as Rio, if the persons in question were orderly disposed." According to this authority, it was not how numerous the North American visitors were, but their bad manners that caused trouble. After admitting that there were some who conducted themselves like gentlemen, he continued:

133

"But we fear so much cannot be said of the California emigrants generally. We know they had been in a high and unnatural state of excitement before leaving home; perchance they have had a long and rough passage by sea, with cramped quarters and rough fare; and making due allowance also for the natural ebullition of spirits on coming to port; yet after all the allowance which the liberal would make, there is still left a score of riot, excess and rowdyism to be acknowledged which ill becomes the American character. Many a Californian has had the pleasure of passing a night in the calaboose in payment of trenching on the public quiet. Some, for crimes of a more serious nature, have been sentenced to the penitentiary for a period of years."

In Hall's view, the visitors made a sorry showing as compared with the Brazilians. "Not a citizen or slave did we see intoxicated . . . or in any way riotous during the week's time we were in port; on the contrary, the inhabitants seemed quietly attentive to their own business—courteous to their foreign guests—and indeed wonderfully forebearing of their follies. . . ."

In general the Yankees were favorably impressed with Rio, and even those who permitted their exuberance to get out of hand had only praise for the hospitality of the citizens. Public buildings, churches, and gardens were opened to them, and the visitors found many of these superior to anything they had known at home. To the northerners the climate, "seldom very hot or very dry, never cold," seemed ideal, and the luxuriant vegetation, the variety and beauty of the flowers and shrubs, aroused their unstinted admiration. "With these natural facilities they seem cheerfully to devote time and expense to adorning their grounds with everything that is lovely to the eye, or delicious to the taste and smell." In particular the botanical gardens in the suburbs, extensive and beautifully kept, delighted the visitors. "No obstruction was offered us in rambling freely over this wide area of rich cultivation; indeed a guide who spoke our language kindly attended us . . . giving us explanations of flowers, or fruits, as we might desire, and all, un-Yankee-like, gratis."

But unalloyed praise was not habitual to the strongly nationalistic visitors. Having paid tribute to the courtesy of the Brazilians, the magnificence of their public buildings, and the area's natural beauties, the diarists proceeded to expose the other side of the shield. One, having devoted several pages to describing the beauty of the city's public and private gardens, was constrained to add: "While we readily concede that the taste and skill of the Brazilian exceed ours in this particular department, yet, in respect to all the great purposes of life, we must think the scale is decidedly in our favor. Nay, we go further; we believe that in agriculture, commerce and invention, indeed in every branch of useful industry, they are, at least, fifty years behind the age."

One of the black marks against the land, in the opinion of those from the abolitionist strongholds at home, was the open trading in slaves to be seen both at Preia Grande across the harbor (where the slave schooners from Africa deposited their human cargoes) and in the great central market in Rio itself. "Here," wrote E. I. Barra, "were offered strong men, robust women and children, for sale the same as donkeys and goats. Some of those offered for sale were not more than four months from their native land—Africa. There they were offered on the altar of mammon—all for glittering gold." Curiously, some of the Argonauts were less repelled by this traffic than by the Brazilians' immense enthusiasm for bull fights; those who out of curiosity viewed one of these spectacles commonly recorded their shocked revulsion at the sport.

One Yankee, L. M. Schaeffer, fresh from a Maryland farm, who reached Rio early in 1849 on the *Flavius*, found nothing at all of which he approved. His unfavorable impressions began even before the whaleboat reached shore; the native oarsmen, he observed, did not know how to handle their craft, and the appearance of the crowd gathered at the dock confirmed his worst suspicions: "A more filthy, sickly, trifling set of beings . . . I have never seen before or since, nor desire to see." He went to a hotel and discovered that although the owner was a New Yorker the accommodations were "miserable." The Emperor's chapel stood near by—"it did not compare with the Baltimore exchange." Other features of the city did not alter his conviction that all things were ordered better in Yankeeland. The houses had not proper cellars, the gutters were in the middle of the streets (obviously the wrong place for them), and the streets themselves "need very much the attention of a sweeper." Schaeffer visited the navy yard, and of course found it vastly inferior to those of home. One warship was on the stocks, "but I should suppose, by the time it was finished, the wood would be pretty much decayed." Water for household use had to be drawn from public wells, "hydrants and pipes being unknown to the Brazilians." Slavery naturally received his attention; these "poor degraded blacks" took the place of drays, and were driven so hard by their masters that "about seven years finishes them entirely." He granted that the central market was large and reasonably clean, but the meat looked to him like horseflesh and it was inexpertly cut. "They want a Yankee butcher among them." "On the whole," concluded this censorious visitor, "Rio is not a desirable place of residence." He returned to the *Flavius* rejoicing at the privilege of "again treading the deck of an American vessel"—the perfect symbol of rampant Americanism.

Notwithstanding their impatience to reach California few begrudged the time spent in Rio, for the opportunity to explore the city, to sample its food and drink and revel in the freedom of life ashore was welcome after so many weeks at sea. Their stay commonly lasted about ten days, while supplies were replenished, minor repairs undertaken, and other preparations made for the next leg of the journey, this one including the hazardous passage of the Horn. As the time of departure drew near, the Californians busied themselves with their individual preparations, laying in fresh fruit, wine, and other products as insurance against the monotony of the ship's fare, writing last-minute letters and depositing them on some vessel about to sail for home, providing themselves with bottles of the potent Brazilian aguardiente, and on the final night in port staying late on shore to enjoy their last contacts with urban life.

These farewell revels were sometimes conducted with so much zeal as to get the participants in serious trouble. The hour of sailing was fixed to take advantage of the outgoing tide, and those not aboard at the specified time were unceremoniously left behind. To be stranded in a foreign city with all one's friends and possessions standing out to sea was of course an unenviable situation, even though the victims had only themselves to blame. But some found themselves thus abandoned through no fault of their own. It is of record that some shipmasters were not averse to slipping away before the announced time, knowing that fewer mouths to feed would favorably affect the profits of the voyage, and aware too that it would be possible to take on other passengers (at the currently high fares) at the next port of call. Thus at Rio and elsewhere there were left stranded "many an unwary passenger, who, without money or baggage, is left to such comfort ashore as the gloomy circumstances may afterwards unfold."

3

USUALLY the abandoned ones had no recourse but to hunt up the American consul, thus adding to the problems of that already overburdened official. For through all of 1849 and most of 1850 the nation's consulates in half a dozen South American ports were thronged with citizens bearing grievances of one sort or another. Many of their complaints were trivial, or outside the jurisdiction of the officials; such visitors were told to compose their own differences or, if this failed, to leave the ship and take passage on another. There was in fact a considerable amount of shifting from vessel to vessel at each port, although it does not appear that many benefited by the change: the passenger who found conditions unbearable on one ship was unlikely to be long content on the next.

But of course not all the grievances laid before the consuls were those of chronic complainers. On certain of the gold ships passengers were imposed on by rapacious owners

and had their lives endangered by unseaworthy vessels
or incompetent skippers. When delegations appeared at
the consulates with legitimate complaints the officials were
often able to bring about their correction, for they had
authority to fine an owner, or to discipline a captain who
had overreached himself, even in extreme cases to relieve
him of his command. This drastic step was taken in the
case of the master of the *Pacific*, which reached Rio in
March 1849 after an eventful and uncommonly contentious
voyage from New York.

The *Pacific* was one of those ships on which, as one of its
unhappy passengers wrote, "anything might happen and
usually did." The latest of its adventures had taken place
while it was entering the harbor at Rio. This was a short
and inconclusive engagement—unrecorded in histories of
naval battles—between the ship and an unnamed German
gunboat. Dr. J. D. B. Stillman, historian of the cruise, thus
describes the encounter:

"Early this morning we found ourselves close in and
running up the lower bay. Met a Prussian gun-brig, beating out. We were before the wind, and should have given
way to the brig. The vessels were approaching—the brig
hailed us twice. Our Captain made no reply, but held on
his course and down came the brig upon us—both vessels
rolling in the heavy swells that were coming in from the
sea; a collision was imminent. The flying jib-boom of the
Prussian made a complete circuit of our starboard quarter, and caught our flag hanging at the spanker gaff. Mr.
Packard [the mate] made an attempt to save it, but it was
beyond his reach, and, leaning over, he caught from the
jolly-boat under our stern a white utensil indispensable to a

chamber set, and which was placed there with others for safety, and, swinging it with all the vigor of his powerful arm, he sent it careening through the air like a bombshell; striking the foresail, it fell in a thousand pieces on the deck of the man-of-war. In an instant, up went our lost ensign, under the Prussian flag, with three cheers from the enemy."

Enraged at the affront, and forgetting that their skipper had been in the wrong in the first place, the passengers demanded that the *Pacific* run alongside the Prussian while they boarded her and recovered the lost flag. This Captain Tibbets prudently refused to do, and the two vessels were soon out of hearing of the abuse being shouted back and forth. The Americans swallowed their chagrin and made plans to reward the chamber-throwing mate when they reached port. It was decided to present him with a vase "of peculiar shape" in honor of his exploit, and to have engraved thereon his family crest.

This comic-opera encounter with the gunboat, however, was not the only concern of the *Pacific's* passengers when the vessel touched Rio; the ship's company had been embroiled in violent quarrels from the very beginning of the voyage. The source of the trouble lay, as on so many other California-bound vessels, in the quality of the food and the manner of its preparation and serving. When repeated complaints to Captain Tibbets and a Mr. Griffin—joint owners of the craft—proved unavailing, the atmosphere grew steadily more explosive. Dr. Stillman, later a prominent physician in San Francisco, and the spokesman for the group, wrote on March 2: "The general temper of the passengers is mutinous and there is danger of violence on slight provocation." He continued: "We paid $300, each, for our passage; by our agreement, we were to have good cabin fare, to eat at the same table with the owners and their families. Instead of this, we were herded together like a mass of convicts, damned and abused from one side of the ship to the other. . . ." Captain Tibbets's despotism, his brutal treatment of his crew, and his callous disregard for the welfare of his passengers were such that the entire company reached Rio determined to square accounts with him.

Dr. Stillman relates the steps by which they went about getting their revenge. "For several days," he wrote on March 19, "my time has been spent . . . trying to have our grievances against Captain Tibbets redressed. We found Lieutenant Bartlett in command of the *Ewing* [a gunboat] here, and he has taken an active interest in our cause. We filed a complaint with our consul, Mr. Gordon Parks, and our minister, Mr. Todd." A hearing was held at the consulate, at which the captain proved conciliatory, affably agreeing to undertake whatever reforms the passengers demanded. An agreement was drawn up, which Tibbets promised to sign the next morning. The committee departed, thinking their troubles over. But that night word reached them at their hotel—they were stopping ashore while their differences were adjusted—that the *Pacific* had got clearance papers and that Captain Tibbets was preparing to sail, leaving his critics behind.

Faced by this emergency, Stillman and his cohorts spent an active night. First they drove to the house of the consul, who lived in the suburbs. They arrived at midnight. "He put a bottle of wine before us and told us that, under the representations of the captain, he had cleared the ship." After some persuasion, however, he was prevailed to take action; the group left bearing an order addressed to one of the Emperor's chamberlains, urging him to use every effort to stop the ship, "even if he had to blow her out of the water." Armed with this, the group hurried to the house of the Brazilian nobleman, aroused the porter, and, again after a lengthy argument, were admitted. That official read Consul Parks's letter and, sitting down at his desk, wrote an order that he instructed his visitors to carry to the commander of a fort guarding the entrance to the harbor. Once more their coach clattered through the streets of the sleeping city. At the waterfront Stillman and his companions aroused a boatsman, hired his craft, and rowed to the fort. There they aroused the commander, delivered the chamberlain's order, and had the satisfaction of seeing an orderly dispatched with instructions to see that the *Pacific* was not allowed to pass. "Having accomplished this," wrote Dr. Stillman, "we returned to our hotel, well satisfied that if the ship *Pacific* attempted to put to sea . . . it would be well for us that we were not aboard."

But this by no means ended the matter. Next day the skipper appeared in the consul's office, where he cheerfully greeted the passengers' committee, blandly denied that he had had any thought of leaving them behind, and suggested that they sign the agreement drawn up the day before. By then, however, Stillman's group had had enough of the affable captain. "The committee . . . resolved to abandon the compromise and make the attempt to remove him from command. . . . The ship is under arrest and the trial comes off next Monday. . . ." But events proved that the beleaguered captain was not at the end of his resources. In the interval he cultivated the goodwill of those on board the *Pacific* to such good effect that when the hearing opened

142

he presented a resolution signed by some forty of the passengers protesting against his removal. When Stillman pointed out that virtually all those signing had earlier signed a petition demanding his removal, the consul refused to attach any weight to the document, whereupon Captain Tibbets threatened to dismantle the ship and abandon the voyage. Unimpressed by this threat, the consul ended the matter by directing that Captain Tibbets be removed from his command. This decision was of course an immense relief to the committee members, who foresaw that they would fare badly indeed if they had to put to sea again in a ship commanded by their enemy. On March 27 the consul came on board with their new skipper, a Captain Estherbrook, and, by Dr. Stillman's account, during the remainder of the voyage the *Pacific* lived up to her name.

4

THE Argonauts' impatience to reach the gold fields was such that they begrudged every hour lost at intermediate ports, even though they realized that on a voyage of such length one or two stops could not be avoided. It is significant, however, that while many regretted the time spent at Rio or St. Catherine's, all welcomed the prospect of a second stop, this time on the Pacific side of the continent. Perhaps the reason was that the second lap of their journey had included the tedious passage of Cape Horn, and the knowledge that this ordeal was safely behind put entire ships' companies in a mood for celebration. At any rate, as they sailed toward Talcahuano and Valparaiso the pages of their diaries usually reflected the holiday spirit in which the Yankees prepared to scramble ashore.

"We landed at Talcahuano, the port of Concepcion, and here I am and it is great country!" wrote one of the young men on the *Leonore*, who went on to describe the attractions of the seacoast settlement, remote and primitive and over-run with Americans. "About a hundred of us ride around on donkeys, and go to bullfights, cockfights, and fandangos. You bet the girls are good looking!"

Talcahuano lay two hundred miles south of Valparaiso; its harbor was adequate and its setting picturesque; it was surrounded by high hills covered with thick forests, a welcome sight after the snowy desolation farther south. "Some of the trees have a shade of light green, reminding us of fields of wheat in Maine," wrote J. Lamson, whose ship dropped anchor there in July 1849. The town itself, at the head of a long bay, seemed from a distance a spot of extraordinary attraction, its white walls and tiled roofs rising steeply upward from the water's edge. But here again closer acquaintance brought disillusion. Lamson continues:

"A number of Chilean boats drew alongside. . . . We speedily filled them, all of us eager to land, our curiosity being highly excited in anticipation of the new and strange things we were about to behold in this pretty town. Judge then of my disappointment when on landing I found my-self in the most filthy and disgusting village I ever beheld. A row of ill-looking houses, huts and shops stretched along the bay for nearly a mile. Three very narrow, parallel streets ran the length of the village, and were crossed at right angles by other streets still narrower, and all filled with mud and filth. . . ."

Stops Ashore

Talcahuano, in short, was typical of all remote seaport towns during the middle of the last century. It had both the vices and the vigor of the frontier, a curious combination of primitive outpost and cosmopolitan trading center. Most inhabitants lived in "little mud huts made of stakes driven into the ground, interwoven with twigs, and plastered over with mud," yet the bay shore was lined with substantial business houses, their storerooms piled high with the products of the country awaiting export and with goods brought in from the world's markets. The owners and managers of these businesses (mostly foreigners, many of them Americans) had large and comfortable houses on the hillsides above.

By the middle of 1849 the heavy California traffic had already given the town a distinctly American flavor. Those newly arrived were impressed by a profusion of signs designed to attract the custom of the Yankees. During a short walk along the waterfront one visitor observed the California Hotel, American Hotel, American House, New Bedford House, New York Restaurant, Eagle Hotel, and others. Some of these establishments had been in existence before the gold-rush traffic began, for Talcahuano had long been a port of call for American whalers. But few of the places lived up to the promise of their names. "I went into several," wrote J. Lamson, "and found them so excessively filthy that despite the keenness of my appetite I could not eat, and made up my mind to go back to the dirty little bark for my dinner." Not all the visitors were so squeamish, however—or perhaps they had better luck in their choice of eating-places. Another emigrant describes a veritable banquet he and his party enjoyed at the Tremont House, operated by a Yankee sea captain and his Chilean

145

wife, which consisted of "macaroni soup, roast beef, roast wild duck, corned boiled beef, potatoes, beets, squash, bread, pudding, wine. . . ."

While hotels and restaurants were numerous at Talcahuano, bars were even more so. The strong wines of Chile and its aguardiente were both plentiful and cheap; and those newly ashore were avid customers. As in most towns frequented by sailors from every quarter of the world, prostitution was a flourishing industry. In general the Argonauts' diaries are silent on this subject, and their reticence becomes understandable when it is recalled that many kept records of their voyage with the idea of sharing them with families and friends at home, and any frank discussion of commercialized vice violated the conventions of a mid-Victorian era. So rigid was this taboo that one looks in vain in Anglo-Saxon narratives for any admission that the Yankees consorted with South American prostitutes. One finds instead—and that but rarely—only such oblique references as this, from Lamson's impressions of Talcahuano:

"As I pushed into the cross streets I saw a great many women seated or standing at their doors, or walking in the streets. Many of them were filthy, though some were neatly dressed, and were rather pretty. They had dark complexions, fresh, florid cheeks, bright, black eyes, glossy hair hanging down their backs in two braids. . . . They had a smile and a word for all strangers, but their smiles were those of a siren. They were all sunk to the lowest depths of degradation and pollution. There were exceptions, and it is said that the married women are remarkably faithful to their marriage vows. . . ."

5

VALPARAISO, a more imposing place than Talcahuano, although its harbor was less good, was the favorite west-coast port of call; more gold ships stopped there than at any other South American spot except Rio. The visitors found much to admire in the city, and little to criticize. Its setting was highly picturesque; one Argonaut described it as being "as theatrical as a stage setting," adding: "a spur from the Andes shoots out to the coast and ends at the promontory where stands the lighthouse. The debris from this spur has formed a low and narrow strip of ground where stands the city. . . ." Unlike most South American streets, Valparaiso's were wide and straight—"as wide as Washington Street in Boston." The leading business establishments were handsomely housed, and, as at Talcahuano, rows of pretentious residences were perched on the cliffside high above the water. The ever patriotic Yankees were gratified to learn that the most conspicuous of these was the home of the United States consul, William G. Morehead. "It is on the extreme edge of a plateau, jutting out from the mountain, and looks down upon the lower town over a precipice three hundred feet high; here the stars and stripes are kept flying from morning to night, the symbol of power and liberty."

"The general style of building is far more pleasing than at Rio," wrote L. M. Schaeffer, a passenger on the *Flavius*, who went on to record his pleasure at finding, upstairs above an American-owned ship-chandlery firm, a well-equipped reading-room where New York newspapers were on file. But another feature of the town aroused this commentator's disapproval: its citizens took a much more frivolous view of the Sabbath than was customary in his pious home town. His denunciation of this laxness, however, was not severe: "I fear the morals of Valparaiso are not of the highest order. Yet a more social, hospitable, and polite people I have never met."

Valparaiso was a seaport and as such had its full share of "boarding houses, brothels and grog shops," although this quarter was more picturesquely situated here than in most cities. T. R. Warren described it thus:

"Rising abruptly above the south end of the city are three conical hills, straggling and broken by volcanic action, and named respectively 'Fore, Main and Mizzen Tops'— their terraced sides occupied by sailors' boarding-houses and gambling-hells of the lowest description. Here jack retires on the receipt of his wages, from which, after being stupefied with bad liquor and beaten and robbed of his money, he is summarily ejected, lucky not to be sent headlong down some of the steep precipices, as many a poor devil has been before him. These tops are the very St. Giles of the coast and the Alastian retreat of all criminals and desperadoes."

The increase in traffic set in motion by the discovery of gold had a marked effect on a dozen seaports on both sides of the continent. Captain George Coffin of the *Alhambra* recorded its impact here:

"I found in Valparaiso many passenger ships bound for California, and the great number of Americans on shore . . . seemed to nationalize the town. Yankees did just as they pleased and the city authorities were powerless to restrain them; but the great California emigration has been a godsend to this place, and they can well put up with the Yankee dare-devil spirit for the sake of the Yankee gold. . . .

"Everything in the line of provisions has advanced fifty percent. In the staple article of flour California has opened a new and extensive demand, and hundreds of acres are now in wheat where last year were nothing but weeds and thistles. . . ."

Like most visitors the gallant skipper of the *Alhambra* paid tribute to the beauty and graciousness of Valparaiso women. The Almendral, chief promenade of the city, was a place of enchantment to travelers newly come ashore after months-long confinement in the crowded and womanless ships. "Here the sparkling black eyes of the señoritas," states Captain Coffin, "dart their bewitching glances through the meshes of their thin gauze headdress, which, with their graceful demeanor, their superb carriage and elegant movement seem to make them appear as ethereal beings." That the young women of Chile were better-looking, better dressed, and far more willing to permit themselves to be seen and admired than those of the east coast was the universal verdict. A passenger on the *Almana* wrote in May 1849: "The ladies are very handsome with their black hair and eyes, and all wear silk stockings." T. R. Warren joined the chorus of praise:

"Chilean ladies are noted for their beauty, and look with lenient eyes upon 'outside barbarians.' . . . They still retain a strong nationality of character, and are as yet free from the exactions of Parisian etiquette, which so illy

149

becomes the Spanish maiden: naturally dignified, with an air as fearless and free from affectation as might be imagined from their remoteness from the world, their charm with their naiveté and piquancy of expression melt you with the tenderness of their glances; with complexions of pure white and red—with full black eye and profusion of glossy locks, and of majestic form, they are most attractive women. . . ."

6

SOME four hundred miles west of Valparaiso lies Juan Fernández, and to this remote island the gold rush brought for the first and last time in its history a period of brisk activity. Not more than fifty ships stopped there during 1849 and 1850, but these must have seemed a great armada to the island's handful of inhabitants, to whom the rare call of a whaler and the twice yearly visits of a supply ship from the mainland had theretofore been their only contacts with the outer world.

The California ships stopped at Juan Fernández mainly because the island, although it was destitute of other supplies, had an abundance of wood, fruit, and water, the last flowing cool and clear from mountain springs and known to mariners as the best to be had on the entire voyage. The method of taking on water was often described by visitors. A wooden flume carried it from springs high on the mountainside and into water deep enough so that the ships' casks could be placed on rafts, towed close to the beach, and filled.

Taking on water commonly occupied the crew during

the first day or two in port; following that, parties were sent into the forest, where they cut enough wood to keep the galley stove supplied until the end of the voyage. While this was going on, passengers explored the island, inspected the caves that had sheltered Chile's most hardened criminals in the days when Juan Fernández had been a penal colony, or gathered the fruit that grew prodigiously in the abandoned orchards.

But to most visitors these were not Juan Fernández's main attractions; curiously, although the island was quite without commercial or economic importance, it was better known to the average Yankee than any of the great cities of the mainland. Most Americans had little exact knowledge of such centers as Rio, Buenos Aires, or Valparaiso, but there were few indeed who did not possess a fund of information—much of it inaccurate—about the topography, climate, and vegetation of Juan Fernández. For of course this was Robinson Crusoe's Island, and the Defoe romance was one of the most widely read books of the day.

Typical of the spirit in which hundreds of young Americans approached this shrine is that of twenty-two-year-old Richard Hale, whose ship, the *General Worth*, dropped anchor in the cove in March 1849:

"We are getting into shape for port—the most fascinating spot, for me, on the face of the globe! Robinson Crusoe's Island! It is to be our next stopping place. What schoolboy . . . but has imagined himself cast away on this very island. . . . Tomorrow I shall see the enchanted isle! Not the picture of fancy but the real ground . . . perhaps the cave that Robinson dug, or the ruins of his little hovel. . . ."

151

When he was ashore at last, the relics of Crusoe's exile proved disappointing—Juan Fernández was not a tourist center and so had neglected to provide an adequate literary shrine—but the "real ground" lived up to young Hale's anticipations. "It is really a lovely spot," he wrote the next day, "the side facing the bay gently rising from the shore to the base of the hills in natural sloping lawns. Behind the mountains are fertile valleys, where grow delicious fruits—pears, peaches, plums, figs, apricots, cherries, strawberries . . . all growing wild, in great abundance, with none to harvest them." E. I. Barra, who reached the island during that same month on board the *Samson*, offered similar testimony, detailing the variety and size of the fruits growing in the little valleys opening into the anchorage. After weeks of subsisting on salt pork and moldy bread, the newcomers fell to with delight. "Peaches were at this time in their full maturity," wrote Barra, "quinces so large that they astonished the farmers who had emigrated from the bleak northern hemisphere; wild oats in the fullness of harvest time; figs to be had for the picking. In a word it was a most beautiful oasis in midocean."

These delicacies were free for the gathering because, while the island had once supported a considerable population of prisoners and their keepers, the penal colony had been abandoned years earlier and the number of inhabitants had shrunk to less than a dozen. These were in charge of an official named Echandea, who was suffering semi-exile for some political offense at home; all save one were Chileans. The lone exception was a Yankee seaman who had deserted from a whaler years before and now acted as harbor pilot—"a smart-looking state-of-Maine man, with a Chilean wife. They occupied one of the cozy little cot-

Ship Panama March 7, 184[9]

Feeling that profane & indecent language is both wrong and ungentlemanly, without excuse & deserving no indulgence, and alike contrary to the precepts of morality & good breeding; & believing also that from association or concert of action comes strength of resistance against pernicious habits; therefore,

We, the Undersigned do agree as gentlemen, that during the present voyage to California, we will not, on any pretext whatsoever, indulge in profanity or vulgarity; & that furthermore, should we at any time be found so far forgetful of ourselves & what is due to us as gentlemen, as to use any of the interdicted expressions, we will not take offence when called to propriety by any one of the undersigned.

Russell S. Boofish
Amos Coroza
Ed. W. Whitman
Horace W. Carpentier
Thomas A. Ayres
Peter Manny
Edward Hacker
Lewis Derrindeau
W. S. Hayden
Thomas Selleck
A. T. Bristol
Leonard L. Gale
John T. Penrand
John L. Fraser
Wm M. Rowlett
Oscar P. G. Hottenbach

Milton Green
William Newell
Caleb Beale
Victor L. Booth
Peter L. Spelten
Raymond Summers
James Palmer
Samuel Strode
Andrew Foot
Charles Holland
H. R. Woodruff
Wm. H. Blackwood
C. A. Curtis
H. A. Baldwin
James P. Gardner

RESOLUTION AGAINST THE USE OF PROFANITY

Signed by passengers on the steamer **Panama** *during its maiden voyage from New York to San Francisco, February 15 to June 4, 1849*

VIEW OF PANAMA CITY

From an old engraving

—Edgar B. Jessup

tages made of straw, with leaf-covered roofs, scattered along the hillside, overlooking the bay."

The inhabitants were not altogether unaware of the island's literary associations, and visitors eager to see relics of Crusoe's exile were directed to a cove a mile or two to the west of the settlement. Few failed to make this pilgrimage, either scrambling over the intervening mountain—a steep, rough climb that occupied an entire day—or borrowing one of the ship's boats and approaching from the water side. In any event they seem to have felt themselves amply repaid; all describe in detail Crusoe's small cave— singularly well preserved after a lapse of nearly a hundred and fifty years—dug into the hillside "on an elevation opening towards the sea, and from which the recluse had a full view . . . of the ocean."

Such was the power of Defoe's story that few had any suspicion that Robinson Crusoe was other than an actual person. One diarist acknowledged—rather grudgingly, it appears—that Crusoe was a fictional counterpart of Alexander Selkirk, but even he shrugs the matter off: the cave he reverently stands before is far more Crusoe's than Selkirk's. Others are bothered not at all by such hairsplitting: Robinson Crusoe was as completely real to them as though, clad in his skins and carrying his grass umbrella, he had welcomed them to his little kingdom. E. I. Barra thus describes his feelings on first entering Crusoe's cove:

"It was here that the poor shipwrecked mariner passed four lonely years of his adventurous life. It was here that he trained his goats, watched the seafowls and the wild beasts that roamed around on the precipitous cliffs. It was on this very spot that he had cultivated his little garden. The poor fellow! I could almost picture him as standing before me, with his unique garments of goat skins, looking with longing eyes, out upon the broad expanse of ocean to, perchance, discover some friendly sail, that might be directed thither-ward by a kind Providence. . . ."

Perhaps it was their own close knowledge of the vast reaches of the sea that gave them a sense of kinship with Crusoe and an understanding of the realities of his dilemma.

Sometimes the first stops on the Pacific were at points farther north, either at Callao or at one of the islands of the Galapagos group. Occasionally the need for supplies or emergency repairs caused ships to drop anchor at obscure places along the way, and these unscheduled stops were often intensely interesting. Thus T. Robinson Warren one day in 1849 found his vessel passing close by the guano islands, a few miles seaward from the port of Pisco, Peru. There he marveled at the clouds of thick yellow mist that rose perpetually from the three rocky islands as gangs of prisoners and wretched Chinese coolies dislodged the powdery fertilizer from its vast deposits and dumped it into waiting ships.

"The guano is first loosened with the pick [wrote War-ren], then shovelled into wheelbarrows and wheeled to the brink of the cliff, and there dumped into a canvas tunnel which leads into the launches below, which are waiting to receive it and convey it to the ship. These tunnels are called mangueras or sleeves, and some of them are immensely large. Under these the large ships haul, the tunnels leading down into their holds, and their loading is thus completed in a day or two."

154

But speed of loading was the only good feature of the guano trade; ships often had to wait many days for their turn beneath the canvas sleeves. Meanwhile the whole area was blanketed with fine dust that penetrated into every cranny of the vessels; moreover, "it has a large element of ammonia in it, so much so, that on going into a ship's hold laden with it, sneezing, coughing, and watery eyes are the penalty." Warren's ship left the spot without regret, few on board being inclined to dispute his opinion that "the working of the guano is a most awful business."

Vastly more attractive was Peru's chief city, Lima, and those on the comparatively few California ships that stopped there set sail again with a new comprehension of Peru's long history, of its tradition of culture, and of the magnificence and antiquity of its public monuments. For Lima lay only a few miles inland from its seaport town of Callao, and nearly every Argonaut who stopped there availed himself of the privilege of viewing one of the most picturesque of South American cities. Churches, bridges, parks and buildings were on a scale designed to open the eyes of those Yankees who believed the southern continent to be a backward land, peopled by an indolent and unenterprising race not many degrees above savagery.

The seven-mile trip from Callao to Lima was made on horse or muleback, the admirable road built during Peru's heyday having been permitted to fall into ruin. The road presented a further hazard in that it was frequented by bandits, and parties from visiting ships were warned to avoid making the passage after dark unless they were strong in number and well armed. This added zest to the expedition, however, and the capital itself was worth whatever danger the visitors encountered on their way to and from it. One of Lima's spectacular landmarks was a great stone bridge spanning the River Rimac, which flowed through the city and divided it in two. Nearly six hundred feet long and supported by graceful arches, this structure for nearly two hundred years had withstood not only a heavy traffic but the frequent earthquakes to which the region was subject. Near the bridge was the Alameda, a great city park—"the most beautiful perhaps in the world" —where the residents congregated on warm evenings, strolling beneath avenues of ancient trees or riding past on horseback or in elegant coaches. As in most cities of Spanish origin and tradition, the focal point of Lima was the plaza, about which were grouped its most impressive buildings: the huge cathedral and an array of other public structures, including the palace, once home of the Spanish viceroys —"a long, low, rambling building, over which waved the Peruvian standard."

"The other two sides of the square [continues Warren] were formed by long rows of buildings, two storys high; the upper story projecting over the sidewalk, forming a colonnade, along which are the shops of the dry-goods merchants, resplendent with all the wealth of French, Italian and Indian stuffs, and so disposed as to make a brilliant display, and to attract the eye of the beautiful Limanian as she saunters under their cool arches. Between the pillars . . . are embroiderers of gold and silver, with here and there an Indian flower-girl, with her bouquets tastily arranged for sale; and outside are the ice-cream vendors, extending along the two sides of the square. . . ."

Small wonder that the Yankees after a day or two in this once rich and still vastly impressive city, observing the well-ordered life of the inhabitants, the luxurious shops and varied amusements, returned to their barren little ships with a new respect for this ancient outpost of Spanish-American civilization.

Northernmost of the stopping-places on the Cape Horn route was a spot quite different from Lima: the islands of the Galapagos group, lying astride the equator, six hundred miles west of the mainland. Comparatively few put in at these remote and rocky islands, but those who did found much of interest to record in their diaries or sketchbooks. The *Canton* dropped anchor off one of the easternmost of the group in August 1849, and Joseph Kendall thus described it in a letter to his young daughter in New York:

"A description of this island will seem to you singular in the extreme. It is without any water, with the exception of one place about eight miles from where we lay anchored. The greater part of the island is utterly scorched by the sun. . . . It is all of volcanic matter, like burnt black cinders, which rattle like a bell at every step one takes. Not a blade of grass is to be seen, but there are some very beautiful shrubs, with aromatic scents, very cheering to my senses."

Although there was a lack of vegetation over much of the islands, Kendall—like many later visitors, including Charles Darwin—was impressed by the abundance of land and marine life. In particular he was charmed by the number of birds, large and small and of many species, and all quite without fear. "Many flew around me and some lighted on the men's shoulders." He was interested, too, in the iguanas, alligator-like creatures from two to three feet long, of which there were countless numbers. "Their appearance is not

157

very inviting, although they are perfectly harmless. I had one put on board . . . and made quite a pet of it."

The chief novelty to the Yankees, however, was the vast colonies of turtles for which the islands were famous, and which added welcome variety to a diet that had grown excessively monotonous. There were two varieties, sea and land turtles, both so large that two men could lift one only with difficulty, and—like the birds—they showed no fear of human beings, whom they permitted to approach with complete unconcern. The *Canton* group gathered specimens of both species and during their stay enjoyed turtle soup and turtle steaks three times a day. When the craft set sail again, her decks were cluttered with sixty of the great creatures, destined to disappear one by one into the ship's galley during the long cruise to San Francisco.

The *Canton* carried away from the Galapagos not only a deckload of terrapin but two young Yankees who had been stranded there since deserting a New Bedford whaler nine months earlier. This pair seemed none the worse for their adventure, for the island's varied wild life had made the problem of survival easy. But the role of castaways had long since lost its allure, and when the *Canton's* skipper agreed to transport them to San Francisco they came aboard with evident relief.

7

IN MANY instances the journey from the west coast of South America to San Francisco was the most trying of the entire passage. Ships beating northward from equatorial waters into the North Pacific were much of the time running counter to the prevailing winds, with the result that often vast distances were covered with but insignificant progress toward the goal. Not infrequently storms arose during which the painfully acquired gains of weeks were nullified in a few hours as the ships were swept southward again by the violent gales. Moreover the Argonauts by then had been at sea for many weeks. Their boredom had increased from day to day to the point where all looked forward with almost intolerable longing to the moment when they could go ashore again, this time permanently.

"Our voyage is becoming prolonged to an excessively wearisome duration," wrote J. Lamson from the *James W. Paige* in August 1849. "More than a month ago we calculated on arriving at San Francisco in ten days; and with a fair wind we could have performed the voyage in that time." But the wind had shifted, blowing continuously from the northeast, and thirty days later the *Paige* was as far from port as ever. "We suffer much from weariness, lassitude, and drowsiness, consequent on our long voyage and almost total inactivity," Lamson wrote a few days later; and went on to report an increase in quarrels with the ship's officers and of bickering among the passengers, all reflecting a nervous strain induced by their slow progress. Then, on September 1, the picture changed: "We have at last got a fair wind, and during the whole day sail directly on our course without tacking. Our spirits begin to revive, and we are not quite hopeless of reaching port. . . ."

In greater or less degree this experience was repeated on scores of ships. On the *Washington Irving*, lying becalmed less than two hundred miles from San Francisco, time hung heavily indeed. Garrett Low commented on the complete boredom induced by looking constantly at the same faces, hearing the same stories, reading the same books, and playing the same games. In their impatience certain of the *Washington Irving's* passengers considered adopting drastic measures in the hope of wooing back the elusive winds. On board was the Reverend Mr. Thorne, whom some professed to believe was a Jonah; the desirability of casting him overboard was under discussion when a breeze fortunately sprang up and the plan was abandoned.

The approaching end of the journey affected different groups in different ways. Some sank deeper in their lethargy; others were stirred to renewed activity. A passenger on the *Tarolinta* confided to his journal his belief that so long a sea journey was a poor preparation for the ordeal ahead. Many weeks of close confinement, with little opportunity for physical exercise, had taken their toll, he feared, and he and his companions would reach the gold fields with their strength and stamina at a low ebb, physically unable to compete with those toughened by the hardships of the overland trails. As a means of overcoming this handicap he advocated daily brisk walks on deck, together with an hour or two of climbing in the rigging and a series of vigorous competitions: weight-lifting contests, wrestling and boxing bouts. Whether or not anything came of this resolve subsequent entries fail to state.

But on most ships a wave of renewed energy could be observed as the California coast came into view. On the *Capitol* the ship's deck presented the appearance of "a small manufacturing village: there was a harness and belt shop, a book bindery, a pistol and knife factory, a shoe-shop, a carpenter shop, and a laundry, all doing a brisk business." Passengers generally found their thoughts centering on the day, now almost at hand, when they would be called on to grapple with the realities of mining-camp life. Whole ship-loads made final inspection of their equipment, repaired their clothing, oiled and polished their weapons, sharpened their tools. Those who traveled in company groups broke out their supplies and set about familiarizing themselves with the operation of their mechanical gold-washing machines, cutting up bolts of canvas and fashioning them into tents, or attending meetings at which, after thorough discussion, final plans were perfected for their impending assault on the gold fields.

Chapter Four: PANAMA AND NICARAGUA

1

ONE of the results of the discovery of gold was that it enormously widened the horizons of countless Americans, causing them to abandon their traditional provincialism and to think and plan on a global scale. Many thousands who had formerly had but slight interest in lands beyond their borders developed a consuming interest in the geography of the entire Western Hemisphere. The maps and atlases of the day were in heavy demand, and in every community young men studied them eagerly, searching for routes that promised to lead to the gold fields with a minimum of delay.

Obviously the shortest course was that leading due west across the nation that had been newly extended to the Pacific. Many chose this without debate, for the distance was less than half that of any other route, and they would avoid having to face the unfamiliar and perhaps dangerous ordeal of a protracted sea voyage. But there were those who took an opposite view. Those who lived near the Atlantic or Gulf coastlines looked naturally to the sea as the easiest and safest means of reaching far-away lands. More, it would avoid the expense and delays of assembling the equipment needed for so long an overland trek: wagons and horses or oxen, supplies to support man and beast during the crossing of the trans-Mississippi wilderness, weapons to protect lives and property from attack by hostile Indians.

But even those who, for what seemed sufficient reasons, elected to make the passage by sea were by no means unanimous in their choice of routes. A study of the maps made it clear that the voyage about Cape Horn was an extremely roundabout means of reaching their goal: nearly fifteen thousand miles of travel to reach a point that, on a direct line, was hardly one fifth that distance. A passage of that length, over a route that included extremes of heat and cold, of dead calms and violent storms, was not one to be lightly undertaken. But these hardships were not its only, or indeed its chief, drawback. In the blunt-nosed sailing ships of the period a round-the-Horn passage to San Francisco could rarely be accomplished in less than five months, and constantly in the mind of every Argonaut was a gnawing fear that the richest rewards would be garnered by those who reached the gold fields first, that every hour of delay diminished his chance of fortune. To many of those poring over the maps there seemed one ideal solution to their dilemma. To travel by ship to Panama, cross the fifty-mile Isthmus, and re-embark on the Pacific side would cut many thousands of miles from the trip and reduce the elapsed time by half.

These '49ers were of course not the first to recognize that the crossing at Panama involved a great saving of time and distance in traveling between the two oceans. For three centuries before Marshall's discovery the Isthmus had been an important link in commerce between the hemispheres. Across it had flowed an active and varied traffic, the fruit of Spain's trans-Pacific trade routes and of her rich conquests in Peru and elsewhere on South America's west coast. From its beginning in the early sixteenth century this commerce had flourished for a century and a half, and because of it the city of Panama had become the chief ornament of Spain's colonial empire, "boasting of temples adorned with gold and silver, and pictures of great value, with nunneries, monasteries, and hospitals, and more than seven thousand houses, many of which were of magnificent construction." At the same time there had sprung up on the Atlantic side of the Isthmus a hardly less impressive town, Puerto Bello, where the treasure gathered from half the world was loaded on galleons and carried to Spain. Over the paved road that connected the two ports had flowed the wealth that for well over a century had made the homeland the world's richest nation.

So tempting a prize did not fail to engage the attention of the freebooters of that piratical age, and in 1671 Henry Morgan, by a swift and bloody coup, captured Panama and Puerto Bello and laid both to waste. Spain's control over the Isthmus was maintained for more than a hundred years after this catastrophe, but meantime her hold on her American possessions had gradually relaxed and one by one her colonies had slipped away. Thereafter the importance of Panama declined year after year until by the middle of the nineteenth century it had sunk into obscurity.

"A little life was still kept up in the ruined town," wrote a contemporary visitor, "through its pearl fishery and the scanty agricultural resources of the province; and a little trade was still carried on with the Island of Jamaica, from whence its foreign goods were imported; but even these were gradually decreasing up to the year 1849, when the discovery of gold in California, and its accompanying emigration from the United States and Europe crossing the Isthmus at this point, gave a sudden and unexpected impetus to business."

How profound this impetus was is recorded by thousands of Argonauts who followed the century-old Spanish trails through the Panama jungles during the next few years.

Even before the gold discovery, the long-stagnant Isthmian traffic had begun to flow again at an accelerated pace. The increase in commerce between the United States and England and the newly liberated countries on the west coast had refocused attention on the advantages of the Panama crossing over the time-consuming passage of Cape Horn. As early as the 1820's small packet brigs were sailing regularly from New York to the Isthmus, connecting haphazardly on the Pacific side with ships that plied the South American coast as far south as Callao. A few years later faster and more dependable communication was inaugurated by a British company, which operated steamships on both oceans, the two routes terminating on their respective sides of the Isthmus. The British government subsidized this venture by means of a mail contract; service was extended down the west coast as far as Valparaiso, and on the Isthmus trains of pack-mules were used to transport mail and freight. The latter was mostly specie; less valuable freight continued to be sent round the Horn in sailing ships.

As time passed, a keen rivalry sprang up between the United States and England for the growing Pacific trade; the Yankee merchants were by no means content to yield this profitable market to their competitors. It was not until after 1846, however, the war with Mexico having given this country a territorial stake on the Pacific, that positive steps were taken to link the two sides of the continent more closely. Properly to administer her new territory, means of communication more rapid and dependable than the overland trails or the time-consuming passage round the Horn were urgently needed.

As a first step in that direction, a treaty was negotiated, late in 1846, between the United States and the Republic of New Granada—of which Panama was then a part—by which this country was granted free transit across the Isthmus and in return guaranteed New Granada's sovereignty. The next year, 1847, the long-standing controversy over the boundaries of the Oregon territory having been amicably settled between this country and England, the plan of establishing regular mail service to California and Oregon was taken up in earnest. The matter was before Congress for many months. Eventually a bill was passed and signed by President Polk authorizing an annual subsidy of $290,-000 for a line of steamers, with semi-monthly sailings, between New York and Chagres. Later a similar bill provided a subsidy almost as large for monthly service on the Pacific between Panama and the California coast, with its northern terminus at Astoria.

The mail contracts were duly awarded, but the men who first received them were unable to fulfill their terms, and both were taken over by others. The Pacific line fell to William H. Aspinwall, a man of ample means and wide mercantile experience; the other went to a group headed by George Law, a capitalist who had previously been identified with large railroad projects. Of the two ventures that on the Atlantic had to all appearances a far better chance of success, for its steamers could draw trade from Central America and the west coast of South America as well as from California and Oregon. The Pacific Mail Steamship Company (as Aspinwall's company was called) on the other hand seemed a dubious gamble, there being, in 1847, little commerce between the country's east and west coasts and no real prospect of more for many years. "The Pacific Company," stated a writer in the late 1850's, "was looked upon by the generality of business men as a certain sequestration of a large amount of property for an indefinite time, with a faint prospect of profit; and the wonder seemed to be that so sound a man as Mr. Aspinwall should have engaged in it."

These pioneer mail contracts required that five steamers, each of fifteen hundred tons, be placed on the Atlantic run, while operations on the Pacific called for three steamers, two to be of not less than a thousand tons and the third of six hundred. Both companies began building the vessels promptly; the first were finished in time to permit through traffic between New York and San Francisco to begin before the end of 1848. In preparation for inaugurating regular service, the first of the Pacific Mail steamers, the *California*, left New York in early October 1848. She was bound on the round-the-Horn voyage to her home port, Panama, there to start monthly round trips to California. Meantime the Atlantic company made ready the *Falcon* and dispatched her to Chagres on December 1, timing her departure so that she would arrive at the Isthmus at about the same time the *California* reached Panama, thus permitting passengers to cross over and re-embark with little delay.

When this pioneer line of mail steamers began operation no one foresaw how soon or how profoundly events in California would affect its fortunes. Although gold had been discovered more than eight months before the *California* left

ACAPULCO

A regular port of call for the Panama and Nicaragua steamers. From Letts's California Illustrated

SAN JUAN DEL NORTE (GREYTOWN)

The eastern end of the Nicaragua route. From Letts's California Illustrated

SAN JUAN DEL SUR

The Pacific terminus of the Nicaragua route, 1859. From Pim's
The Gate of the Pacific

THE SAN JUAN RIVER, CONNECTING LAKE NICARAGUA
AND GREYTOWN

*Showing the type of native boats used by the first Argonauts on the
Nicaragua route. From Pim's* The Gate of the Pacific

New York, and although accounts of its extent had been published all over the East, the news had caused so little interest that the steamer left port with her cabins empty; no through passenger for California was on board and the ship carried less than half a dozen passengers of any sort. Nor had the excitement begun when the *Falcon* left almost two months later; her passenger list numbered less than thirty, the majority of whom were booked for passage to inter- mediate ports in the United States, chiefly to Savannah and New Orleans. The *Falcon* was already three days at sea when President Polk's message of December 5, 1848 touched off the rush, and it was not until the craft reached New Orleans that her passengers learned the news.

Then at last the belated scramble began. In New Orleans the *Falcon's* half-empty cabins were filled to their utmost capacity. She reached the Isthmus in mid-December with two hundred passengers aboard, all but a few bound for the gold fields. With the *Falcon's* arrival off Chagres, Panama entered yet another phase of its singularly checkered his- tory, one that was destined for two full decades to make the Isthmus one of the world's most traveled thoroughfares.

2

DURING the first stages of the migration it was not clear which of the sea routes was to claim a major share of the traffic. In mid-January 1849 Horace Greeley's *Tribune*, which had constituted itself a sort of oracle on all matters pertaining to the discovery, published what it termed the first comprehensive survey of the exodus. "There has been, and there still exists," it began, "a great diversity of opinion as to the number of persons who have left for California since the beginning of the excitement." After stating that most guesses placed the number at more than ten thousand, it added that a day-by-day search through the newspaper files for the month beginning December 14 and a listing of every vessel to sail for California from United States ports, with the number of passengers on each, fixed the total of those at sea on January 14, at 2,212.

The routes followed by this advance guard were divided as follows: thirty-six vessels bearing 1,164 passengers and 518 crew members had set out for the trip round the Horn; one ship with thirty on board had cleared for Vera Cruz (where its passengers planned an overland trek across Mexico), and seven—four of them steamers—had headed for Chagres, with combined passenger lists totaling 530. Thus at the earliest stage of the rush the number going round Cape Horn exceeded those crossing at Panama by more than two to one, and this proportion held through the spring and early summer of 1849. After that, as the hardships and delays of the Panama crossing were one by one eliminated, a steadily greater number took the shorter, faster route. By the middle of 1851, three of every four traveling between the two coasts crossed either at Panama or Nicaragua, whereas the once heavy traffic round the Horn had declined to a thin trickle. But it was many months before any but the most primitive accommodations were available on the Isthmus, and those who first made the crossing encountered an almost unbroken series of hardships and delays.

Ships from the north first touched the Isthmus at Chagres, a forlorn village on the shore of an inlet once guarded by the Spanish fortress of San Lorenzo, long since reduced to ruin.

"Chagres at this time [wrote Hubert H. Bancroft] was a town of about seven hundred inhabitants, dwelling in some fifty windowless, bamboo huts, with thatched, palm-leaf roofs, and having open entrances, and the bare ground floor. The town was surrounded by heaps of filthy offal, the greasy, stagnant pools bordered with blue mud. It is situated on a small but exceedingly picturesque and almost land-locked bay, well nigh buried by the foliage that skirts its banks and rolls off in billowy emerald toward the hills beyond. . . ."

But despite its picturesque setting Chagres had a long-standing and well-deserved reputation for its pestilential climate, and newcomers were advised to tarry there only until means could be found to transport themselves and their belongings up the river to higher ground. This was often a difficult task. How it was accomplished by one pioneer group is described by Elisha Oscar Crosby, who reached Chagres on the steamer *Isthmus* in January 1849:

"I associated with ten or twelve of our passengers, and we hired a large bungo, for our baggage, and a smaller one for ourselves from the natives, and the same day got our 'traps' from the steamer, and stowed them as best we could, on these dugouts, and commenced our ascent of the Chagres River, the natives rowing or paddling, with an oar like a long handled shovel, or poling by long poles resting on the bottom of the river, and occasionally getting into the water and dragging our boats along. We got up from Chagres five or six miles that evening, and camped on the bank of the river. . . ."

J. M. Letts, who arrived on the bark *Marietta* less than a month later than Crosby, found the little port already badly overcrowded. Anchored in the roadstead some hundreds of yards from shore—shallow water preventing a nearer approach to land—lay the *Falcon*, and the same day the *Marietta* reached port, the *Crescent City*, a side-wheel steamer bringing one hundred and thirty passengers, also dropped anchor, "together with several sailing vessels, bringing, in all, about one thousand passengers."

The descent of so many on the little settlement naturally caused a vast confusion, and this was compounded by the fact that each new arrival was determined to get ashore and on his way with the least possible delay. The northerners had of course no clear notion of what they might encounter on shore, and they had prepared themselves for any emergency.

"It was amusing [wrote Letts] to see the passengers preparing to make their advent to land. It is well understood that no one started for California without being thoroughly fortified, and as we had arrived at a place, where, as we thought, there must be at least, *some* fighting to do, our first attention was directed to our *armor*. The revolvers, each man having at least two, were first overhauled, and the six barrels charged. These were put in our belt, which also contained a bowie knife. A brace of smaller pistols were snugly pocketed inside our vest; our rifles were liberally charged; and with a cane in hand, (which of course contains a dirk), and a *sling shot* in our pockets, we step off and look around for the enemy."

The newcomers, as it proved, had no need for their heavy armaments. But although the natives were the reverse of warlike, the Yankees soon found that they did not lack resourcefulness in other fields. With hundreds demanding transportation up the river and with only a few native bungos to carry them, the boatmen were in excellent bargaining position, a fact that they were not slow to realize. With the first parties to land they quickly concluded deals by which they agreed to transport them as far as Gorgona —a distance of some forty miles—for a flat fee of ten dollars per passenger. Later, the competition having become brisker, they demanded—and received—four to five times that amount. The exorbitant charges naturally caused resentment among the emigrants and much ill will resulted, and occasional violence. Bayard Taylor, who made the crossing in July 1849, questioned the boatman who took him from Chagres to Gorgona, and heard the natives' side of the controversy. "Ambrosio told me that they would serve no one well who treated them badly. 'If the Americans are good, we are good,' the latter stated. 'But if they abuse us, we are bad.' " Taylor was inclined to think that much of the trouble was brought on by the Yankees themselves, whose arrogance in dealing with the natives was as marked at Panama as in the South American ports where the round-the-Horn contingent stopped.

"Many blustering fellows [he wrote] with their belts stuck full of pistols and bowie knives, which they draw on all occasions, but take good care not to use, have brought reproach on the country by their silly conduct. It is no bravery to put a revolver to the head of an unarmed and ignorant native, and the boatmen have sense enough to be no longer terrified by it."

As always in such circumstances, the majority of well-behaved travelers had to pay for the excesses of the few. Having been cheated once, the boatmen had their revenge on the usually innocent customers who next engaged them. One of their favorite devices was to accept from the unwary payment for the passage to Gorgona and, while their passengers were gathering up their belongings, to make a deal with another group and set off up the river, leaving the first party stranded. Sometimes this process was varied: the boatmen would conclude a bargain with one group and be on the point of departure when a new party approached offering a larger sum. Thereupon the boatmen would play one group against the other, and if those in the boat failed to meet the higher bid they and their belongings were unceremoniously put ashore and the successful bidders took their place. This process might be repeated several times before the bungo finally got under way. Nor was that all. Many boatmen, having been paid in full at the beginning of the trip, stopped halfway up the river and refused to continue without a substantial additional payment. This form of extortion became so frequent that new arrivals were advised to pay only half the boatmen's fee, withholding the balance until the end of the trip.

These practices, along with some petty thievery and their constitutional indolence, failed to endear Panama's native boatmen to the generality of the Argonauts. E. S. Capron, who made the crossing in 1853, found nothing to admire in the native population, whom he judged to be composed mainly of Negroes and Indians. He added that many by intermarrying with the whites had produced a mixture having "a few of the good and many of the bad qualities of both. . . . Ignorance, treachery, dishonesty, cowardice, and indolence are universal characteristics. The devotion to gambling amounts to a perfect mania."

Another, who had lost in transit a valuable piece of baggage, commented feelingly: "The experience of thousands will attest that it is unsafe—indeed it is downright rashness —to entrust property to the custody of the natives or Spaniards."

Yet another, Theodore T. Johnson, who arrived in February 1849, found Chagres a sorry place indeed, a huddle of bamboo huts with peaked roofs of palmetto leaves standing in the midst of an odorous swamp, its streets "filled with a confused mixture of dogs, hogs and naked children, Negroes and Creoles." Johnson came on the steamer *Crescent City*, the passengers on which, desperately anxious to push on to California, were so incensed at the indolence and high charges of the native boatmen that Johnson reports them taking up this cry: "Whip the rascal, fire his den, burn the settlement, annex the Isthmus!"

Much of the northerners' dissatisfaction stemmed from the urgency of their desire to get on to California in the van of the rush. Their impatience, already strong, was increased by occasional meetings with miners traveling eastward, who, having reaped a fortune in the diggings, were homeward bound with their profits. Bayard Taylor reports one such encounter soon after he stepped ashore at Chagres:

"A returning Californian had just reached the place, with a box containing $22,000 in gold dust, and a four pound lump in one hand. The impatience and excitement of the passengers, already at a high pitch, was greatly increased by his appearance. Life and death were small matters compared with immediate departure from Chagres. Men ran up and down the beach, shouting, gesticulating, and getting feverishly impatient at the deliberate habits of the natives; as if their arrival in California would thereby be at all hastened. The boatmen, knowing very well that two more steamers were due the next day, remained provokingly cool and unconcerned. They had not seen six months of emigration without learning something of the American habit of going at full speed."

Few of the Yankees who landed on the Isthmus knew the language of the country, but all became familiar indeed with one Spanish word: *mañana*.

3

THE distance from Chagres to Panama City by river and trail was roughly sixty miles. In the first months of the rush the crossing was made in about five days. The meandering Chagres River, by turns broad and sluggish, narrow and turbulent, was the sole avenue of traffic for the first two thirds of the journey; the final twenty miles, involving a passage over the hilly southern edge of the Isthmus and the descent to the Pacific, was made on foot or, more commonly, on muleback.

The trip was long and strenuous, and most Argonauts reached its end weary and footsore and dirty, but little the worse for the adventure. There were virtually no accommodations along the route. In general the traveler had to carry his own food, sleep in his own blankets—either in the

CHAGRES IN 1851

Here the Argonauts debarked for the passage across the isthmus to Panama City. From Letts's California Illustrated

PREPARING BREAKFAST ON THE CHAGRES RIVER

The journey up the river usually consumed three days, with overnight stops en route. From Letts's California Illustrated

SAN PABLO

A way-station on the Trans-Isthmian Railroad. From Otis's Illustrated History of the Panama Railroad

PASSENGERS BOARDING THE TRAIN AT ASPINWALL

The eastern terminus of the Panama Railroad. From Otis's Illustrated History of the Panama Railroad

open or in the bamboo huts of the natives—and endure alternately blistering heat and torrential rains, meanwhile contending with swarms of mosquitoes, fleas, and other insects, and running the ever present hazards of malaria, dysentery, cholera, and Panama fever. But compensating for the hardships and dangers, he lived for a few days a life totally unlike any he had known before, familiarizing himself with the exotic tropical fruits, the curiously luxuriant jungle vegetation, the bright-hued birds and flowers, and the monkeys, alligators, and other Panama fauna.

Few who made the journey failed to find it fascinating. Bayard Taylor, a seasoned traveler, pronounced it "decidedly more novel, grotesque and adventurous than any trip of similar length in the world." He added: "It was rough enough, but had nothing that I could exactly call hardship, so much was the fatigue balanced by the enjoyment of unsurpassed scenery and a continual sensation of novelty."

Some of the novelties were of a nature that few travelers would willingly have repeated. Taylor's first stop was at the village of Gatun, half a dozen miles upstream. Through the good offices of his boatman, Ambrosio, he was able to rent a hammock in one of the native huts, "a single room, in which all the household operations were carried on." His description continued:

"A notched pole, serving as a ladder, led to a sleeping loft, under the pyramidal roof of thatch. Here a number of the emigrants who arrived late were stowed away on a rattling floor of cane, covered with hides. After a supper of pork and coffee, I made my day's notes by the light of a miserable starveling candle, stuck in an empty bottle, but

had not written far before my paper was covered with
fleas. The owner of the hut swung my hammock meanwhile, and I turned in to secure it for the night. To lie there
was one thing, to sleep another. A dozen natives crowded
round the table, drinking their aguardiente and disputing
vehemently; the cooking fire was on one side of me, and
every one who passed to and fro was sure to give me a
thump, while my weight swung the hammock so low, that
all the dogs on the premises were constantly rubbing their
backs under me. . . ."

Also at Gatun, perhaps in this very hut, another group
witnessed an example of the natives' casual domestic habits.
George Schenck and two companions stopped for cups of
coffee, which were duly set before them and into which they
emptied the contents of the bowl of sugar on the table.
Schenck goes on:

"Some other passengers came along after us, and I
thought I would watch and see how they managed about
their sweetening. . . . I presently saw one of the natives,
a girl of about sixteen or seventeen years . . . go out and
get a piece of sugar-cane, and commence chewing it, and
occasionally she would eject the juice from her mouth into
the coffee while it was being prepared outside the hut.
Swain asked me if I was going to have some more coffee. I
declined. . . ."

Beyond Gatun the current grew swifter, and all the
strength and skill of the boatmen were needed to maintain
an average progress of a mile an hour. Hubert H. Bancroft
thus pictures the long bungos as they were laboriously
polled or towed past a succession of rapids:

178

"Taking their stand upon the broadened edges of the canoe on either side, one end of their pole upon the bottom of the river, and the other placed against their shoulder, smoking with perspiration, their deep chests sending forth volumes of vapor into the vapory air, their swollen sinews strained to their utmost tension, and keeping time to a sort of grunting song, they step steadily along from stem to stern, thus sending the boat rapidly over the water, except where the current is strong. The middle of the channel, where the water is deep and the current rapid, is avoided as much as possible; yet with every precaution the men frequently miss their purchase and the boat falls back in a few minutes as great a distance as it can recover in an hour. . . ."

After an hour of this back-breaking work the boatmen tied up their craft and plunged into the stream to cool off; at intervals, too, they disappeared into the jungle, to return a few minutes—or a few hours—later carrying bottles of native brandy, from which they took frequent pulls to fortify themselves for the task ahead. But drinking en route was not confined to the natives; many Yankees believed that a supply of wine or stronger beverage was a necessary safeguard against the diseases prevalent on the Isthmus. Thus it was no uncommon sight on the Chagres to encounter entire boatloads following an erratic course upstream, with passengers and natives alike giving voice to their hilarity in loud bursts of song. One emigrant was amused to observe how quickly the boatmen picked up such popular melodies as *Oh! Susanna* and *Yankee Doodle*, singing them at the top of their ample lungs, and with of course no idea of the meaning of the words they were mispronouncing.

The passage up the Chagres usually continued three days, with intermediate overnight stops at native villages along the way. Normally the boat trip ended at Gorgona, although when there was ample water in the stream it was sometimes possible to persuade the boatmen to push on another four miles to Cruces. Both towns were extremely lively places, with crowds of natives and emigrants thronging the streets night and day and making so much noise that few found it possible to sleep. For it was here that the travelers paid off their boatmen (generally with much haggling) and immediately started a new series of wordy negotiations for transportation to Panama City.

Like the Chagres boatmen, the overland packers shrewdly fixed prices according to the current demand for their services. The distance was only twenty miles, but the route was through a rugged country and the trails were rough and narrow and frequently knee-deep in mud. The chief means of transit for men and goods were the diminutive but sturdy Panama mules, scores of which were constantly moving over the route, bearing burdens out of all proportion to their size. The cost of renting the animals was, of course, subject to violent fluctuations. Bancroft, who made the passage in March 1851, found the prevailing price for saddlemules "from ten to twenty dollars." Taylor and his party, who had crossed nine months earlier, paid "ten dollars the head for riding animals, and six dollars for each one hundred pounds of freight." During the same month H. D. Pierce, whose party numbered about twenty, including three women, paid two hundred and fifty dollars for the thirty mules required to transport them and their considerable freight down out of the hills. Others who chanced to reach Gorgona or Cruces when the stream of emigration had temporarily slackened were able to hire mules and their attendants for as little as five dollars each.

This part of the journey, while difficult and tiring, was likewise full of interest.

"The trail from Gorgona [wrote Bancroft] . . . was rough in the extreme, and led through a greatly diversified country. Two miles brought us across the table land, then we entered a dense forest, from which the sun was wholly excluded by the overhanging branches. Thence we followed a path successively over soft, uneven ground, through shady cañons, and mountain passes murky in their gloomy solitude, up and round precipitous hillsides cut by travel into steps and stairs, on which and into well-worn holes the careful and sagacious animal placed his foot tenderly, knowing that an inch or two on the wrong side would send him sliding down the steep slope. . . . Often we passed through ravines which had been washed out by rain, and so narrow at the bottom that on entering on either end persons must shout in order to notify others who wished to come from the opposite direction. . . . Some of these gullies have been worn down thirty feet and more by centuries of travel and are so narrow at the bottom that a loaded mule can hardly get through. . . ."

The trail from Cruces, while longer and rougher than that from Gorgona, had the advantage of being open in all weather, whereas the Gorgona route speedily became impassable during the frequent tropical downpours. This was because the Cruces route followed the ancient Spanish trail connecting Panama with Puerto Bello. It had once been paved over its entire length, and, notwithstanding centuries of neglect, enough of the stonework remained to give the mules a precarious footing. Henry Sturdivant, who passed that way early in 1851, found the trail "a gutter of mud between rocks on a shelf at the top of a precipice." His party had a difficult passage, with only one spot en route offering shelter from the heavy rains. This was a place called the Half-Way House, "a miserable little tent about twelve feet square." Sturdivant thus sums up the journey:

"After being jolted to almost paralytic unconsciousness on the mules, alternately burned by the tropic sun and soaked by the tropic showers, and liberally bespotted by the mosquitoes and other nameless visitors of the previous three nights, the Argonauts hailed Panama with delight."

4

TRANSIT across the Isthmus was difficult enough during the first months of the rush, but it was not long before measures to speed traffic and to provide some degree of comfort to the travelers were being put into effect. The management of the steamship lines operating between the Isthmus and the east and west coasts were responsible for most of the improvements. These recognized that the Panama crossing was the weakest link in their entire route and that its hardships and delays were causing many to reject it in favor of the overland trails and the much longer voyage round the Horn.

As early as mid-January 1849 Aspinwall purchased and

sent to the Isthmus a little 250-ton steamer, the *Orus*. She was put on the run up the river, where she operated as far as the depth of the water permitted, substantially reducing the distance that had to be covered in native bungos. Later that year a new and lighter craft was put in use, on which passengers were carried to within a few miles of Gorgona. A number of other small side-wheel steamers were presently added to the run, and by the summer of 1850 only a few of the emigrants traveled in the native bungos.

Meantime work on the trans-Isthmian railroad was getting under way. This project was not, as might be assumed, inspired by the discovery of gold; indeed, it had been under consideration for more than a decade before the rush began. The route was surveyed as early as 1841; in 1845 a French company was organized to build the road, and the government of New Granada granted it exclusive rights to operate trains across the Isthmus for a period of ninety-nine years. One of the crises characteristic of French politics, however, prevented the financing of so large an enterprise, and a few years later New Granada canceled the agreement. Meantime, the United States government having in 1847 subsidized the establishment of mail steamers on the east and west coasts, the obvious advantages of a connection by rail between the two lines again brought the railroad project to the fore. A party of engineers was accordingly dispatched to the Isthmus early in 1848 charged with locating a feasible route, and at the same time negotiations were conducted at Bogotá by which the American company received from the New Granada government a contract similar to that once held by the French. A number of bills were introduced in Congress seeking aid in building the line, but strong opposition developed and in the end all were defeated. While this was going on, however, the gold rush had got under way and the projected railroad, no longer regarded as a poor investment, was easily financed by the public sale of stock.

The survey was completed early in 1849, and in the fall of that year the first construction contract was let. The original plan was to begin with the section from Gorgona to Panama City, thereby permitting passengers to travel by river boat from Chagres, then take the railroad for the final twenty miles to the Pacific. But the task of transporting supplies and heavy construction equipment that far inland proved slow and costly, and, the contractors having gone broke, a new start was made, this time on the Atlantic seaboard. Manzanillo Island, on Navy Bay, some four miles from the mouth of the Chagres, was selected as the terminus, and at this point presently sprang up the town of Aspinwall, which became familiar to many thousands of coast-to-coast travelers during the next twenty years. Aspinwall was on water deep enough to permit steamers to tie up at its docks, thus eliminating the use of lighters, but that was about the sum of its advantages. The town was surrounded by pestilential swamps, shut off from the cooling sea breezes, and in general presented an aspect that most travelers found depressing in the extreme. Bancroft describes the place as it was in 1851:

"Travel the world over and in every place you may find something better than is found in any other place. Searching for the specialty in which Aspinwall excelled, we found it in her carrion birds, which cannot be surpassed in size or smell. Manzanilla island may boast of the finest vultures on the planet. Originally a swamp, the founda-

HIGH AND DRY

A San Francisco street in 1851, showing the hulls of abandoned vessels converted into storeships.
From Marryat's Mountains and Molehills

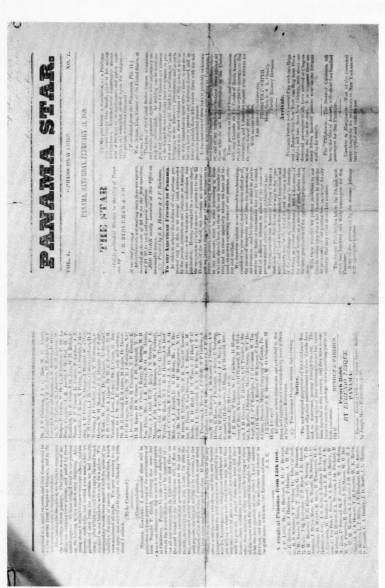

VOLUME 1, NUMBER 1 OF PANAMA'S FIRST NEWSPAPER

Beginning on February 24, 1849, the Panama Star was published weekly by American emigrants marooned on the isthmus "as a means of temporary relief from the monotony of our situation."

tions of the buildings were below the level of the ocean, and dry land was made by filling in as occasion required. The result in this soft soil of filth and vegetable putridity may be imagined. The very ground on which one trod was pregnant with disease, and death was distilled in every breath of air. . . . Glued furniture falls in pieces; leather molds, and iron oxidizes in twenty-four hours."

Bancroft saw the place at its worst period, while the process of building a habitable town in the midst of a steaming tropical jungle was at its height. Later visitors found it less obnoxious, although few pronounced it a positive beauty spot. One British traveler passing through in 1853 dismissed it as "a typical Yankee frontier town, raw and unlovely." By then the docks had been completed, and several large warehouses, besides the railroad company office and a scattering of small shops, hotels, and frame residences. This visitor reported that a great deal of building was still going on: a new iron wharf extending into the bay, extensive railroad repair yards, and the City Hotel. This last long remained Aspinwall's chief architectural glory, with a dining-room seating two hundred, a sixty-foot bar, and—by crowding cots side by side the length of its long outer balconies—its ability to provide sleeping-quarters for five hundred guests.

The name of this booming town was long a matter of controversy. When its construction first began, it was christened in honor of the New York magnate who headed both the Panama Railroad and the Pacific Mail Steamship Company, and as Aspinwall it was known to the traveling public for a generation. The government of New Granada never recognized that name, however, and on the official maps it was called Colón. But not until some forty years later did the name Aspinwall disappear from common usage.

The Panama Railroad, one of the engineering triumphs of the 1850's, was five years building, during which its planners met and overcame a succession of knotty problems: crossing by trestles and fills miles of tropical swamps, bridging the swift Chagres River, and hacking out a road-bed through long stretches of jungle and across the rugged terrain on the Pacific side. It was not until January 1855 that the line was completed and through trains began operating from ocean to ocean. Meantime as sections were completed—to Gatun, to Bohío Soldado, to Barbacoas, finally to Gorgona—the picturesque river trip was gradually shortened, then eliminated entirely.

Completion of the railroad not only speeded the Isthmian crossing, but also drastically reduced its cost. In January 1849 a writer to the *New York Herald* thus listed his expenses for the sixty-mile crossing: rental of canoe from Chagres to Cruces, $25; mule from Cruces to Panama, $12; for carrying 180 pounds of baggage from Cruces to Panama, $44— a total of $81, plus meals and lodging during five days of travel. By February 1852, after the railroad had reached Bohío Soldado, the fare by train to that point was $5, with an additional $2.50 for the short river trip to Gorgona. The remaining twenty-mile overland trek was still expensive, the usual rental being $16 for each mule and $10 per hundred pounds for freight. This section remained a bottleneck during the two years while the railroad from Gorgona to Panama was building, although most of its worst features were gradually eliminated. In the summer of 1853 California-bound passengers were advised on reaching Gorgona or Cruces to consult steamship company agents stationed there, who would recommend responsible carriers. Travelers were further cautioned to insist that the contractor bind himself to deliver at Panama all goods entrusted to him, under penalty of forfeiting one half his fee. In October of that year the Pacific Mail Company signed an agreement with Hurtade & Hermonos, "largest mule owners on the Isthmus," making them exclusive agents for transporting the company's passengers and their baggage. "Annoyance and uncertainty attending the present system of procuring mules will thus be obviated," stated the *Panama Herald*, which added that passengers could then buy tickets from New York through to San Francisco at fixed rates, and that the contractors would take charge of all baggage when the steamers reached Panama or Aspinwall, "so that the risk of loss and late delivery will be avoided."

That these risks were considerable both before and after Hurtade & Hermonos commenced operations is clear from the many complaints of travelers, expressed in their journals and in letters to newspapers on both coasts. These constitute a long record of possessions lost or stolen, of trunks rifled en route, and of passengers forced to miss their steamers because of the failure of their belongings to arrive on time, or of having to embark with only the clothing on their backs and with a well-founded suspicion that their missing property would fail to follow on the next steamer.

Not only was carelessness and petty theft rampant on this section of the route; bands of brigands were active all during the early years, and their raids on the pack trains often yielded rich hauls. California miners returning home with hoards of gold dust were the most frequent victims. Many avoided this hazard by entrusting their treasure to the steamship or express companies, which undertook for a fee to carry it safely across the Isthmus, but even this precaution was sometimes futile. Panama newspapers reported frequent raids on the specie trains of the carrying companies. On August 7, 1850 one of the Howland & Aspinwall convoys was attacked, the bandits making off with $30,000. In December of the same year another train, operated by Zachrisson, Nelson & Company, was set on a few miles out of Panama and $120,000 in gold dust taken, although this time most of the loot was recovered. Only when the treasure was in the form of gold bars was it comparatively safe, for its weight was then so great that the bandits were usually forced to abandon it in the jungle to avoid capture.

The completion of the railroad in 1855, after five years of effort and the expenditure of six and a half million dollars—a record sum for forty-seven miles of single-track road—brought to an end the pioneer phase of Isthmian travel. Thereafter passengers rode from ocean to ocean in reasonable comfort and with so little delay that those arriving in the morning at one port could make the crossing, embark on the waiting steamer at the other side, and be at sea again before nightfall. Two trains were operated daily from each terminus; the running time was a little more than three hours, and the fare for adults was twenty-five dollars, with half-price for children under six. Freight was fifteen cents a pound. These high tariffs were much criticized, but all attempts to reduce them failed, and it was only when bitter competition with the Nicaragua route brought on periodical rate wars that the public benefited by occasional bargains.

Thereafter, until the transcontinental railroad was completed in 1869, the Isthmus enjoyed a heavy traffic east and west, with an average of thirty thousand passengers crossing each year, plus a huge tonnage of freight. During all this period the Panama Railroad had the distinction of returning to its owners profits far greater than that produced by any other of the world's railroads of anything like comparable length.

5

DURING the height of the gold rush a horde of California-bound emigrants daily swarmed ashore at Chagres, all determined to make their way to the far side of the Isthmus without delay and there re-embark for the final climactic dash to the diggings. To a man they were harried by a fear that unless they hurried, the fortunes they envisioned would fall to others. It was in this headlong spirit that thousands thronged the beach at Chagres, bidding against one another for passage up the river, and, having hired a boatman, loaded themselves and their belongings into his bungo and triumphantly set off.

Four or five days later these same men straggled into Panama, tired and unkempt from the rigors of the trail, from loss of sleep and exposure to tropical heat and rains, and from combating the indifference and extortions of the natives. They usually arrived late at night (having left Gorgona at daybreak), and so near exhaustion that few had any curiosity at all as to what manner of place they were entering. Swaying on the backs of mules as weary as themselves, they grew aware of a change in the character of the country: the trail flattened out and became a roadway, cultivated fields could be discerned on either side, and traffic increased as produce carts and water-carriers joined the parade of pack-mules. Then, states Bancroft, "houses, two and three stories in height, of wood and adobe, supplant the remoter reed huts, and following the current of gold-seekers we leave behind the shops outside the walls, cross the moat, and passing under the arched and towered gateway of Puerta de Tierra, with its old stone cross and bell, we enter Panama."

Relics of the days when Panama had been the axis of Spain's New World empire were everywhere visible to the newcomers, and would receive their curious attention in the days to come. But the arriving Argonaut's first thoughts were centered on a more immediate problem: food to allay his hunger and a place to lay his head. More often than not, neither was available. The city's hotels were generally filled to capacity, with guests occupying cots crowded ten to the room (and paying well for the privilege), and such restaurants as existed were seldom able to serve more than a fraction of the crowds that queued up outside their doors.

Finding that accommodations within the town itself were hopelessly jammed, later arrivals set up camp in the tree-covered fields outside the ancient walls, improvising shelters with whatever materials came to hand and preparing their meals over campfires. During the first weeks of the rush these fields were sparsely settled, but the tide of emigration grew swiftly, with first scores, then hundreds arriving daily, and soon the entire perimeter of the town was a vast encampment, swept by dust clouds and overrun with lizards and tropical insects. Vultures circled overhead and bands of dogs pawed through the refuse that littered the ground. Indifference to sanitary conditions, combined with overcrowding, exposure, and a climate naturally dangerous to the northerners, had the expected result. Disease was widespread, frequently reaching epidemic proportions. Thousands fell victim to dysentery and yellow fever. An almost total lack of medical attention or care made the mortality high, for in general the stricken emigrant was left to shift for himself, his fellows ignoring him either from fear of contracting the disease or from sheer indifference. Of this callousness toward their suffering countrymen J. D. Borthwick, who made the crossing in 1853, wrote:

"There was a great deal of sickness, and absolute misery, among the Americans. . . . The deaths were very numerous, but were frequently the result of the imprudence of the patient himself, or of the total indifference of his neighbors, and the consequent want of any care or attendance. The heartless selfishness was truly disgusting."

Frank Marryat, making an east-west crossing in 1852, himself contracted yellow fever during the journey and spent the last few miles of the ride into Panama clinging to the back of his mule, falling off periodically, and being bodily lifted on again by his companions.

"Our party arrived at Panama half dead with fatigue [he wrote], draggled with mud, and shivering in the torn clothes that for nearly sixty hours had been drenched with rain. I was placed in bed; the other male passengers—all of whom had arrived in good health—made themselves comfortable, and thought no more of the . . . rain or mud. In less than ten days *they all died of yellow fever but one*, and I alone of those attacked recovered."

It was not until letters began to appear in New York and other northern newspapers telling of these hazards to health—one called Panama "one of the worst pest holes in the tropical world"—that a true picture of conditions on the Isthmus reached the public. The steamship companies tried to minimize the danger, having a well-founded fear that it would tend to divert traffic to other routes. Passengers carried the disease aboard the ships, and voyages up both the east and the west coast were sometimes made with cabins jammed with the desperately ill, and burials at sea daily occurrences. After such runs steamer officials commonly attributed the deaths en route to "various fevers," "isthmus diseases," and similar ailments, carefully avoiding the dreaded words "cholera" and "yellow fever."

But it was of course impossible to suppress entirely the fact that the Isthmus offered a serious hazard to the health of the unacclimated Yankees. Steps to improve conditions were taken by the transit companies and others. "There is a hospital attended by American physicians, and supported to a great extent by Californian generosity," wrote a visitor in 1851, "but it is quite incapable of accommodating all the sick." Knowledge of the causes and control of tropical diseases was then extremely limited, and professional treatment—when it was available at all—was confined to putting the victim to bed, dosing him with quinine, and restricting his diet to liquids. Gold-hunters stranded at Panama sometimes used their enforced idleness writing letters home giving advice on how those planning to follow might safeguard their health. One offered this prescription: "Keep out of the sun by day and out of the air and dew at night. Drink hard spirits in moderation and while drinking eat no fruit. Wear light flannel next to the skin and light outside garments." Another advised travelers to remain away from the coastal areas, prolonging their stay in

Gorgona, Cruces, or other hill villages as long as possible and descending on Panama only when their ships were ready to sail.

But this program, sound in theory, had a serious defect: the number of ships leaving Panama for the gold fields was totally inadequate to accommodate more than a small fraction of those clamoring to board them. Thus, while a heavy stream of emigrants descended on Panama from the Atlantic side, only a thin trickle was able to re-embark, and the consequence was that the already crowded town daily grew more so. This influx of course wrought a marked change in the place, transforming it almost overnight from a moldering village that for generations had been drowsing under the hot sun into a confused, noisy, and incessantly active seaport where, according to one unwilling guest, "one finds nothing to admire and much to deplore, where everything conspires to make one's stay there the reverse of pleasant, and where each passing day intensifies one's longing to be at sea again."

Part of the Argonauts' dislike of Panama City was certainly due to their natural impatience at the long, long delays nearly all experienced there. Idle and frustrated, the unwilling guests could find in the town no redeeming features at all. "No place can be more dirty, dingy and dilapidated than Panama," wrote E. S. Capron in 1853. "The streets are narrow and paved with rough stones, which have been worn, without being repaired, for ages." Others were critical of the rubbish-strewn sidewalks, of the natives' habit of living under the same roof with their domestic animals, and of their primitive carts and produce-laden donkeys. All this seemed lamentably unenterprising to the brisk and energetic Yankees. But the average Yankee

193

was also thrifty, and the usurious tribute exacted by local merchants and tavern-keepers, the grogshops and gambling-houses, completed his disillusion. David Lake, from Topsfield, Massachusetts, who made the crossing late in 1851, put up at the California House for the first few nights; then, considering the charge of a dollar and a half per day excessive, he "built a shanty with the branches of a tree" at the edge of the town and lived frugally and in reasonable comfort until he was able to sail north. Panama to his mind was "a miserable place." T. Robinson Warren reached the spot toward the middle of 1849 and found it already taken over by the Americans.

"Hundreds of desperate looking men [he wrote] armed with knife and revolver, were thronging the streets, whose vernacular announced them indubitably as Yankees. Over the doorway of almost every house were signs in . . . English . . . while almost every available apartment was filled with monte, roulette, and faro tables, around which were crowds of betters. . . . The hotels and dwelling-houses were full to overflowing, and every tenement was occupied. The hotels, if such they could be called, were huge old native houses, utterly unadapted for the purpose; the barn-like rooms, damp, windowless, and overrun with vermin, looked more like prison vaults than sleeping apartments, and instead of the weary traveller—half dead from exposure and jaded from his long mule-ride—being assigned to an apartment where he could retire to rest . . . he was ushered into one of these tomb-like rooms, and told to choose his bed from among some fifty cots ranged along its walls, and in tiers throughout its length—his dressing-room and toilet appointments being an open corridor furnished with a gross of tin basins, any quantity of filthy brown soap, and a huge sheet (for a towel), suspended on a roller, and a cracked looking-glass. . . ."

6

ON JANUARY 17, 1849 the steamer *California*, having left New York the previous October, dropped anchor off Panama after a difficult and uncommonly slow passage round the Horn. Her coming, long awaited by impatient throngs at Panama, touched off a bitter feud between the Pacific Mail's agents, Zachrisson & Nelson, and some fifteen hundred emigrants who were determined to board her. Because the little vessel, by the utmost crowding, could accommodate only about two hundred and fifty (fifty in the cabins and one hundred and fifty in the steerage), it was clear to all that a great many would have to be left behind. That there was a limit to the capacity of the 1,000-ton *California* was generally recognized. But what the marooned Yankees could neither understand nor forgive was the fact that on her passage up the west coast the vessel had put in at Callao and—news of the gold discovery having reached that port—Captain Forbes had been persuaded to fill his empty cabins with some seventy Peruvians.

It was the presence of these foreigners on the ship, occupying space they themselves sorely needed, that aroused the resentment of the waiting Yankees. But that was only one of their grievances. Many had taken passage on the steamer *Falcon* with the understanding that they were to re-embark at Panama on the *California* and so make a quick trip to the gold fields. Through tickets to California had been offered them when they came on board at New Orleans, but only a few had bought them, the majority thinking it would be an easy matter to find passage up the coast after they reached Panama. Not until they reached the Isthmus did they repent their failure to provide themselves with transportation at the beginning of the voyage. The result was a concerted rush on the Panama agents of the Pacific Mail, hundreds offering passage money and demanding assurances that they would be taken on the *California*. Faced by this dilemma, the company's agents tried hard to work out as equitable a system as the circumstances would permit. Those holding through tickets were given priority on the remaining space aboard the *California*. Other tickets to a number far beyond the steamer's normal capacity were then sold on a basis of first come, first served, with the understanding that those near the head of the list would be taken on board the steamer; those who remained behind were to be sent north on the *Philadelphia*, a sailing ship chartered by the Pacific Mail, then due from the east coast with a cargo of coal.

The failure of the *California* to reach Panama as soon as planned—she had been delayed at Rio for lack of coal—added to the general uncertainty and unrest. Letters detailing the emigrants' grievances blossomed in Atlantic coast newspapers through the first weeks of 1849. A writer in the *New York Tribune* told of fears that the *California* had been lost en route and that the company planned to send all passengers north on windjammers.

"However [he added], to get on at the slow progress of a sailing vessel ill suited men bound to make a fortune

196

in the gold region. . . . Grounds of blame were invented for the conduct of Messrs. Zachrisson & Nelson . . . and a few hundred men, having nothing else to do, impatient of a moment's delay, wrought themselves into not a little excitement on the subject. Therein originated the meetings which will be famous in the newspapers of New York."

Far from lessening the tension, the eventual appearance of the *California* had an opposite effect. The presence of the South Americans on the ship was regarded as something in the nature of a national affront. A second letter to the *Tribune*, published on March 9, stated:

"Many Americans here are very indignant that these people were on board, but the Captain of the steamer assures them that he will take just as many Americans as though the Peruvians were not on board, he intending to let them sleep on deck, which he would *not* allow an American to do. . . ."

Even this assurance had no great effect. Yet another *Tribune* letter tells of threats by the angry Americans to use force. It begins:

"You are already apprised that the great excitement about the gold of California has induced an unexpected number of persons to come across the Isthmus, *en route* to the mines. Many of these cannot be accommodated on the steamer, and this with other circumstances has generated a state of feelings which will be better understood by what I am about to report. . . ."

This correspondent proceeds to describe a mass meeting held at the American Hotel on the evening of January 19, at which three hundred emigrants planned various reprisals against Captain Forbes, the local agents of the steamship company, and the contingent of Peruvians ensconced on the ship. The tension was eased, however, by the reading of a circular issued by General Persefor F. Smith, then on his way to assume command of the military forces in California. In it he made clear that aliens would be unwelcome in the gold fields.

"The laws of the United States [the circular stated] inflict the penalty of fine and imprisonment on trespassers on the public lands.—As nothing can be more unreasonable or unjust, than the conduct pursued by persons not citizens of the United States, who are flocking from all parts to search for and carry off gold belonging to the United States in California; and as such conduct is in direct violation of law, it will therefore become my duty, immediately on my arrival there, to put these laws in force, to prevent their infraction in future, by punishing with the penalties prescribed by law, those who offend. . . ."

This assurance that foreigners would not be allowed to plunder the diggings while hundreds of deserving Yankees were stranded at Panama cooled the temper of the crowd, some of whom had been advocating forcibly ousting the Peruvians from the *California*. In the end the counsels of moderation prevailed and the meeting, which might well have ended in a Donnybrook, broke up after adopting resolutions condemning the steamship company for transporting aliens to California and warmly commending General Smith's enunciation of the principle of Yankee gold for the Yankee miners. The threat of force thus averted, the *California* took on some two hundred and fifty bona fide Argonauts and on February 1 weighed anchor and steamed north, with more than four hundred aboard. As many again were left behind; some of these were loaded on the *Philadelphia*, which, having been emptied of its coal and refitted with tiers of bunks, sailed a week later.

Meantime the migration was reaching full tide, with new shiploads debarking daily at Chagres to augment the impatient throngs at Panama. Three weeks elapsed after the departure of the *California* before her sister ship, the *Oregon*, completed her round-the-Horn passage and dropped anchor on February 23. By then there were twelve hundred waiting on the Panama beaches, and of these the *Oregon*, which had a large number of through passengers, was able to take on only about two hundred. The third and last of the Pacific Mail steamers, the *Panama*, followed two months later, sailing north on May 18 with another two hundred and—so rapidly had the influx grown—leaving behind nearly ten times that number. Congestion on the Isthmus remained severe for two or three months longer, to the vast discontent of the emigrants, who found themselves stranded in an alien city, with both their patience and their capital melting away and all the while exposed to the danger of tropical fevers and consumed by the fear that while they waited in idleness the gold fields were being plundered by others. Some, despairing of finding other transportation, bought small open boats and hopefully set sail for the north; others abandoned all hope of reaching California and, returning to the Atlantic side of the Isthmus, took passage for home.

Panama remained a badly overcrowded city through all the first half of 1849; then gradually the crowds thinned out. One reason for this was that news of the hardships and delays of the crossing were widely published in Eastern newspapers and had the effect of diverting the bulk of the traffic to other routes. Another was that the three Pacific Mail steamers were then plying on regular schedules between Panama and San Francisco, with sailings timed to make reasonably prompt connections with ships arriving on the Atlantic side.

By the beginning of 1850 the Panama route was again enjoying public favor. With the hazard of weeks-long delays eliminated, it offered the shortest passage to the gold country, although the trans-Isthmian trek still involved hardships that many chose to avoid. But improved facilities along the route—steamships on the Chagres River and company-operated pack trains between Gorgona and Panama City—before long reduced both its discomforts and costs. Meanwhile the building of the railroad was being pushed with all speed, and when it was completed Panama's pioneer era drew to a close. During the next dozen years it was the chief avenue of traffic between the two coasts, and the thousands who passed that way each month looked on the once difficult crossing merely as a pleasant break in the long sea voyage.

7

THE thousands who swarmed up the Chagres and struggled down the hilly trails to Panama City were of course only part of the mighty procession streaming toward the gold fields. Many chose the overland trails, and the endless file of sailing ships headed round the Horn were evidence of the popularity of that route. But both these had obvious dis-

THE WAY THEY CROSS THE ISTHMUS

From a series of lithographs satirizing the Gold Rush, issued by N. Currier in 1849

—California Historical Society

EMIGRANTS ASCENDING THE CHAGRES RIVER, 1849

From a sketch by Charles Nahl   —The Bancroft Library

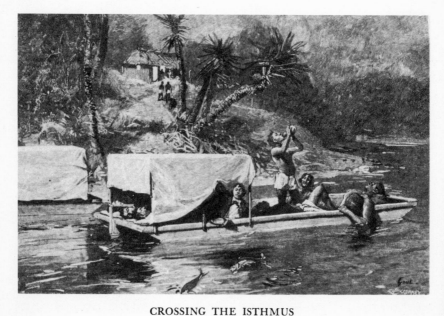

CROSSING THE ISTHMUS

A stop en route. From a sketch by Charles Nahl
                                        —The Bancroft Library

advantages, the chief of which was that they consumed a great deal of time, and in the eyes of the California-bound time was precious.

Poring over their maps, the embryo Argonauts worked out a variety of combination land-and-sea routes that seemed, on paper at least, to offer a practical solution to their demand for a swift passage. The Panama route was in the beginning the most widely followed of these compromises between the all-land and all-water journeys. But it was not long before reports began drifting back telling of a lack of transportation north from Panama City, of thousands waiting for ships that never came, while week by week their capital melted away and scores fell victim to tropical diseases.

Through the spring and summer of 1849, news of conditions at Panama was widely circulated all through the Eastern states, causing thousands to look for an alternate crossing that would avoid the hazards of the Isthmian route, yet retain its chief advantages; that is, a narrow land crossing sandwiched between two comparatively short sea voyages. As the year advanced, a growing number came to believe that they had found the answer. Five hundred miles north of Panama the tapering extremity of the continent again narrowed, bringing the two oceans close together and presenting no serious physical obstacles to travel between the two coasts. To be sure the isthmus at Nicaragua was much wider than that at Panama—the most feasible route was about 165 miles long compared to the latter's 60—but balancing this were certain advantages. For one thing, it shortened the distance from New York to San Francisco by almost a thousand miles, and the saving was even greater for ships touching at New Orleans. Moreover, the crossing was broken by Lake Nicaragua, more than a hundred miles long, which lay near the western side of the isthmus and was separated from the Pacific by a ridge of hills less than a dozen miles across. Lake Nicaragua's outlet, however, was to the east, through the meandering 120-mile-long San Juan River, which empties into the Caribbean at San Juan del Norte.

This crossing had been known to the Spaniards for more than three hundred years, having been discovered in the early sixteenth century by explorers searching for an ocean-to-ocean trade route that might be used as a substitute for Panama, which then suffered from frequent raids by British freebooters. Hence, by gold-rush times, the region already had an involved history. Its towns had been overrun and leveled time and again by contending factions among the Spaniards themselves and by the British. In 1780, in retaliation for Spain's support of the revolting North American colonists, Horatio Nelson, then a twenty-one-year-old captain in the British Navy, landed at San Juan del Norte and led a party up the San Juan River to Lake Nicaragua. There he destroyed the Spanish fort, Castillo Viejo (its ruins were visible to Argonauts passing that way seventy years later), and subdued a Spanish garrison on one of the islands in the lake. But he presently encountered a far more formidable adversary. An epidemic of tropical fever claimed the lives of all but ten of the two hundred men he had led into the interior, and the future admiral himself was so severely stricken that he remained an invalid the rest of his life.

With the disintegration of Spain's American colonies Nicaragua shared the same fate as her rival farther south; both crossings lapsed into almost complete inactivity.

Not until the first quarter of the nineteenth century did they again begin to attract the attention of the great maritime powers. By then the growth of interocean commerce had led France, England, and the United States to consider the possibility of a canal somewhere in Central America, for each nation recognized that to build and control such a waterway would give it control of the trade between the hemispheres.

The result was an international tug of war that lasted three quarters of a century and intermittently engaged the attention of half the world, with diplomats, promoters, financiers, and engineers jockeying for advantage, seeking to further their own projects and to defeat those of their rivals. From the first, Panama and Nicaragua were rivals in this struggle. Both had their proponents and critics, and the controversy that resulted persisted from decade to decade. The venerable Panama versus Nicaragua argument in fact continues to this day, for even the completion, in 1914, of the waterway to the south by no means silenced those who advocate a second crossing in Nicaragua.

The gold rush of course enormously stimulated interest in these canal projects. Among those who were presently studying maps of Nicaragua was a canny and resourceful New Yorker, Commodore Cornelius Vanderbilt. Having amassed a fortune as a shipowner and by his control of the New York ferry system, Vanderbilt was ready to embark on larger enterprises. He had seen two rivals, George Law and William Aspinwall, inaugurate steamship service between New York and California with the help of liberal government subsidies. But in its initial stages this venture had interested him not at all; the territory it was designed to serve was a vast wilderness and in the normal course of events it would be decades before a substantial coast-to-coast traffic could be developed. But then came the discovery of gold and almost overnight Aspinwall's and Law's dubious enterprises had become by far the most profitable steamship routes in the world.

Eying the lucrative traffic that had fallen to his competitors, Vanderbilt considered means of cutting himself in on the profits, or better still of outmaneuvering them by cornering the trans-Isthmian business for himself. What better way to accomplish this than by building a canal across Nicaragua? Such a waterway would be a brilliant achievement, a business and engineering coup that at one stroke would confound his rivals and satisfy his own flair for the dramatic. For the man who controlled a Nicaraguan canal would also control the vast California traffic then just getting under way. It would eliminate the long circuit of South America and obviate the necessity of the transshipment of passengers and goods at Panama; Aspinwall's and Law's steamers would have to abandon Panama in favor of the shorter Nicaragua route, and Vanderbilt's monopoly would pile up tremendous profits for years to come.

Fascinated by this grandiose scheme, the Commodore set plans in motion designed both to explore its possibilities and, should investigation prove that a canal was practicable, to gain commitments from the Nicaraguan government granting him the exclusive right to build and operate it. Vanderbilt was by no means the first in the field, for canal projects had been regularly put forward for many years. But Nicaraguan politics, traditionally unstable, were then so erratic that, although concessions were granted to virtually every group that applied, these were just as regularly repudiated when one government lost power and another succeeded it. So, beyond a few preliminary surveys and many rose-tinted estimates of the canal's costs and its probable profits, nothing had been accomplished.

But the matter had been under discussion so long in Congress and elsewhere that by the fall of 1848 Nicaragua was well known throughout the United States, and those planning to join the California rush gave thought to this route along with others. The lack of dependable means of transportation between Nicaragua and California caused most to avoid going that way during the first months of the rush. As early as February 1849, however, one shipload was already at sea headed for Nicaragua and hopeful of reaching the mines well ahead of those traveling by more circuitous routes. The promoter of this venture was a George Gordon, of Philadelphia, who had organized "Gordon's California Association," chartered a small brig, the *Mary*, and for a modest $260 offered first-class passage "from New York to San Juan de Nicaragua, from thence per Steam Boat *Plutus* to Granada, on Lake Nicaragua; or, navigation permitting, to Managua, Matiares or Nagarote on Lake Leon, as may be most convenient for landing; and a passage from Realejo, on the Pacific, to San Francisco with Hammock, Bed, and Bedding for the voyage and Camp accommodations during detention on land, en route."

How to transport the *Mary's* passengers from Realejo to San Francisco promised to present some difficulty, but this hurdle too Gordon took in his stride. He had, he announced, appointed an agent on the Pacific side of the Isthmus with authority to charter ships at Panama, Acapulco, or other west-coast ports and to dispatch them to Realejo to pick up the Nicaragua emigrants and carry them north. But the chance of finding idle ships in west-coast ports in the spring of 1849—when the hundreds marooned at Panama were offering almost any price for passage north—must have seemed remote even to the optimistic Gordon. His advertisements of the new route ended on this note of caution: "In the unexpected event of vessels not being procured, $75 of the passage money and 60 days' provisions will be refunded to each passenger at Realejo, which will procure passage on the mail steamers which will pass there." The fact that Realejo was not a scheduled stop for Aspinwall's Pacific Mail steamers was ignored; perhaps Gordon hoped that if enough emigrants patronized his route influence could be exerted to force the Panama steamers to stop and pick them up.

In any event, Gordon's promise of a quick passage to California attracted so many that when the *Mary* sailed from New York on February 10, she carried a capacity load of 136 passengers, among them a considerable group of recent Yale graduates. At first the expedition ran smoothly enough. The *Mary* dropped anchor at San Juan del Norte, where the party debarked and waited while the little steamer *Plutus*, which had been brought along in parts, was reassembled and made ready to carry the group up the San Juan River and across Lake Nicaragua. Three weeks later, it having grown clear that the *Plutus* lacked the power to cope with the numerous rapids of the river, the party had to resort to native bungos, just as their fellows were doing on the Chagres. The trip up the river and across the lake to Granada took them until mid-April, where another long wait ensued before, mounted on muleback, they proceeded by easy stages to Realejo. There they encountered further protracted delays. It was not until July 20 that they got transportation on a small brigantine, the *Laura Ann*, and hopefully set sail for San Francisco.

But the trials of these pioneers of the Nicaragua route were by no means over. The *Laura Ann*, badly overcrowded and with meager supplies of food and water, encountered adverse winds and made so little progress that after three weeks she was forced to put in on the barren coast of Lower California. Only the arrival there of a Peruvian ship prevented an extremely serious situation, for the *Laura Ann's* provisions were exhausted and nearly all her crew had deserted the moment she dropped anchor. With supplies bought from the South American ship, and her leaky water casks refilled, the interrupted journey was resumed. She finally reached San Francisco in early October, more than eight months after the party had left New York.

The vicissitudes of "Gordon's California Association" seem for a time to have discouraged others from essaying this same route, and during all of 1849 the sea-borne emigrants streamed on to the south, either to Panama or round the Horn. But meantime Nicaragua had not been forgotten. Commodore Vanderbilt's canal project had been in the public eyes for months. Moreover, some practical progress had been made. As a first step, Vanderbilt had sent a trusted agent to Nicaragua, well supplied with funds and charged with persuading the native government to grant his company exclusive rights to operate a canal "or other system of transportation" across the isthmus. This emmissary proved an able negotiator. Aided by the United States consul, he succeeded in securing the hoped-for contract, and on uncommonly liberal terms. By it Vanderbilt's corporation, the American Atlantic and Pacific Ship Canal Company, agreed to pay the Nicaraguan government

$10,000 a year during the construction period, plus $200,-000 in the company stock and twenty per cent of the net profits after the canal was in operation. This arrangement was to continue for eighty-five years, whereupon title to the property would pass to the Nicaraguans. Moreover, the document contained this shrewd proviso: in the event detailed surveys indicated that the cost of building a canal would be prohibitive, the company was authorized to substitute for it "a railroad, or rail and carriage road, and water communication between the two oceans." Thus Vanderbilt hoped to assure himself of a monopolistic control of trans-Nicaraguan traffic, regardless of whether or not the canal ever materialized. He thus found himself in a position to enter actively into competition with the Panama route for the heavy California trade.

But when the terms of this agreement were made public they immediately set off international repercussions. Great Britain too had long had ambitions to dig a trans-Nicaraguan canal and, in order to further her plans, had established a protectorate over a strip of territory on the Caribbean side of the country, known as the Mosquito Coast. Early in 1848, before the gold discovery had become known, her position had been strengthened by a diplomatic coup in which the natives of the region, abetted by the British, had revolted and proclaimed their independence. The port of San Juan del Norte was occupied by the rebels, and the British established a custom house there, renaming the village Greytown. Thus, with a British-controlled puppet nation occupying the only feasible outlet to the Caribbean, England was in a position to block any canal project of which she did not approve.

This clash of interests brought on heated debate in both

THE TRIALS OF CROSSING THE ISTHMUS

From Marryat's Mountains and Molehills

NIGHT SCENE ON A GOLD-RUSH STEAMER, 1850

From a drawing by Gilbert Gaul, after a sketch by Charles Nahl, in the Century Magazine, April 1891

the United States and Great Britain and severely strained relations between the two powers. The matter was the subject of long discussions between Secretary of State John M. Clayton and Sir Henry Lytton Bulwer, the British Minister; meantime, pending their outcome, the treaty negotiated at Nicaragua in the interest of Vanderbilt's company was not sent to the Senate for ratification. While the negotiations were in progress, Bulwer let it be known that should the American company relinquish its claim to exclusive control of the canal, British capital would be made available to help finance it. This did much to soften the opposition of the Vanderbilt group, who by then foresaw that the enterprise would be immensely costly. The Clayton-Bulwer Treaty was accordingly signed and Vanderbilt set off for England for conferences with London bankers looking toward the joint financing of the canal, which would be open to the traffic of all nations.

This mission was a failure; the British financiers refused to underwrite the venture on the ground that its cost would be excessive. Vanderbilt thereupon abandoned, for the time being, his plan for a canal. But by then the gold rush was in full tide and his interest centered on plans for gathering in a share of the rich trade flowing across the Isthmus of Panama. He returned from England and hurried down to Nicaragua to speed preparations for putting a land and water crossing into operation. There he spent several weeks inspecting the proposed route, traveling by steam-powered river boat up the San Juan River and across Lake Nicaragua to Virgin Bay, then proceeding on muleback over the range of rugged hills that lay between the lake and the Pacific.

Convinced that this route presented no insuperable difficulties, he returned to New York and prepared to enter actively into the coast-to-coast trade. Two light-draft river steamers were built to convey west-bound passengers as far as Virgin Bay. Meantime a road was being cut from the latter town to the Pacific, where a second port, christened San Juan del Sur, was established. To transport the Argonauts to Nicaragua, Vanderbilt put on the New York to Nicaragua run the best and fastest of his steamers, the 1,500-ton *Prometheus*, then newly completed. A second steamer, the *Pacific*, of 1,100 tons, was dispatched round the Horn to establish service on the west coast, plying between San Juan del Sur and San Francisco. Later other vessels were added to the fleet, as were also larger steamers for the run on the river and lake. The road from Virgin Bay to San Juan del Sur was rebuilt, planked over its full length, and fast horse-drawn stages were put in service over this twelve-mile highway.

The preliminaries over, through service was inaugurated in the early summer of 1851, and on July 4, San Franciscans uproariously celebrated the arrival of the first Vanderbilt steamer, the *Pacific*, designed to challenge the monopoly of Aspinwall's Panama line.

8

MEANTIME other groups, not waiting for Vanderbilt to get his steamship lines in operation, had essayed the Nicaragua crossing. Some of these pioneer passages were tedious in the extreme. One was the west-east trek of H. D. Pierce, a homeward-bound New Yorker, who had been in California since August 1849. In early October 1850 he sailed from San Francisco on the brig *Swift Shure* and landed at Realejo after a seven-week trip during which supplies had run low and sickness made heavy inroads among the eighty-seven passengers. Then began a long journey of some three hundred miles to San Juan del Norte. The first part of the route was from Realejo to León, with overnight stops at native villages along the way. Pierce traveled by cart, "being carried with my baggage when I chose to ride," and paying six dollars for the privilege. "The country is beautiful but a perfect wilderness," he commented, ". . . inhabited by Monkeys Birds & Serpants & beasts of prey." Having passed through miles of uninhabited jungle, he and his party were agreeably impressed with Nicaragua's capital, León, "a large and ancient town containing 40,000 inhabitants. . . ." He continues:

"The Cathedral is an imence building being 350 feet long & 170 wide. The roof is built on Many arches, & the whole structure is brick & stone Morter & Sement. It was 18 years in building & cost $1,800,000. The view from the church is verry extensive. There are 13 Churches. There are many ruins in & about the Citty. No commercial or Mecanical opperations are carried on, except Shoe Makers & some small traders. . . . The Natives are verry friendly & think much of the Americans. . . ."

The road from León to Granada was extremely rough— "not an hours work has been done on it . . . only to cut the Brush out of the way. It crooks & dodges about to Shun trees & mudholes." But the beauty of the route, much of which passed along the shore of Lake Managua, won the admiration of the group, and at the town of Masaya they had a mild adventure.

"Arived . . . before dark [wrote Pierce] & put up with the rest of the company at the house of a wealthy old Spaniard. . . . There was about forty in our party, & in the evening our host had a fandango for our amusement. It was Supposed that we had a large amount of Gold & the old man & his family were much alarmed by a report that the Soldiers & Natives were going to attack the house & cut our throats. Our guide allso was alarmed, so after they had barred the doors & windows, at his request we kept a watch all night. All passed off quietly & they were relieved when morning came. . . ."

Two days more brought the party to Granada, where they hired native boatmen and laid in provisions for the voyage along the shore of Lake Nicaragua. This took six days, the travelers camping on land at night and by day enduring alternate periods of heavy rain and scorching sun. Arriving at San Carlos (which they found dingy and uninviting, its inhabitants "most wretchedly poor"), on December 4, the group began the 120-mile descent of the San Juan River to the Caribbean. Two more days of passing over a succession of swift rapids brought them at last to San Juan del Norte. Their hope of finding a ship in the harbor on which they might take passage home having proved futile, the group resigned themselves to another period of waiting.

"The inhabitants [states Pierce's diary entry for December 6] are composed of Germans French English & Musketoes or natives which predominates. The Americans have well nigh eat them out of house & home . . . as they raise nothing about here. Went to board with an old German Lady at $1.25 per day. From the lake to this place there is not a house nor any improovement of any kind except such as is made by the Alligators. . . ."

Their stay at San Juan del Norte lengthened to two weeks, while other parties straggled in from the west, filling the forlorn and rain-swept town to overflowing. At last, the expected steamer having failed to appear, the stranded group appealed to the British consul, asking that the frigate *Inflexible*, then in the harbor, be pressed into service to carry them to Chagres. This was done; the warship took on Pierce and five hundred of his fellows and steamed off, meeting the long-expected passenger steamer soon after it had cleared the harbor. "We paid one ounce each for about 30 hours run," commented Pierce. At Chagres most of the group were able to get passage on the *Crescent City*, which landed them at New York on January 8, 1851, three full months after they had left San Francisco.

Somewhat similar was the journey of J. M. Letts, who left California on November 28, 1849, on the *Edward Everett*, landed at Realejo, and followed much the same route to León and Granada. There the party engaged bungos to carry them across the lake to San Carlos and so down the river to San Juan. This journey too was not without incident. Letts details numerous encounters with the natives, who, like those of Panama, were not averse to levying tribute on the supposedly rich Californians. The driver who contracted to take them from Realejo to León was so adroit a financial manipulator that Letts commented: "with a suitable pair of pantaloons, and a clean shirt, he would have done honor to Wall-street." His favorite exploit was to conceal his oxen in the jungle and announce that they had become lost. Thereupon a confederate would appear and offer—for a substantial fee—to find them. The first time this happened the Yankees cheerfully paid, but when he tried to duplicate the exploit they proved less gullible.

"In the morning [wrote Letts] our driver went out in search of the team, but soon returned, pronouncing them *unfindable*. . . . [He] was accompanied by a worthy, of about his own age and personal appearance. We sent the driver out again . . . but his companion remained. After loitering for half an hour, he proposed going out in search . . . thought he could find them for five dollars; we, as if wishing to drive the best bargain we could, asked him if he could not find them for less; he came down to four, three, two, and one dollar, and finally to twenty-five cents. We took him, tied his hands behind him, then tied him to a tree; we then cut half a dozen good sized saplings. He . . . seemed to look on this as a crisis in his affairs. We asked him where the oxen were, he said 'just over the hill'; we asked him if the driver knew it, he said, 'Si, Senor.' "

The oxen speedily materialized and the journey continued.

A second encounter occurred a few days later:

"On our arrival at San Carlos we were required to submit to custom-house regulations, the officer insisting upon searching our trunks. To this we demurred, having passed through the entire country without submitting to such an ordeal. The officer seeming anxious to compromise the matter, demanded $5 instead from each; the Americans who had preceded us submitted to this extortion, but we were determined to resist. The officer became more moderate coming down—down—down—to a *real;* upon our refusing to pay this, he made a move in the direction of the cannon which was near; we, however, were first to possess it, and things for a moment wore a warlike appearance. The officer, not wishing to bring things to a crisis, held a consultation with our 'Padrone,' and came to the conclusion that all was right, that as we were Americans he would treat us with due consideration."

Letts's party was among the last to make the journey by these primitive methods, for on their passage down the San Juan River they passed Vanderbilt's little steamboat, the *Director*, making its way upstream to inaugurate steam traffic on Lake Nicaragua.

9

VANDERBILT'S opposition steamers were welcomed with enthusiasm by travelers on both coasts. For many months the public had been critical of the high fares and indifferent service of the Pacific Mail, which from the beginning had enjoyed a virtual monopoly of steamer traffic. That the new company would offer serious competition is evident from the San Francisco newspapers of the period, which from early in 1851 had been reporting Vanderbilt's preparations to put the Nicaragua crossing in operation and detailing the supposed advantages of the route over that via Panama. Of course these included the fact that it substantially shortened the distance from coast to coast and reduced to a mere twelve miles the land journey. Yet another superiority was claimed for it, one that weighed heavily with those familiar—either from personal experience or by hearsay—with the hazards of the Panama crossing: the climate of Nicaragua was said to be cool and invigorating and the country free of the diseases to which the traveler was exposed farther south. These roseate claims were not all borne out. Many of those passing over the route complained bitterly of oppressive heat during the daytime and of swarms of insects at night; and malaria, yellow fever, and even cholera were by no means unknown.

Numerous other complaints began to be heard once the new line was in operation. These were mainly because Vanderbilt, avid for a quick share of the profits, had his steamers in service long before proper provision had been made to handle the heavy traffic that was shortly flowing across the Isthmus. The result was that the early travelers encountered hardships and delays far more onerous than those at Panama, where the crossing by then could be made in tolerable comfort. The result was that through the summer of 1851 some San Francisco journals, reversing their previous stand, published letters detailing the shortcomings of the Nicaragua route, while others sought to refute the charges. Thus on September 7 the *Alta California* printed a letter from a Dr. Rabe commenting on certain rose-tinted descriptions of the new route written by Vanderbilt's San Francisco agent, R. J. Vanderwater. Rabe wrote that the passengers who had left New York on the *Prometheus* had had a slow and difficult passage indeed; they arrived in San Francisco fourteen days later than had they gone via Panama. He added:

'TWEEN DECKS ON AN EARLY PANAMA STEAMER

This combination dining-room and social hall was the only place where passengers could congregate in bad weather. Redrawn from a sketch made by Charles Nahl in 1850

—The Bancroft Library

THE BURNING OF THE "GOLDEN GATE"

Off Manzanillo, Mexico, July 27, 1862. From Harper's Weekly, August 23, 1862

"As to the 'twelve mile road'—that is coming—and so is Christmas. As to the 'hotel at Rivas that shames all Panama'—it certainly shames the Devil. One more matter: people are not to be gulled now-a-days by 'forty running hours'; the time consumed in transit from point to point was five days; and we were not even encumbered by baggage."

The letter that prompted Rabe's outburst had been published in the *Panama Star* of August 11 and reprinted in the *Alta* two weeks later. It gave this all too bright picture of the first large party to cross Nicaragua under the Vanderbilt auspices:

"I was a passenger on the *Prometheus*, from New York, July 14th last. We reached San Juan del Norte on the 23rd; left there by the iron steamer, *Sir Henry L. Bulwer*, on the 24th; ran about 45 miles up the San Juan River; and came to anchor for the night. On the 26th, having walked around the portage (300 yards) we took bungos, ten miles to the Toro rapid, where we got on board the steamer *Director*, for Virgin Bay; arrived there at daylight Sunday, 27th, but finding no signal of the arrival of the steamship *Pacific* at San Juan del Sur, we passed up the lake ten miles, to the city of Rivas, a place of 10,000 inhabitants, where we remained until Thursday, and then came on board the *Pacific;* left San Juan on Friday, at 2 P.M. . . . Hereafter the ships and boats will meet regularly, and the passengers will pass over the Company's road to Virgin Bay, (12 miles and 18 chains) which it is true, is now only a mule road, but it is being laid with plank, and will soon be a good wagon road. However, with all the obstacles incident to a

217

first trip, I came from ocean to ocean, in exactly 40 hours running time. . . ."

A round-robin letter signed by passengers on a west-east crossing made in the fall of 1851 offered prompt re-buttal to the above. "In the first place," it stated, "we were informed, by Vanderwater, the agent of the line at San Francisco, that we would be put through in . . . twenty-two or three days . . . that we could cross the Isthmus in two or three days—that everything was arranged, and a good road." But the party arrived at San Juan del Sur to find the road all but impassable and no mules to carry them and their belongings to the lake. After three days they made their way as best they could to Rivas, where they stopped another six days; then, no steamer arriving to pick them up, they set off across the lake in native bungos—"at the imminent danger of our lives." Five days of travel brought them to San Carlos. "We then started down the river, and we were compelled to row all night, and we got to Greytown in some thirty-six hours." There a final piece of bad luck awaited them. The steamer on which they held tickets had already sailed and they faced the alternatives either of taking passage, at their own expense, on another ship or of awaiting the next Vanderbilt steamer. There was an epidemic of fever raging in Greytown, and nearly all the group chose to pay their own fares to New York, which they reached forty-five days after they had left San Francisco. Vanderbilt's agent at Greytown could offer them no assurance that the company would return the cost of the unused part of their tickets, which added to their already strong sense of injury. One account of their tribulations ends on this note:

218

"And we here invoke the travelling community, if they value comfort, health, convenience and life, touch not the unclean thing, but deal with honorable men, who, if you are detained, will indemnify you, as they have heretofore done, by paying you a reasonable amount."

10

AT NICARAGUA as at Panama means of speeding passengers across the isthmus and of caring for them en route were provided as fast as possible. Improved landing facilities were installed at the two ports. Larger lake and river steamers were put in operation, and adequate but by no means luxurious hotels were built at points where overnight stops must be made.

A graphic picture of the Nicaragua crossing after it had been long in operation was provided by Mark Twain in a series of letters to the *Alta California*, written in 1866. Twain left San Francisco on December 15 on the steamer *America*, Captain "Ned" Wakeman commanding. The ship reached San Juan del Sur on the 29th, but there had been an outbreak of cholera in the town and passengers were not allowed to land until the next day. Mark admired the port's natural setting but was not impressed by the place itself. "We found San Juan to consist of a few tumble-down frame shanties—they call them hotels—nestled among green verdure and overshadowed by picturesque hills." His group of eight pre-empted one of the mule-drawn wagons for the trip to Virgin Bay. These did not much resemble the swift and handsome vehicles of the company's advertisements.

Twain described his as a "faded mud wagon . . . with four little sore-backed rabbits hitched to it." The road, however, was in excellent repair, and the three-and-a-half-hour journey was pleasant, although Mark deplored the profusion of roadside signs put up along the way by the enterprising Yankees. "There was some round abuse indulged in . . . of . . . such people, who invade all places with their rascally signs, and mar every landscape one might gaze upon in worship, and turn to a farce every sentimental thought that enters his brain."

Like many northerners before them, the males of the group were not oblivious of the Nicaraguan maidens, whom they encountered, stated Twain, "about every two hundred yards throughout the journey." His admiration for these sepia-colored damsels ("buff colored, like an envelope") inspired him to several pretty flights of eloquence that included tributes to their beauty, their grace, their well-rounded figures—"they are singularly full in the bust, the young ones"—their black hair, white teeth and ever ready smiles. Even their behavior, which by northern standards was sometimes lamentably lax, Twain could not bring himself to condemn too severely: "They are virtuous according to their lights," he commented, "but I guess their lights are a little dim." Two young women who sauntered by were both of such pulchritude that the impressionable Mark's praise reached new heights of extravagance: "—such liquid, languishing eyes! such pouting lips! such glossy, luxuriant hair! such ravishing, incendiary expressions! such grace! such voluptuous forms! such precious little drapery about them! such—" At that point he was brought up short by his companion, an uncouth and

unromantic fellow, who interposed: "But you just prospect
one of them heifers with a fine tooth—"

Twain's descriptive talents were not all expended on the
comely Nicaraguan girls. The *America's* four hundred passengers, pressing forward over the hill road between ocean
and lake, presented, in his words, "the wildest, raggedest
and most uncouth procession I ever saw." He was reminded
of a pageant in which all the actors wore fantastic mas-
querades.

"The steerage passengers travelled on muleback,
chiefly, with coats, oil-skin carpet sacks, and blankets
dangling around their saddles. Some of the saddles were
new and good, but others were in all possible stages of
mutilation and decay. There were not a dozen good riders
in the two hundred and fifty that went on horseback, but
every man seemed to consider that inasmuch as the animals belonged to 'the Company,' it was a stern duty to
ride them to death. . . . Such racing and yelling, and beating and banging and spurring, and such bouncing of
blanket bundles, and flapping and fluttering of coat-tails,
and such frantic scampering of the multitude of mules,
and bobbing up and down of the long column of men, and
rearing and charging of struggling ambulances in their
midst, I never saw before, and I never enjoyed anything
so much."

The hundred-mile crossing of the lake was made in
twelve hours, in a comfortable steamer and over a route
made delightful by the unsurpassed loveliness of the scenery.
At San Carlos the travelers were transferred to "a long,
double-decked shell of a stern-wheel boat, without a berth

or bulkhead in her—wide open, nothing to obstruct your view except the slender stanchions that supported the roof." In this they traveled down the channel of the San Juan, past the ruined castle of Lord Nelson fame, and on to within thirty miles of Greytown before the craft was tied up for the night. "Those who had hammocks swung them, and those who hadn't made beds of their overcoats, and soon the two dingy lanterns, hung forward and aft, shed a ghostly glimmer over the thick-strewn and vaguely defined multitude of slumberers." Next morning many complained of the discomfort of sleeping on the unyielding decks—"but these little troubles were soon forgotten when the galley-boys came up . . . and disclosed the happy truth that we had not only the usual tea and coffee and sandwiches for breakfast, but also cheese!"

Twain dealt at length on the meals supplied them by the transportation company during the crossing. "On the lakeboat, they fed us on coffee and tea, and on sandwiches composed of two pieces of bread enclosing one piece of ham. On this boat they gave us tea, coffee, and sandwiches composed of one piece of ham between two pieces of bread. There is nothing like variety."

The party reached Greytown on December 31, having spent something less than twenty-four hours traveling from the Pacific side. This port impressed Twain no more than had San Juan del Sur. It consisted of about two hundred frame houses "and some nice vacant lots," with an extremely mixed population numbering eight hundred, most of whom were engaged in selling goods or services to the Yankees. Usually transients were obliged to spend a night there before boarding the steamers, and the consequence was that every second householder was in the hotel business. Beds cost a dollar each, which Mark considered no bargain. "It does not cost much to keep a Greytown bed in order; there is nothing to it but a mattress, two sheets and a mosquito bar." Having spent the last night of 1866 on one of these austere couches, Twain boarded a small boat early the next morning and, in a heavy downpour, was rowed through the heavy surf and, soaked to the skin, clambered up on the deck of the steamer *San Francisco*, which sailed at noon. That evening the passengers, sitting "under jeweled skies," passed the time by singing:

God save the good ship as onward she flies!
We're homeward bound! homeward bound!

"That is well enough," Mark wrote. "I like that."

Chapter Five : STEAMSHIPS

1

By NO means all the California Argonauts traveled on sailing ships. The age of steam had been revolutionizing ocean travel all during the decade before the gold discovery. By an odd coincidence the beginning of the westward rush coincided almost exactly with the departure from New York of the first of a fleet of thousand-ton steamers initiating monthly runs between Eastern ports and the nation's new west-coast possessions.

The government mail subsidy that made these pioneer lines possible was fixed by act of Congress in March 1847, and during the eighteen months that followed, contracts were let, steamship companies were organized, ships were built, and provision was made for fueling and supplying and servicing them at the remote Pacific ports.

The first Pacific Mail steamer to be completed was the *California*, a 1,050-ton side-wheel steamer, with accommodations for sixty saloon passengers and one hundred and fifty in the steerage. She was dispatched round the Horn from New York in early October 1848 and was scheduled to reach Panama on January 4. There she was to pick up such passengers as might be carried by the *Falcon*, of the United States Line, which sailed from New York for Chagres on December 1. Both vessels left with all but a few of their cabins empty, for although nearly a year had passed since Marshall's discovery, recognition of its significance had come slowly to the east coast. But once the movement got under way, it grew with amazing speed. The *Falcon* left New York on December 1, carrying less than a hundred passengers; eighteen days later when she sailed from New Orleans she carried more than twice that number. The *California*, which had set off from New York two months earlier than the *Falcon*, had but six passengers, none of them bound for California. Delays en route made the *California* two weeks late in reaching Panama City. When she dropped anchor off that port on January 17, she was besieged not only by the *Falcon's* passengers but by hundreds who had come on the *Crescent City* and on numerous sailing ships. "The isthmus was fairly swarming with gold seekers," wrote Bancroft, "some 1500 in number, all clamoring for . . . a passage on the *California*."

Of course not all these could be accommodated, but so many were crowded on board that this first steamship to ply the route between Panama and San Francisco made her maiden voyage with a passenger list far exceeding the most sanguine calculations of her builders. With more than four hundred on a ship designed to carry only a few more than half that number, the task of providing meals and sleeping-space for all taxed the ingenuity of officers and passengers alike. A correspondent for the *New York Herald*, Stephen H. Branch, described the livestock carried in pens on the deck: hens, sheep, goats, cattle, and pigs—all destined to find their way into the capacious pots of the galley. Providing meals for so many was of course a problem, since neither galley nor dining-room space permitted serving all at the usual hours. As in most sailing ships, passengers were divided into companies; each appointed one or more of its number to carry pans of food to some appointed spot on the deck, where the group consumed it, using such utensils as they chanced to have at hand. It is not surprising that many found the food, prepared and served under such conditions, unappetizing, and there were those who complained that there was not enough of it.

One passenger, Elisha Oscar Crosby, fared better than most. Crosby, a young New York attorney who had taken the trip for his health, carried a letter to Zachrisson & Nelson, the Pacific Mail's Panama agents; this he duly presented, asking to be put aboard the *California*, then about to sail. He adds:

"Mr. Nelson very kindly and considerately took me in charge, and furnished me with a box of provisions, and a large Mexican Hammock for he said he could do little else than to put me on board; that there were only accommodations for 25 persons . . . and how the passengers were to manage was more than he could tell. But he said . . . that . . . what I could not get from the general mess I must take out of my box. . . . He also advised me to take the Hammock, which I did, and had it hung in the rigging of the steamer, and slept there most of the way from Panama to San Francisco."

As to how the *California's* passengers occupied themselves, and what were their sleeping-arrangements, details are meager, although it is known that wherever space could be found additional berths had been built while the ship lay off Panama. But the Argonauts had been inured to so many hardships during their stay on the Isthmus, and were so delighted to be taken aboard at all, that they were inclined to overlook whatever discomforts they encountered en route.

The *California* left Panama on February 1 and reached San Francisco an even four weeks later. Not only was the voyage slow, it was full of variety. Five stops were made en route: at Acapulco, San Blas, Mazatlán, San Diego, and Monterey. At Acapulco insubordination among the firemen caused much uneasiness, many fearing that the crew would desert in a body and so bring the voyage to a premature end. But the difficulty was finally adjusted, and the sailors—who were as anxious as the others to reach the gold fields—remained on the job, only to jump ship the moment the anchor was dropped in San Francisco Bay. Both at Acapulco and Mazatlán passengers went ashore en masse, partly to see the country but mainly to forage for provisions. "The steamer was also replenished," wrote Crosby, "with everything that could be procured in the way of fresh provisions, such as vegetables, fruits, live beef, sheep, pigs and poultry."

Monterey was reached on February 24, and there a new difficulty arose. The ship reached that port with the supply of coal in its bunkers practically exhausted. While the passengers roamed about the town, crew members went into the thick woods on the hillsides, where they foraged for fuel to keep steam in the boilers during the final hundred miles of the journey. This went on for three days; then, after huge stacks of wood had been assembled on the beach and some of it carried on board, a reserve supply of coal was found in bags under a storeroom floor. The passengers were summoned on board and on the evening of the 27th the journey was resumed. Next morning the *California* passed triumphantly through the Golden Gate, ending the first steamer voyage between the two coasts.

2

IT WAS of course the steamers' speed that made them desirable in the eyes of the Argonauts. Even in the earliest days they reduced the coast-to-coast time of the fastest sailing ships by more than half. In the summer of 1849 Bayard Taylor found some seven hundred men waiting at Panama, all determined to take passage on the two small Pacific Mail ships then on the San Francisco run. The only steamer in port was booked to capacity, and those lucky enough to hold tickets on her were being offered—and refusing—six hundred dollars each for them, twice their original cost. The Pacific Mail's Panama agents were, naturally, still under heavy pressure, and there were always those among the impatient throng who advocated taking forceful possession of the ships. "A few days before we came," wrote Taylor, "there was a most violent excitement on the subject, and as the only way to terminate the dispute, it was finally agreed to dispose by lot of all the tickets for sale." Each man's application was accordingly numbered and a drawing was held. But there were only fifty-two places available for the more than three hundred who entered the raffle, and the disappointed ones were not mollified.

Even those lucky enough to hold the coveted tickets admitting them to the steamer were not at the end of their trials. Embarking at Panama was a slow and tedious process, and if the weather chanced to be rough it was attended with considerable danger. Because of shallow water close to shore, the Pacific Mail ships anchored more than a mile from the beach and passengers and their baggage had to be ferried out in small boats. This traffic was in the hands of native boatmen, who congregated before the town's hotels as the sailing hour approached, noisily soliciting patronage. Having concluded a bargain, they seized the passenger's belongings and made off for the beach, the owner following anxiously behind. At the water's edge the traveler climbed on the native's back, was carried through the surf, and was deposited in a bungo, which lay just beyond the breakers. This process was repeated until the frail craft was so loaded with men and goods that it seemed in imminent danger of swamping, whereupon oars were unshipped and the long pull out to the steamer began. Those who had made these precarious bungo trips rarely failed to record their relief at finding themselves safely on board ship.

The days that followed were hardly less memorable, for life on the pioneer Pacific steamers had no precedent.

"A voyage from Panama to San Francisco in the year 1849 [wrote Taylor] can hardly be compared to sea-life in any other part of the world or at any previous period. Our vessel was crowded fore and aft: exercise was rendered quite impossible and sleep was each night a new experience, for the success of which we were truly grateful. We were roused at daylight by the movements on deck, if not earlier by the breaking of a hammock-rope and the thump and yell of the unhappy sleeper. Coffee was served in the cabin; but, as many of the passengers imagined that, because they had paid a high price for their tickets, they were conscientiously obliged to drink three cups, the late-comers got a very scanty allowance. . . ."

The avidity with which this shipload of pioneers descended on the tables at mealtimes aroused Taylor's wonder, if not his admiration. Two meals were served daily, breakfast and midday dinner, and the opening of the 'tween-decks dining-room was announced by the ringing of a bell. "At the first tingle . . . all hands started as if a shot had exploded among them; conversation was broken off in the middle of a word; the deck was instantly cleared, and the passengers, tumbling pell-mell down the cabin-stairs, found every seat taken." When platters of food were placed on the tables the speed with which it disappeared amazed the journalist. "There was a confused grabbing motion for a few seconds, and lo! the plates were cleared. A chicken parted in twain as if by magic, each half leaping into an opposite plate, a dish of sweet potatoes vanished before a single hand; beefsteak flew in all directions; and while about half the passengers had all their breakfast at once upon their plates, the other half were regaled by a 'plentiful lack.' "

Having observed this phenomenon twice a day throughout the voyage, Taylor set down this philosophical comment:

"Among our company of two hundred and fifty, there were, of course, many gentlemen of marked refinement and intelligence from many parts of the Union—enough, probably, to leaven the large lump of selfishness and black-guardism into which we were thrown. I believe the controlling portion of the California emigration is intelligent, orderly and peaceable; yet I never witnessed so many disgusting exhibitions of the lowest passions of humanity, as during the voyage. At sea men completely lose the little arts of dissimulation they practise in society. They show their true light, and very often, alas! a light little calculated to encourage the enthusiastic believer in the speedy perfection of our race."

Hubert H. Bancroft, who made the trip two years later than Taylor, found the situation much the same. Although by then more and larger steamers had been put on the run, the number demanding passage was still far in excess of facilities for handling them comfortably. "No man knows himself, much less his neighbor," Bancroft commented, "until he has made a voyage in an overcrowded ship in hot weather." His catalogue of the annoyances of the voyage is a long one, the chief of which was the enforced close association day and night with the noisy, the profane, and the boorish. Gamblers, braggarts, and "brazen faced . . . young women" made life difficult for sober-minded travelers, who looked on in silent disapproval as these took possession of the ship, "seeming to vie with each other in rendering themselves disagreeably conspicuous."

"To the refined and sensitive [he added], such an infliction, from which there was no escape for days and weeks, was torture. Of all the miseries I ever experienced on shipboard, sea-sickness, tempest, filth, and fever included, by far the worst has been the crowd, among whom there were always some supremely disgusting persons whose presence one could not escape. . . ."

But the picture was not all dark, as Bancroft himself admits. During a large part of the voyage the ships kept close

232

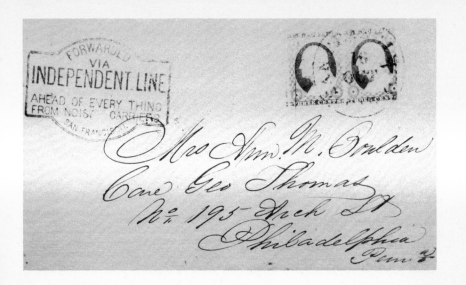

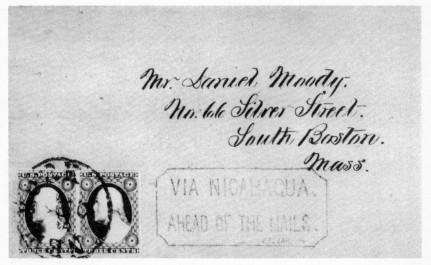

"AHEAD OF THE MAILS"

Examples of propaganda stamps on letters carried by pioneer steamers competing with those of the Pacific Mail, which held the government mail contract. During the early 1850's much mail was sent from San Francisco by "pick-up operators" who gathered bags of letters and, for a fee, forwarded them via opposition steamers to New York, where they were deposited in the post office. —From the collection of Edgar B. Jessup

THE 1,275-TON PACIFIC MAIL STEAMER "TENNESSEE"

The Tennessee *operated between Panama and San Francisco from March 1850 until she was wrecked a few miles north of the Golden Gate on March 6, 1853.* —Wells Fargo History Room

DEPARTURE OF AN ATLANTIC STEAMER, 1854

Throngs crowded the San Francisco dock to witness the twice-monthly sailings of the Pacific Mail steamers. From the Pictorial Union, July 4, 1854. —California State Library

to shore, and it was pleasant on balmy days to sit beneath the deck awnings and watch the changing panorama of palm-fringed shores and rolling green hills extending inland to lofty mountain ranges. At such times a spirit of sociability permeated the ship. "Gossips took heart; matrons smiled serenely; paterfamalias grew jocund; attention turned toward comfort, reading and amusements. Gallants mixed huge pitchers of iced punch, and therewith regaled the ladies." Moreover, by 1851, in deference to the greater number of women and children among the passengers, some of the more flagrant abuses of earlier days had been prohibited. Professional gamblers who through 1849 and 1850 had taken over the public rooms, spreading out faro and roulette games on the tables of the dining-saloon, were required to ply their trade less openly. But although gambling was officially prohibited it was by no means eradicated. Bancroft reported "plenty of card-playing in the state-rooms, where the occupants could gamble to their heart's content, and lesser games obtained on capstan, bench, and skylight." He observed too an epidemic of wagers: "on daily distances, on the time of arrival at any point, on the height or weight of any person or thing, on the time in which coat and boots could be taken off and put on, and on anything that happened to strike the fancy, however absurd." Clearly, time passed slowly on these pioneer voyages!

Most of the discomforts stemmed of course from the necessity of crowding on board as many passengers as could possibly be carried. When a ship designed to accommodate, in first and second cabins and in the steerage, a total of six hundred put to sea with a thousand on board, much in the way of conveniences and privacy had to be sacrificed. All through the early 1850's letters detailing the grievances of disgruntled travelers appeared in newspapers on both coasts. Many of the complaints were of conditions that could not well be avoided; others were well founded. Meals hastily prepared and served at unseasonable hours were to be expected, but that the food itself should be limited in quantity and sometimes half-spoiled or vermin-infested was less easily excused.

There were numerous such charges, not all of them against the quality of the food. One man wrote that on the entire trip from Panama to San Francisco, a matter of fourteen days, the linen on the bunks in the first-cabin staterooms was not once changed. Another complained that the dining-saloon was constantly in filthy condition, with floor unswept, plates carelessly washed, and both tablecloths and waiters' coats badly needing immersion in soap and water. Still others pointed out that sanitary facilities were totally inadequate, that one bathroom did service for all the first- and second-cabin passengers, and that the steerage—which held some two hundred—had none at all. A passenger on the *North Star* on the run from New York to Aspinwall stated that "there were four water closets for the use of about three hundred people of the first and second cabins."

During the first few days out of Panama the heat below was often intense. The consequence was that most passengers slept on deck, some swinging hammocks from the rigging, others getting such rest as they could on the hard deck planks or in the companionways. After a night spent on a pile of ship's gear a passenger on the *California* wrote next morning: "Got up, neck, back, and arms nearly broke rubbing on the bars, ropes, etc." Another stated:

"Everywhere the ship is crowded; the passengers on each side of the machinery, the upper and lower forward decks, the long steerage extending from the bows far aft on both sides of the engine—all are full, and many of the berths are occupied by two passengers each. . . ."

Excessive overcrowding, combined with the heat of the tropics, induced a widespread relaxation of the period's mid-Victorian standards of modesty. One writer thus describes the scene at night on one of the Panama steamers:

"Although it is very dark, you will observe that the benches around the ship's rail are filled with human beings. Some are stretched out at full length, others half reclining. You will see as you inspect these benches females in the close embrace of the sterner sex, their heads reclining in the most loving manner on the shoulders of their male protectors. You will naturally enough suppose them to be husband and wife or sister and brother. They are in some cases, but more frequently are not, but only a couple whose acquaintance dates back to the ship's sailing. . . . Around the mainmast is a dark mass composed of forty or fifty persons, of all ages and both sexes, heaped together en masse, and all apparently sound asleep. . . ."

Going below, this observer found an even greater informality:

"Directly at the foot of the steps, lying on her back, is an Irish woman weighing not less than two hundred and fifty pounds. She is almost without clothing, so great is the heat. Around her, like a litter of pigs, are five children, the eldest being about five years of age. Every berth is filled. Women can be seen in this second cabin who have apparently lost all sense of decency, who at home would cover the legs of a piano, so particular were they in regard to anything appearing naked."

3

THE design of the early gold-rush steamers all followed much the same pattern. The upper decks were clear from stem to stern, except for a deckhouse slightly forward of amidships, which sheltered the officers' quarters and navigation room. When the weather permitted, the passengers gathered here to take their exercise, to play games, or, in southern waters, to take their ease beneath canvas awnings. Companionways fore and aft gave access to the lower levels, that nearest the bow leading to the forecastle, and a second opening into the dining-saloon, a long narrow room that extended two thirds the length of the ship. Light and air were admitted to this chamber by skylights and ventilators set into the deck above. The long tables with their immovable chairs were used not only for meals; between times passengers gathered about them to read, write letters, or talk. This was the social center of the ship when, in northern latitudes, the deck above became too chilly for comfort.

Ranged about the sides of the dining-saloon were a series of doors opening into the first-class staterooms. These were tiny, crowded compartments, each containing from two to four berths, together with washstand, mirror, and space for storing baggage. The rooms were carpeted; curtains hung before the berths, assuring a degree of privacy, and each had a porthole admitting light and air. These cubicles were often stifling hot in the tropics, particularly those above the engine room or boilers. Later, on ships specially designed for this run, windows replaced the portholes, and in some cases air-ducts were installed, through which air was forced by the forward motion of the ship. Second-cabin accommodations were commonly in the after end of the ship. The chief difference between first and second class was that sleeping-chambers in the latter were much larger, each containing a dozen or more berths, sometimes as many as fifty. Second-cabin passengers had the same privileges as those going first-class and ate the same meals, although they were often relegated to later messes.

The steerage was deep in the ship and well forward. Here, in dark, crowded quarters, filled from floor to ceiling with tiers of berths, passengers lived in noise and confusion, with no hope of privacy. In the earlier steamers there was no segregation of the sexes; men, women, and children were crowded indiscriminately into a single large compartment, where the only open spaces were narrow aisles between long lines of berths. These were usually built in groups of three both vertically and horizontally, so that the person occupying that fartherest from the aisle was obliged to climb over the other two to get in or out.

The space allotted to each steerage passenger was small indeed. The berths were mere pieces of canvas stretched between wooden frames six feet long and eighteen inches wide, and the distance between one and its neighbor above or below was a scant two feet. Passengers were obliged to furnish their own bedding and eating-utensils. Their food was served them direct from the galley, outside which they lined up at mealtimes to have their plates and cups filled. They ate lying down in their berths or standing in the passageways.

Letters protesting such conditions became so numerous in newspapers that steamship-owners on both coasts were forced to make certain improvements. Many passengers claimed that they had bought steerage tickets on representations by the companies that the quarters were convenient and comfortable, and hence not only men traveling alone, but women, children, and family groups had embarked with no foreknowledge of what they would encounter. Responding to the public clamor, the companies installed tables at which steerage passengers could sit at mealtime, and supplied them with cutlery and plates, and on some ships a separate room was partitioned off for the use of women and children who were traveling unaccompanied by males. For these accommodations passengers paid as high as $150 for the passage from Panama to San Francisco; later steerage passage dropped to $100, where it remained for several years.

Steamer fares in general fluctuated wildly during the first five or six years. At Panama during the early months of 1849 the pressure for space was so great that tickets changed hands for as much as $1,000. The established rates were high enough. First-cabin fare was $300 from Panama to San Francisco, with steerage half that sum. On the Atlantic, first-cabin tickets from New York to Chagres were $150, and the steerage was $75. Thus the cost from coast to coast was $450 and $225 respectively, and this did not include the expense of meals and lodgings, boat and mule hire while crossing the Isthmus. These rates remained unchanged until the beginning of 1850, when other ship-owners, eager to share in the traffic, began to offer competition to the pioneer Pacific Mail.

Not the earliest but certainly the most serious threat to

the Aspinwall company's monopoly was Vanderbilt's Nicaragua line, which entered the field in the summer of 1851. The Commodore's method of luring patronage from the steamers operating out of Panama was not only to advertise that the new route was far shorter and that Nicaragua's climate was healthful and salubrious, but to post fares well below those of his competitors. Cabin rates from San Juan del Sur were fixed at $100, as against $250 charged by the Pacific Mail for the Panama to San Francisco run. During the rate war that resulted, fares dropped sharply on both routes. There were periods when it was possible to travel from New York to San Francisco in the first cabin for as little as $100, as against $450 during the earlier period. Neither company, however, could long sustain such superlative bargains. From late 1851 onward coast-to-coast fares were generally stabilized, with tickets on the better steamers averaging around $300 in the first cabin, $200 in the second, and $150 in the steerage. In 1855, however, an outbreak of cholera at Nicaragua having sharply reduced travel over that route, Vanderbilt again resorted to price-cutting to fill his empty steamers. First-class passage from New York to San Francisco was slashed to $180, and the steerage went down to an all-time low of $50.

About that time, too, the volume of emigration began to fall off, and steamers that had formerly carried from eight hundred to a thousand passengers on each trip now left port with no more than three or four hundred. Competition for this diminished traffic periodically caused the operators to resort to rate wars. In September 1854 three steamers of rival lines were simultaneously loading at San Francisco: the Pacific Mail's *Sonora*, Vanderbilt's

Cortez, and the *Yankee Blade*, owned by the Independent Line. In their bids for patronage existing rates again tumbled to points far below cost. The *Cortez* offered first-class passage to New York for $200, the *Yankee Blade* cut this to $175, and the *Sonora* advertised $150. Second class was $150 on the two first named, with the *Sonora* again undercutting to $100, while steerage passage was $50 on the *Yankee Blade* and *Sonora* and $80 on the *Cortez*. All three companies lost heavily, but the unquestioned bargains they offered stimulated in the Californians a brisk desire for travel. All three vessels left with full passenger lists, the *Cortez* carrying six hundred, the *Sonora* seven hundred, and the *Yankee Blade* nearly a thousand.

4

MORTALITY on the steamers was far heavier than among those who made the round-the-Horn passage on sailing ships. One reason was that while the time in transit was far shorter, the steamers carried many more passengers and crowded them even more closely together than was usual on the windjammers. This naturally increased the hazard of epidemics by multiplying the chances that persons carrying contagious diseases might be aboard and by placing them in daily close contact with numerous others.

But even more serious was the fact that steamer passengers had of necessity to break their journey by a land crossing, either at Panama or Nicaragua, thus exposing themselves for some days to the disease-ridden tropical swamps. Knowing next to nothing of the nature of the

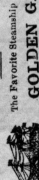
STEAMSHIP ADVERTISEMENTS

Throughout the 1850's, rival steamship lines regularly advertised the advantages of their ships and routes in the San Francisco newspapers.

—Edgar B. Jessup

CARD ADVERTISING THE ADVANTAGES OF TRAVEL VIA THE PANAMA ROUTE

—Edgar B. Jessup

dangers they faced, and consequently taking few precautions to avoid infection, the unacclimated northerners fell easy victim to a variety of maladies: malaria, jaundice, dysentery, yellow fever (commonly called Panama or Chagres fever), or cholera. Having contracted one or another of these diseases, the sufferer could hope for little in the way of treatment. In the earlier period hospital facilities were nonexistent at both Panama and Nicaragua, and when doctors chanced to be available, lack of experience in coping with such illnesses and lack of drugs and nursing rendered them impotent to give more than superficial aid. Hence these dangerous fevers were in most instances permitted to run their course; those who died were placed in ever growing "American" cemeteries at one or another of the ports, and the survivors either returned home or continued on to the gold fields.

But it often happened that persons infected with highly contagious fevers had already embarked on the northbound steamers before they were stricken. When that happened, the result was usually an epidemic that was not brought under control until numerous others were infected, with the melancholy accompaniment of daily burials at sea. The annals of many such trips are grim indeed. Toward the end of 1852 Frank Marryat, having barely survived a siege of yellow fever at Panama, took passage on an unnamed steamer for San Francisco. Because the epidemic was still raging on shore, the ship left port hastily, with insufficient supplies and crowded with passengers.

"I had secured a dog-hole of a cabin [Marryat wrote] and was no sooner on board than my wife, worn out by fatigue and anxiety, was attacked by a violent fever. There were two young doctors on board, but both were attacked shortly after we started. Then the epidemic . . . broke out among the passengers, who—crowded as thick as blacks in a slaver—gave way to fear, and could not be moved from the lower deck, and so lay weltering in their filth."

Marryat went on to report that with neither medicine nor nurses available, and little food, conditions grew steadily worse as the voyage progressed. "From the scuttle-hole of our small cabin we could hear the splash of the bodies as they were tossed overboard with very little ceremony." On the fifth day out their already desperate situation was further complicated by a storm so heavy that the overburdened steamer lost her maneuverability and received so severe a battering that she sprang a serious leak.

"When we commenced to work the pumps they were found to be useless, for the coal had started and the pumps become choked. This new danger drove the epidemic out of the passengers' heads, and they at once proceeded to throw overboard the cargo (and with it my luggage), and then they bailed by means of tubs and buckets. . . . For two days and nights we were in suspense as gang relieved gang at the buckets. . . . All were black and filthy with the coal dust, now mixed with water in the hold. . . . Then the gale broke, and as the ship became easier, the leak gave way before the exertions of the coal-begrimed passengers; we steamed into Acapulco, still bailing out the black water from the hold, and felt ourselves safe, at least, from shipwreck. A favorable change had taken place in my wife's health, and I determined on remaining at Acapulco until

I could procure a passage on a safer and more commodious vessel."

Less happy was the outcome of other voyages. In August 1852 the Pacific Mail's *Golden Gate*, having taken on a full complement of passengers, including several companies of the Fourth Infantry bound for the Presidio at San Francisco, was found to have several cases of cholera. The disease spread with appalling rapidity. Eighty-four of the soldiers died before the ship cleared Panama Bay, and there were almost daily fatalities all the way to San Francisco, where she arrived on August 19.

Both cholera and yellow fever were intermittently present on many other northbound steamers. On the same day—September 1, 1854—the *Sonora* and the *Yankee Blade* reached San Francisco from the Isthmus; each reported deaths en route from the plague, the *Sonora* having lost eight passengers and the *Yankee Blade* six. Vanderbilt, never loath to turn the misfortunes of his competitors to his own advantages, thereupon pressed with renewed vigor his claim of the superior health and safety of his Nicaraguan route; in their advertising his agents in San Francisco adopted the slogan: "Less disease via Nicaragua." In the summer of 1855, however, an outbreak of cholera at San Juan del Sur exploded the myth that passengers traveling by that route were immune. On July 16 the *Sierra Nevada* reached San Francisco from that port, having buried thirty-one passengers during the ten-day voyage. Two weeks later the same line's *Cortez* lost twenty en route, all inmates of the steerage. The epidemic thereupon died out; the next Vanderbilt steamer, the *Uncle Sam*, arrived on August 13 with all her capacity load of seven hundred and fifty in good health. But this was only a respite; when the *Uncle Sam* steamed into the harbor at the end of her next voyage, she was virtually a death ship. Cholera had broken out soon after she cleared from San Juan and had raged unabated through the entire trip; one hundred and four had died en route and another nine succumbed after she reached port. This was the heaviest loss reported on any single voyage on steamers plying the Pacific. A larger proportionate mortality, however, was sustained on the *Philadelphia*, which on its run from Panama to New York in 1852 suffered an outbreak of cholera so virulent that more than a third of its hundred and fifty-five passengers perished on the way.

Such epidemics were, of course, not all confined to the steamers. There were occasional outbreaks of cholera or tropical fevers on the many sailing ships making regular trips between Panama and the Golden Gate during the first months of the rush. San Francisco newspapers seldom reported the mortality on the incoming sailing ships, but the records of two have been preserved. In April 1852 the *Blonde* reached port having lost 18 of her 300 passengers, and she was followed soon after by the *Sir Charles Napier*, which had suffered even heavier losses on her ninety-day passage from the Isthmus, 36 of her 210 passengers having been buried at sea.

5

SICKNESS was not the only sea hazard faced by the California-bound. The Argonauts were exposed to other dangers, including the ever present possibility of the most dreaded of marine disasters, shipwreck and fire. These perils were greatest on the steamers, for while the gold-rush sailing ships did not escape entirely, comparatively few were wrecked, the reason being that, except when they were entering or leaving port, they laid a course far off shore, where an error of a few miles in fixing their positions was of little consequence, and the danger of running aground was practically nil.

The steamers, on the other hand, particularly those on the Pacific, were seldom out of sight of land from the time they left Panama Bay or San Juan del Sur until they tied up at the San Francisco docks. By thus hugging the shore-lines they substantially shortened their runs and effected considerable savings in fuel and other supplies, but this placed an added burden of responsibility on the ship's officers by making faulty judgment or inaccurate naviga-tion liable to dire consequences. Moreover, their task was complicated by the fact that existing charts were incomplete and sometimes misleading, and in the first years lighthouses, buoys, and other navigational aids were completely lacking.

In view of these handicaps, the safety record of the pio-neer Pacific steamers reflects credit on the vigilance and skill of their navigators. From 1849 to 1860 the Pacific Mail carried, at a conservative estimate, a quarter of a million passengers, all without the loss of a single life by ship-wreck. In the main this was credited to the fact that the line's captains were chosen with great care—most of them were former officers of the United States Navy—discipline was rigid, and the crews were well trained.

From time to time the wisdom of such precautions was demonstrated. During 1853 two of the line's finest vessels, the *Tennessee*, and the *Winfield Scott*, ran aground; both were lost. The *Tennessee*, northward bound from Panama with a full passenger list, encountered thick fog off San Francisco and, mistaking for the Golden Gate an inlet a few miles to the north, piled up on the sandy beach. The sea was calm and for two days she remained there, little damaged, while passengers, mail, and freight were removed and preparations were made to pull her into deep water at the next high tide. But at that point the period of good weather ended. "During the night," stated the *Alta*, "the rollers came in heavily on the beach, lifting the ship up from four to five feet and thumping her heavily on the sand as they ran back. When morning dawned it was discovered that she was much out of shape, her back broken, butt ends started and bottom probably bilged; she was then taking in a great deal of water; her connecting pipes were all broken, rendering her engines entirely useless."

This account of the final abandonment of the *Tennessee* is typical both of the florid journalism of the period and of the public's interest in the steamers that formed their chief link with home:

"Her officers and crew felt as if they were attending the funeral obsequies of a dear and valued friend. She was a favorite craft and one of the best sea boats that plowed the Pacific Ocean. She was the home, the pride and refuge of her officers and crew, and many a tear as salt as the brine that surrounds her shattered hull has coursed unbidden from manly eyes, and sprung up involuntarily from the bold and courageous hearts of those whose pride and delight she was as they gazed on the last resting place of the gallant ship. . . ."

The *Tennessee*, the first Pacific Mail steamer to be lost, went aground on the morning of March 6, 1853. Nine months later, on December 2, the *Winfield Scott*, having cleared from San Francisco a few hours earlier, struck the island of Anacapa, one of the group off Santa Barbara, "in fog so thick it was impossible to see the ship's length ahead." The impact stove in the vessel's bow, and, rapidly filling with water, she was again run ashore. She remained afloat until all on board were rescued, then sank in deep water with the loss of much valuable mail and express matter. Anacapa Island was barren and desolate, but blankets and food had been taken off the ship, and the marooned group settled down with such patience as they could muster to what promised to be a long wait before their plight could become known. But once more luck favored them. On the morning of the second day the *California* was sighted entering the Santa Barbara channel. "A gun was fired from the island as a signal. She did not hear the gun but the smoke was seen, and attention being attracted to the island which was crowded with people, they immediately went over and took off the ladies, whom they brought up here. . . ."

On neither the *Tennessee* nor the *Winfield Scott* were any lives lost, and newspaper accounts of the disasters pay tribute to the efficient behavior of their officers and crews. This was not invariably the case. On July 6, 1851 the 600-ton *Union*, owned by one of the Pacific Mail's competitors, the Independent Line, ran aground on the Lower California peninsula while southward bound from San Francisco. The *Union* was a total loss, although here again passengers and crew were rescued, and much of the cargo, including a large amount of treasure, was brought safely ashore.

The vessel struck at three o'clock in the morning, when the
sea was calm and the weather clear. Her loss under such
circumstances puzzled San Franciscans until survivors arrived and told their stories. They reported that the Fourth
of July had been observed so thoroughly, and that the
celebration had been so long continued, that on the night
of the 5th no watch was maintained on deck and the helms-
man had fallen asleep at the wheel.

The Independent Line suffered a second and more
serious loss three years later when the *Yankee Blade*, completed only the year before, and one of the largest and fastest
steamers on the Pacific, was lost off the southern California
coast. This fine 1,800-ton craft was a victim of the owners'
demand for speed, of a wish to make the run from San
Francisco to Panama in a few hours less than competing
boats. Eager to save a mile or two of distance, the *Yankee
Blade's* captain laid a course too close to shore while rounding Point Arguello and crashed at full speed into a sub-
merged reef off the point of the headland. The force of the
impact so damaged the ship that hope of saving her was
abandoned at once and all effort was directed toward
landing her nearly nine hundred passengers. The weather
was clear and the sea calm, but a lack of discipline was at
once evident among the officers and crew. In the resulting
confusion one of the lifeboats capsized as it was being
launched, with the loss of all but four of its twenty-one
occupants. The ship struck in mid-afternoon; between
then and nightfall some two hundred were landed on the
beach, whereupon rescue work was suspended until the
next morning. For those still on board the night was one of
terror and peril. A heavy wind came up and the ship began to go to pieces. Both the captain and the first officer

Pacific Mail Steamship Company's

Through Line to

CALIFORNIA,

CARRYING THE U. S. MAIL.

By Steamers of the PACIFIC MAIL STEAMSHIP CO. on the Atlantic and Pacific,

AND

By the Railroad of the PANAMA RAILROAD Company, via ASPINWALL and PANAMA, to SAN FRANCISCO.

Leaving the Company's Pier, No. 42, North River, Foot of Canal Street, New York, on the

1st, 11th, and 21st

OF EVERY MONTH,

AT TWELVE O'CLOCK, NOON.

When these dates fall on Sunday, the departure will be on the Saturday preceding.

BAGGAGE.

100 lbs. Baggage allowed each adult Passenger. For all over this weight, 10 cents per lb. must be paid to the Purser on board.

No MERCHANDISE nor BEDDING will be taken as BAGGAGE. BAGGAGE CHECKED THROUGH, over the entire route, in charge of BAGGAGE MASTERS, who also attend to ladies and children without male protectors. Baggage received the day before sailing, from passengers who prefer to send down early.

An experienced Surgeon assigned to each Ship. Medicines and Professional Services Free of Charge.

FOR PASSAGE TICKETS,

Or further information, apply at the only office of the Companies authorized to engage passage in this city, (established 15 years,) where State-rooms and Berths on both Atlantic and Pacific Steamers can be secured.

C. L. BARTLETT & CO., Agents,
16 Broad Street, Boston.

(OVER.)

Special Reduced Rates!

☞ FOR THIS TRIP ONLY. ☜

FROM NEW YORK, Nov 1 1866

THE P. M. S. S. CO'S STEAMSHIP,

GOLDEN CITY

CONNECTING AT PANAMA WITH THE

Through Passage Rates,

From New York to San Francisco,

(INCLUDING PANAMA R. R.)

First Cabin, (outside room,) - $300
" (inside room,) - 250
Second Cabin, - - - - - 150
Steerage, - - - - - - - 75
Children between 6 and 12 years 1-2 fare
Children from 2 to 6 years, - 1-4 fare
Children under 2 years - - - Free

U. S. Soldiers having honorable discharges are taken at one-half the regular rates: $300, $200, and $100.

APPLY FOR TICKETS, with Berths and State-rooms, to

C. L. BARTLETT & CO.
Agents for New England,
16 BROAD ST., BOSTON.

(OVER.)

A PACIFIC MAIL CIRCULAR ISSUED IN BOSTON IN 1866

—Edgar B. Jessup

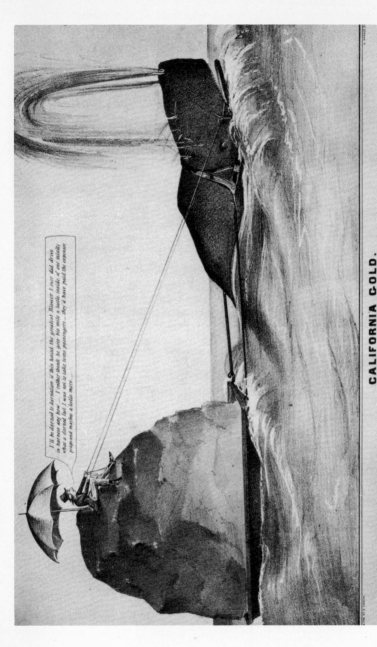

The caption reads: "An accurate drawing of the famous hill of gold, which has been put into a scow by the owner, and attached to a Sperm Whale who is now engaged in towing it around the Horn, for New York."

—California Historical Society

had remained ashore and the result was that all discipline
was lost. Steerage passengers, together with such crew
members as remained, broke into the liquor stores, drank
heavily, and embarked on a campaign of looting and ter-
rorism, rifling the first-cabin staterooms and attacking
those who sought to interfere. The ship's purser, Samuel
Vought, later described the scene:

"Confusion in the wildest sense prevailed, for there
were those who had prepared to swim ashore stiffening with
cold; those who had sought to drown their fear in too frequent libations . . . while some, with calm resignation,
had prepared themselves for the worst, and waited their
fate in peace. Thus we passed the dismal night, made still
more solemn by the churchlike tolling of the bell, which
seemed to beckon us to our funeral."

At eight o'clock the next morning a small coastwise
steamer, the *Goliah*, southward bound from San Francisco,
chanced by. Despite the heavy seas she lowered her boats
and after a day-long struggle succeeded in taking on board
some six hundred. With her heavy load the *Goliah* proceeded
to San Diego, discharged the survivors, and returned to
the wreck, where she picked up nearly three hundred
stranded on the beach. This group had meantime fared
badly.

"Before leaving the wreck [wrote Vought] we sent
ashore all the provisions to be found, awnings and poles
for tents, and clothing, etc. . . . But it is to be regretted
that the actual sufferers never received the provisions sent
them, for a party, composed mostly of the ship's firemen
insensible to humanity, and holding the advantage by

having in their possession a large quantity of firearms and ammunition, took for themselves almost everything that went ashore, and money was seen in their possession, which they could not have obtained honestly. . . ."

The ship was of course a total loss. Thirty passengers lost their lives and the survivors all their possessions. In addition, some $153,000 in specie stored in the *Yankee Blade's* vault was never recovered.

Heavy as were these losses, it was Vanderbilt's opposition line that fared worst. This company then operated six steamers on the Pacific; in a period of fifteen months, from February 1852 to April 1853, four of them were wrecked. First of the series was the *North America*, a new 1,500-ton vessel, northward bound from San Juan del Sur with a passenger list of nine hundred. On February 27, 1852 the ship was approaching Acapulco, running close inshore on a calm moonlit night.

"The evening was beautiful [stated one of the passengers], the atmosphere clear, the moon bright and stars twinkling in all their brilliancy. About 11 o'clock the first mate thought he saw something on shore and called the captain who immediately came on deck, mounted the wheelhouse and took a survey of the coast. At this time we were running outside the surf, and unless the captain was blind or crazy he must have seen that we were too close to shore, and therefore should have kept her off; but instead of this he changed her course toward the shore, when she immediately struck."

Although she went aground on a sandy beach and seemingly sustained little damage, efforts to refloat her were

futile; the surf, striking her broadside, drove her steadily
higher on the beach. The passengers were all safely landed,
together with enough supplies to sustain them on the fifty-
mile overland trip to Acapulco. This trek was successfully
accomplished, most of the party—including fifty women
and about ninety children—traveling on muleback. Hubert
H. Bancroft, who reached Acapulco on another steamer a
week later, reported that nearly all the group were without
funds and were subsisting on charity. Passengers on the
Tennessee contributed seven hundred dollars to their relief.
Meantime news of their plight had reached California, and
in Stockton and San Francisco mass meetings were held
to raise funds for them. The Vanderbilt line was bitterly
criticized, both for the wreck itself and for the company's
failure to provide means by which the marooned passengers
could complete their journey. "As a matter of course,"
wrote Bancroft, "the captain was greatly blamed for the
accident, some charging him with culpable negligence,
others with ignorance of the coast, and others with inten-
tionally running his ship ashore." Of the company's failure
to send prompt aid he added: "One hundred and twenty
thousand dollars, it was stated, had been paid by the *North
America's* passengers; through no fault of theirs, they had
been thrown on a foreign and unhealthy shore, and now
the company were loath to spend a few thousand dollars
to save their lives."

Less than four months later, on August 17, Vanderbilt
lost another of his first-line vessels. The *Pioneer*, a speedy,
1,800-ton screw-driven steamer, launched a year previously,
was run aground on one of the southern California beaches.
Sent out from the east coast to replace the wrecked *North
America*, the *Pioneer* had had a difficult passage round the

Horn. While she was coaling at one of the ports en route, she ran on a reef and sprang a leak severe enough to necessitate keeping her pumps in continuous operation during the remainder of the voyage. Notwithstanding this, she had taken on a full load of passengers at San Juan del Sur and proceeded north. The *Alta California* tells the sequel:

"After leaving Acapulco her machinery became a little deranged and it was soon discovered that she was out of coal and two of the flanges of her propeller had been carried away. In this crippled condition, without coal and without propelling power, she was overtaken by a heavy head sea; and although the pumps of her engine, together with all her side pumps worked by fifty men, were in constant motion, the water made so fast that it was deemed absolutely necessary for the preservation of the lives of the passengers, to run the ship into some place of shelter where they could be landed without risk. She was, accordingly, run into St. Simon's Bay on the evening of the 16th. The water on the following day having gained on them so fast as to reach the furnaces, extinguished the fires. To prevent her sinking she was run on shore where she soon after filled."

Having lost the two finest ships of its fleet, the Vanderbilt line enjoyed six months of immunity before disaster struck again. Then, on February 16, 1853, the *Independence*, 615 tons, proceeding northward from San Juan, ran aground on Santa Margarita Island, off the coast of Lower California, and sank with a heavy loss of life. Here too the stories of survivors were critical of the judgment and skill of the ship's officers. The *Alta* (which had long supported the Pacific Mail and opposed its chief competitor) printed this probably biased story in its issue of April 1:

"On the morning of the 16th, about a quarter past five, a good many of the passengers had turned out to give the crew a chance to wash the decks. A number of them pointed out some rocks ahead and informed the captain that they were running dead on; to which he curtly replied, 'mind your own business'; at the same time declaring that what they took to be rocks *were nothing but whales*. The weather at the time was extremely clear, and not hazy, as the captain reports. A few minutes after that, the ship struck. . . . The engines were backed, the ship went off, and they found she was rapidly filling. . . . Shortly after, the ship was pointed head on to the beach where she no sooner struck than fires burst out."

The attempt to beach the ship failed when she struck a ledge some distance from shore. With fires started in the damaged furnace room spreading rapidly, there began a concerted struggle to escape. Lifeboats were found to be lacking such essential equipment as oarlocks, and those boats that successfully gained shore failed to return, their crews refusing to venture again into the heavy surf. Meantime on the burning ship wild confusion prevailed. One of the survivors, Ezra Drown, described the scene in detail:

"Men of wealth were offering huge fortunes to be saved. . . . Wealth and poverty were on an equality, and sank together to rise no more. Females could be seen clambering down the sides of the ship, clinging with death-like tenacity to the ropes, rigging and larboard wheel. Some were hanging by their skirts, which unfortunately, in their efforts to jump overboard, were caught, and thus swung, crying piteously and horribly, until the flames relieved them from their awful position by disengaging their clothes, causing them to drop and sink. . . ."

Of the three hundred on the *Independence*, one hundred and twenty-five were lost. The survivors, marooned on the barren island without food or water or shelter, and with no means of knowing how long they might have to wait for rescue, had their already desperate plight complicated by an outbreak of looting. "At a time when money had no value," commented Drown, "could be seen the sacrilegious pillaging and plundering of the dead—old men and young men were stripping the bodies of clothing, securing the contents of their pockets, and actually quarreling, yea fighting over a corpse for the plunder!" In fixing responsibility for the tragedy, Drown wrote—and the *Alta* printed—this sweeping indictment of the ship's captain: "That he was insane no one will say, would to God we could. That the act was deliberate and intentional, can and, we believe, will be, successfully established."

Even the loss of the *Independence* did not end the Vanderbilt line's remarkable succession of misfortunes. Less than a month later, in early April 1853, the 1,100-ton screw steamer S.S. *Lewis*, eighteen days out from San Juan del Sur with 385 passengers, missed the Golden Gate in a thick fog and, shortly before daylight, ran aground at Bolinas Bay, eight miles to the north. This time passengers and crew were landed safely and much of the cargo was salvaged, but the ship itself was a total loss—a circumstance that permitted the unfriendly *Alta* to end its story with this comment:

"As there were no lives lost and no distress occasioned by the disaster, other than the temporary inconvenience to the passengers and the anxiety of their friends, this loss may be considered as rather beneficial to the traveling public than otherwise, as the *S.S. Lewis* could not be considered wholly seaworthy."

6

MORE capably managed than her arch rival, the Pacific Mail for a long time was happily free from major wrecks. But when disaster finally struck, it was on a scale exceeding that of all former sea tragedies on the Pacific.

On July 21, 1862 the *Golden Gate*, a 2,100-ton side-wheeler, which for more than ten years had been one of the favorite ships on the Panama run, left San Francisco with 242 passengers, a crew of 96, and in her vaults $1,400,000 in treasure. Among those on board was André Chavanne, who had reached California from his native France in 1851 and during the next decade had risen to control of valuable mining properties. Chavanne later penned one of several accounts of what befell the *Golden Gate*. His narrative begins:

"The trip was a happy and successful one up to Sunday evening, July 27. During that day, the sea was smooth, the heat excessive. All the passengers were lightly clad, the ladies elegantly dressed. Since morning we had been sailing close to shore so as to view the picturesquely shaped rocks and the green grass that capped the hilltops. We were about fifteen miles north of Manzanillo, near Colima, on the southwest coast of Mexico. We were to call at this port and remain there a few hours."

At half past four that afternoon, while the first-class passengers were at dinner, word was brought to the captain's table that the ship was on fire. The *Golden Gate's* master, William H. Hudson, together with R. H. Peterson, the Pacific Mail's fleet captain, who chanced to be on board, hurried out to investigate. Captain Peterson's statement opens:

"We immediately left the table; he [Captain Hudson] took the deck, while I ran to fight the fire, which originated between the forward smokestack and the cabin galley. I saw the forward part of the upper engine room in a blaze. . . . The engineer was attaching the hose, while I ran to the paddle-box calling on all I met to follow and pass down the buckets of water that were always there. This was done and I dashed water in around the smokestack till I was driven from it by the smoke and heat. I then ran to the upper deck, 'aft, to see that they were getting the hose along from the after deck pump; and as this was being done, I . . . heard Captain Hudson say that he had headed the steamer for the shore, which was distant some three and a half miles. Jumping down below, I saw at a glance that we were a doomed ship, as the flames flared up from the engine-room hatch; met Mr. Waddell, who said his men below were cut off and would be burned, and we decided to knock down the bulkhead, in the after freight room, and if possible save them; this was done, and Waddell himself, when prevented by the fire from coming up, jumped overboard from the after freight-port and was saved. . . ."

Meantime the flames, fanned by the rapid movement of the ship, which by then was making at top speed toward the beach, spread with appalling rapidity. Within a few minutes the entire center of the ship was afire, isolating passengers and crew fore and aft. The scene was one of vast confusion. Survivors, forced steadily toward the bow or stern, endured the smoke and heat as long as possible, then jumped overboard, although the ship was still several miles from shore. Many of those who leaped from the bow were swept beneath the churning paddle-wheels, while those who dropped off the stern were speedily left far behind; in either case few survived.

Chavanne, with many others, had congregated at the vessel's after rail, from which the advancing fire had caused them one by one to go over the side until at last he was alone.

"The swirling flames were over me and all around me [he wrote]. I could hardly breathe, the smoke hurt my eyes, the heat was becoming intolerable, the fire was already reaching me. Still I hesitated! I could not make up my mind to add another victim to those I could see struggling before me."

At the last moment he saw a number of lines hanging over the ship's side and trailing in the water. He leaped toward the nearest of these and, "with a precision and an agility of which I would have been quite incapable at any other time," succeeded in grasping it. It was his hope that he might hold on until the still moving ship got near enough to shore to give him a reasonable chance of swimming the rest of the distance. But smoke, flames, bits of canvas, and finally "a shower of burning tar" forced him to slide down into the water.

"Endeavoring to take advantage of everything that would postpone my abandoning the vessel, I hoped I could

257

be towed by tying around my body the rope to which I was hanging. I had already begun to carry out that idea, but had barely touched the water when its resistance, so much greater that the ship was going faster, snatched the rope violently out of my hands, spinning me around."

Then began a struggle that for courage and tenacity has few equals in the annals of sea disasters. Chavanne found himself surrounded by scores of men and women who were "struggling in every direction, grappling with one another . . . drowning one another in ferocious embraces." For the first half-hour he devoted himself to keeping out of the reach of these terrified fellow victims, knowing that only thus had he a chance to survive. In this he succeeded, but the effort consumed time and strength he had hoped to expend making for shore. Now, with darkness falling and the cries of other survivors growing weaker, he found that he had been carried so far out to sea that the shoreline was no longer visible. He had put on a life preserver when he left the ship, and during his swimming about he had come on another. "I succeeded in securing it and was, from then on, able to float more easily and to take some rest, of which I was in great need."

Clinging to these, and with intervals of rest, he started swimming toward land, guided by the still-burning bulk of the beached steamer, some four miles distant. After he had been five hours in the water, the cries of the last of the victims in his vicinity—that of the women—ceased and silence descended, filling him with a deep sense of his isolation. As the night advanced, a brisk wind came up, whipping the sea into swells and vastly increasing the difficulty of clinging to his improvised raft of life preservers.

The struggle continued all night, Chavanne, cold and approaching exhaustion, doggedly paddling in what he hoped was the direction of land. When at length daylight came he was confronted by a new and discouraging development: the shore, which he had supposed to be close at hand, was visible only as a faint line on the horizon. "I understood I had been carried away a great distance during the night, by currents that undoubtedly were carrying me still further all the time."

This discovery disheartened Chavanne only momentarily; soon he again started struggling toward shore, pausing from time to time as weakness overcame him, then grimly striking out again. Thus he passed the hours of the morning and on into the afternoon. His one hope now was to reach a position close enough to shore to permit him to keep it in sight and thus avoid again losing his bearings when darkness descended. Of this period he wrote:

"I kept swimming without looking about me any more. I stopped only to catch my breath; but I could not remain long without moving. It seemed to me that by resting, my limbs lost their suppleness and became numbed. I moved continuously and mechanically. My head was sound, my idea clear; but my heart ached at the idea that very soon I would have no strength left to make headway. During one of the short periods of rest I fancied I heard a noise in the water. Turning my head around quickly, I saw two boats coming toward me."

Chavanne was rescued, after twenty-three hours in the water, by a small Mexican schooner that had come upon him far out at sea at a point forty miles from where his Odyssey had begun. On his urging, the craft cruised about

until long after nightfall in the hope of finding other survivors, but although a number of floating bodies were
sighted, the quest proved fruitless. The next morning he was
put ashore at Manzanillo, seemingly not much the worse
for his grueling ordeal. There he joined a group of survivors
who had been brought in from the beach opposite where
the steamer had been run aground. The reunion was a
gloomy one, for their ranks were sadly thinned.

"Among the people who had been saved [wrote he]
many were in deep despair. Husbands, wives, children,
brothers were missing. The number of victims exceeded
two hundred. . . . We had lost two thirds of the passengers
and a third of the crew."

Of the 338 on board, 223 had perished; $1,400,000 in
specie was also lost. Of all the disasters to gold-rush ships
it was the most costly in life and treasure.

Chapter Six : THE ARRIVAL

1

HOWEVER the journey was made, whether aboard the slow-moving barks and brigs and schooners of the passage round the Horn or on the vibrating, paddle-driven steamers scurrying north from Panama, the near approach to California brought new animation to passengers and crew alike. The lethargy brought on by weeks of inactivity, of endlessly following the same routine, and of confinement in cramped quarters was shaken off, and from stem to stern the little ships fairly hummed with activity. For now at last the Argonauts were close upon the goal toward which they had been striving for months, to gain which they had faced the real and imagined dangers of the unknown and, in many cases, sacrificed their savings and heavily mortgaged their futures. Any way one looked at it, it had been a colossal gamble, with a lifetime of ease awaiting the lucky ones, and with the hazards correspondingly high. What they found in California, how they met its opportunities and disappointments, would inevitably affect the future course of their careers.

Their first sight of the California shoreline brought too a return to the customs and institutions of home, the more welcome because of their recent contacts with an alien civilization in the countries to the south. For this land toward which they were heading was now a part of the United States and, however strange it might seem in other respects, there would be flying above it a familiar flag, symbolizing the laws and customs of the homeland. John Linville Hall expressed a sentiment common to many as, on September 13, 1849, the *Henry Lee* neared the Golden Gate:

"Our approach to the American soil acted upon our feelings as upon the exile's first glimpse of the heaven-pointing spire of his own village church, and the paternal roof which sheltered him in childhood. What sensations thrill his soul! how animated his countenance! how sparkling his eye! how elastic his step! . . . The tumultuous feelings that arise are only to be experienced by him who, after being tossed for months upon the briny deep, lands upon the outskirts of his own vineyard."

But to those aboard the sailing ships the last few hundred miles were often the most tedious of the entire journey. For the prevailing offshore winds were unfavorable for vessels beating northward, and these usually spent days in long, oblique runs that netted only a few miles of forward progress. Sometimes, indeed, they encountered head winds so heavy as to force them far off their course, wiping out in a few hours the painfully acquired gains of a fortnight. J. Lamson of the *James W. Paige* recorded one of many such instances:

"*August* 24 [1852]: Our voyage is becoming prolonged to an excessively wearisome duration. More than a month ago we calculated on arriving at San Francisco in ten days;

and with a fair wind we could have performed the voyage
in that time. Now, after having trebled it, we seem as far
from port as ever. During the last fortnight the winds have
been blowing from the north-east, and we have sailed sharp
on the wind, in expectation of falling in with the northwest trades. . . . We are now about nine hundred miles
west of the coast of California, and in a latitude only four
degrees north of that of San Francisco. . . ."

The *James W. Paige*, like many another gold ship, had
laid a course far to the northwest, hoping thus to avoid the
head winds nearer the coast. By this route the vessels continued hundreds of miles north of their intended destination
until they encountered the steady trade winds common in
these latitudes and so approached San Francisco from the
northwest. But on the *James W. Paige* another full week
passed before the long awaited trades materialized and
meantime passengers and crew were sunk in the depths of
despondency, bored alike with themselves, their ship, and
their companions. "We suffer much weariness, lassitude,
and drowsiness," wrote Lamson. But a day or two later a
favorable wind sprang up; the ship, with sails full and lines
taut, laid a course direct for the Golden Gate. Immediately
all was animation and good cheer.

J. M. Letts describes the *Niantic's* approach to land in the
summer of 1849. On the morning of July 3 weeds and
floating logs were observed and later that day the summer
fogs cleared long enough to permit taking an observation,
which fixed their position some sixty miles off San Francisco.

"The passengers are all engaged in packing up [wrote
Letts]. The retorts, crucibles, gold tests, pickaxes, shovels,

and tin-pans, are put into a separate bag, and laid on the *top;* each determined to be the first off for the mines. Each one having conceived a different mode of keeping his gold, one would exhibit an ingenious box with a secret lock, another, a false bottom to his trunk, a third a huge belt, while a fourth was at work on a fifteenth buckskin bag, each of 20 lbs. capacity. . . ."

Making receptacles to contain their anticipated hoard of treasure engaged the attention of passengers on many ships during the last days at sea. Enos Christman, aboard the *Europe,* wrote: "As we approach the place of our destination the boys are busying themselves in making various bags, shot pouches, etc., out of old boot legs." But the safe storage of their dust was not the only concern of the Argonauts about to land. Soon they would step ashore in a rough frontier country where dangers of many sorts were to be expected; it seemed the part of prudence to be prepared for any emergency. E. I. Barra, who made the voyage on the *Urania,* reported:

"We now have the prospect of arriving . . . in a short time, and the passengers are now preparing to invade an unknown country, where they expect to encounter Indians and wild beasts. The deck is looking like a veritable arsenal. Guns, pistols, bowie-knives, powder flasks, and other death-dealing apparatus that a man may need in a new, unexplored country, can be seen in the process of being cleaned and prepared for action when needed."

The final days at sea brought hazards more real and immediate than those conjured up in the minds of the over-imaginative. During most of 1849 and well into the next year a mighty fleet converged on San Francisco, with as

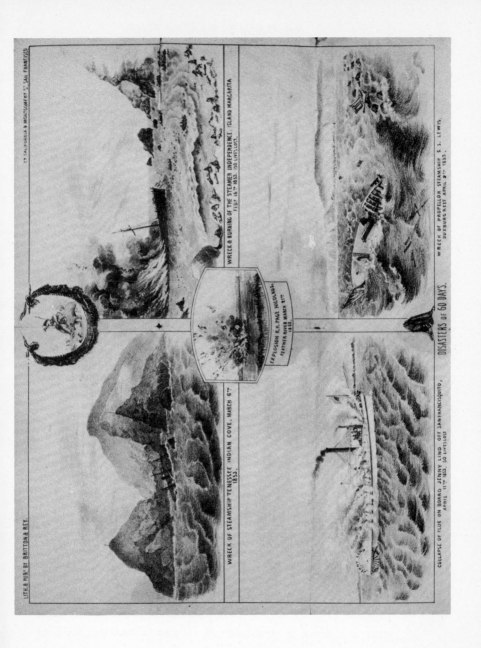

LITH.& PUB.R BY BRITTON & REY.

C? CALIFORNIA & MONTGOMERY S? SAN FRANCISCO

WRECK OF STEAMSHIP TENNESSEE INDIAN COVE, MARCH 6TH 1853.

WRECK & BURNING OF THE STEAMER INDEPENDENCE, ISLAND MARGARITA FEBY 16TH 1853. 150 LIVES LOST.

EXPLOSION R.R. PAGE INCLANA FEATHER RIVER MARCH 12TH 1853.

COLLAPSE OF FLUE ON BOARD JENNY LIND OFF SANFRANCISQUITO, APRIL 11TH 1853. 30 LIVES LOST

WRECK OF PROPELLOR STEAMSHIP S. S. LEWIS, DUXBURG REEF APRIL 9TH 1853.

DISASTERS OF 60 DAYS.

THE HAZARDS OF OCEAN TRAVEL IN PIONEER DAYS

*A letter-sheet issued at San Francisco in 1853 picturing five marine
disasters in near-by waters during a period of less than two months*
—Society of California Pioneers

MR. GREENHORN'S FIRST DAY ASHORE

A letter-sheet, published by Cooke & Lecount in 1850, detailing the trials of the emigrant upon landing at San Francisco

—Society of California Pioneers

many as twenty vessels passing into the harbor in a single day. Cautious skippers maintained a sharp lookout in these crowded offshore waters, particularly during periods of bad visibility, but despite their vigilance collisions were frequent. The bark *Anna Reynolds* was involved in such an accident on the night of November 18, 1849, some thirty miles off the Golden Gate. Nelson Kingsley described its effect on the sleeping passengers:

"About 3 o'clock we were all suddenly awoke by a tremendous crash forward as if every splinter that could be broken loose from us was about to be severed. I sprung out, and found that the ship we saw yesterday was upon our decks crushing our bulwarks in a terrible manner, with her bow, at every surge of the sea. It appears that, from bad management from us both, the watch who were on the lookout, were looking the wrong side for danger. As we had just tacked ship we were on the larboard tack. Our boys were looking to the windward when the affair took place. . . ."

Both ships—the other was the *Amerika*, a German craft— suffered heavy damage to their rigging and bulwarks, but when after twenty minutes and with great exertion they were forced apart, it was found that both were still sound below water and still navigable, and they proceeded on their way.

Not all the gold ships were so lucky. Entering the harbor was a hazardous operation during the first year or two, calling for skillful seamanship even under favorable weather conditions. To find the bay at all was sometimes difficult; its narrow entrance had been overlooked by numerous early explorers of the coast, thereby delaying its discovery for close to two centuries. Once found, to negotiate its winding channel, which narrowed to less than a mile at its inner portal and through which strong currents flowed at each turn of the tide, tested the skill of the sailing ships' captains even when wind was favorable and the visibility good. But there were often periods when the elements conspired to make an already difficult feat of seamanship vastly more so. At most seasons of the year, but more particularly during the summer months, heavy curtains of fog frequently enveloped the coast, sometimes so thick that it was impossible to see a ship's length ahead. Incoming vessels could escape this peril only by putting out to sea again and awaiting the return of clear weather.

Not all the gold ships overcame these multiple hazards. During the early months of the rush marine disasters off the harbor's entrance were reported but rarely in San Francisco's pioneer newspapers, and the record therefore is far from complete. It is known, however, that many ships, having successfully negotiated thousands of miles from their home ports, were lost almost within sight of their goal. These include, besides the steamships already mentioned, the following sailing craft: the *Flying Dragon, Carrier Pigeon, Noonday, Dashing Wave,* and *San Francisco.* Undoubtedly there were others, but their names and the circumstances of their destruction have been lost.

2

VIEWED from the decks of the in-bound ships, California failed in most cases to measure up to the golden Eldorado of the miners' imaginations. What they expected to find is not always clear, and perhaps they themselves had no precise picture of this land which had been so long in their thoughts, but almost unanimously their journals record their disappointment as the barren headlands and treeless coastal hills first came into view. Richard Hale, who arrived on the *General Worth* on May 6, 1849, tells of all hands crowding the rail to view the "promised land," then adds sadly: "But with all the glamor our wildest enthusiasm can paint it, it is yet only an uninviting stretch of waste land." Another thought the straw-colored hills, so unlike the wooded coastline of his native Maine, looked "austere and forbidding," and Bayard Taylor, arriving in the summer of 1849, and scanning the coast through the ship's spyglass, found it "brown and sterile . . . nourishing only . . . some stunted shrubs." On the other hand, the diarist of the *Henry Lee* paints a much less depressing picture in this passage, dated September 12 [1849]:

"As we near the land a more accurate view of its surface is discernible, which is altogether more inviting than any we have seen since leaving our homes. It rises into gentle slopes and is covered with verdure, upon which hundreds of horses and cattle can be distinctly seen feeding. But few trees, and those scattered . . . in clumps, are in view. . . ."

But even those who had been unimpressed with the coastline found much to admire in the harbor itself. As their ships passed through the narrows, few failed to express wonder at the panorama that unfolded before their eyes: the spaciousness of the landlocked bay, its surface broken here and there with islands, between and around which were pleasant vistas of oak-covered hills rolling down to sandy inlets.

". . . on the larboard hand [wrote E. I. Barra] the green hills and deep valleys of the Marin shore came into full view, gladdening the eyes of every person on board. . . . On our starboard bow we saw a bluff jutting into the bay on the apex of which were two or three small brass cannon. Rising far above the cannon was a tall flagstaff from the top of which waved the glorious flag of our country. . . ."

Passing Alcatraz Island and rounding Telegraph Hill, Barra came in sight of the town itself, and of Yerba Buena Cove, its surface crowded with shipping.

"As we sailed into view . . . [he continues] our eyes were greeted with a sight that they never have encountered since. Shipping in such numbers that it was absolutely impossible to enumerate them; they . . . looked to us as if they were piled up one on top of the other."

These were of course the ships that had brought the first mighty wave of emigrants from the far ports of the world. Having served their purpose, they had been deserted by passengers and crew and left to fall into ruin. But not quite all had been allowed to disintegrate in the mud of the cove; some were adapted to useful purposes by the merchants of the expanding town.

"A peculiar feature of the harbor . . . [wrote J. Lamson in the fall of 1852] and one that struck me very forcibly on our first approach, was the great number of dismantled ships that lay thickly scattered around it. These ships had a

268

very old, ruinous, antiquated appearance, and at first sight, gave me an impression, that this new-born city had been inhabited for ages, and was now going to ruin. Most of them have their lower masts standing, and supported by a few ropes and chains . . . [they] have been made subservient to a valuable purpose, having been converted into store-ships. . . . Some of them had doors cut into their sides, with short flights of steps from the water. Some were run aground near the shore, and wharves and streets were built around them, where, with houses erected on them they could scarcely be distinguished from the surrounding stores."

Seeing on every side what fate awaited the ships that had preceded them into the harbor, many felt a momentary pang as they realized that the craft that had been their home for so long was soon to join this forlorn armada. The final leave-taking of the ships themselves, and of the companions of the voyage, always held a note of sadness. Enos Christman, writing in his journal on February 11, 1850, expressed this universal feeling of regret:

"We expect to be landed tomorrow, and this is our last day on the *Europe* after a voyage of about twenty thousand miles and 222 days since we left Philadelphia. Although we have fared miserably aboard the *Europe* we have been at home on her so long that we feel a strong attachment as the time approaches for us to bid her farewell. Often when tossed, rolled, and turned almost upside down, we have cursed her, and the day that placed us upon her. But now when the prospect is that we are to live in tents on shore, we may yet feel the loss of her. . . ."

A feeling of good fellowship pervaded nearly every gold ship during the final hours of the voyage. The resentments engendered during months at sea were forgotten while all contemplated the climactic new phase of their adventure that was about to begin. Often it was the skipper himself who fostered this comradely spirit, hoping to regain the good opinion of his charges by a sudden show of concern for their comfort and well-being. Sometimes his conciliatory move took the form of ordering the cook to break out long-hoarded delicacies, with the result that during the last few days what had been spare and monotonous meals became by comparison veritable banquets. These measures, however, were not always successful.

"This is the last Sabbath we expect to spend on board the bark [wrote J. Lamson in September 1852], and as we expect to separate in two or three days, a meeting was held in the main cabin, the object of which was to settle disputes and restore harmony between the officers and passengers. It proved, however, a failure. Several short addresses were made . . . a prayer was offered, and a parting hymn sung, and we broke up with very little change of feeling."

Of like mind was Frank Marryat, who arrived from Panama in June 1850:

"I must confess I felt great delight when we made the mountains at the entrance of San Francisco Bay; I had been cooped up for forty-five days on board a small barque, in company with one hundred and seventy-five passengers, of whom one hundred and sixty were noisy, quarrelsome, discontented, and dirty in the extreme. . . ."

But not on every ship were the hardships and discomforts such that the passengers could not, as the time for parting grew near, forget past animosities, and, letting bygones be bygones, take leave of one another in a spirit of friendship. Nor were all the skippers tyrants, obsessed with their own importance and prone to abuse the authority given them under the maritime laws. Many used with discretion their wide powers and, while acting with firmness in all matters affecting the safety of the ship, yet refrained from subjecting passengers and crew to the petty restrictions that on less fortunate craft led to bitter resentments. That a harsh and tyrannical captain could make life insupportable for a hundred passengers, engendering quarrels that kept their ships in turmoil for months on end, is made clear by a reading of scores of Argonauts' diaries. And the same source provides ample testimony that the opposite was true. The skipper who, while maintaining his authority at all times, yet treated those in his charge with consideration commonly ended the voyage with the respect of everyone on board. John Linville Hall thus salutes the *Henry Lee's* skipper as the craft dropped anchor in the bay:

"The men sprang up the rigging, as the captain gave orders, with an alacrity and animation that cannot be equalled; and when the final command was given to 'stand clear, let go anchor, he turned to the passengers and crew and said, 'Well, gentlemen, I have done my best for you.' He said truly, and the involuntary shout of gratitude that bursts simultaneously from every heart bore ample testimony that the truth he spoke was felt and acknowledged. Our voyage has been protracted by headwinds and calms, and attended with storms and gales. Dangers . . . have

271

been warded off by the indefatigable vigilance of our noble captain, whose ear has ever been alert to catch the very first intimation of its approach. Not for this alone do we feel grateful, but for the sociability, the gentlemanly and dignified deportment and forbearance in the most trying and vexing situations, which he has ever manifested towards us will live in all our memories, as well as his nautical and mechanical skill. . . ."

3

THE Argonaut's first contact with California life usually began before he had set foot ashore. For hardly had his ship come into view round Clark's Point when small boats could be observed putting out from the beach, and by the time the anchor had been dropped she was surrounded by a crowd of boatmen, all noisily competing for attention. Operators of one-man ferries shouted offers to carry passengers ashore with speed and safety, and at a flat fee of three dollars a head. Agents for the town's auction house, were eager to know what merchandise the ship carried. If she chanced to have any articles currently scarce on shores the runners called out bids that seemed incredibly high, meantime holding aloft bags of gold dust as tokens of their responsibility. Often too these unofficial welcoming committees included a sprinkling of employers on the lookout for carpenters, blacksmiths, clerks, cooks, waiters, and offering to pay for a day's work sums that equaled a liberal week's wages at home. Finally, there were those who, having no business to transact, were drawn out to the ship

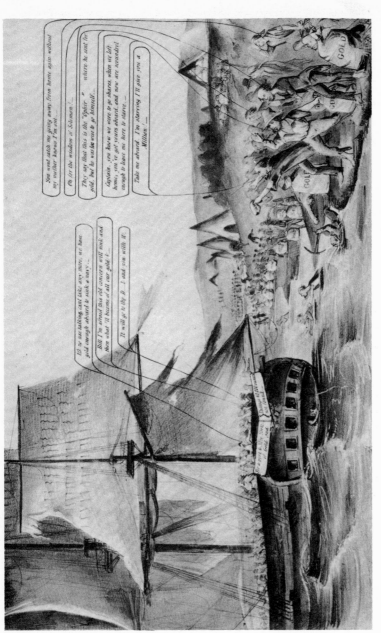

THE WAY THEY COME FROM CALIFORNIA

An N. Currier lithograph picturing the plight of the gold-laden Argonauts when they sought to return home

—California Historical Society

THE SAN FRANCISCO WATERFRONT IN 1851

From an old photograph showing scores of abandoned ships lying in the harbor

Society of California Pioneers

by their longing for news from home, hoping there might be on board someone from their native town or village.

Captain George Coffin, who brought the *Alhambra* into port in October 1849, reported that he was immediately besieged by men who desperately needed help to keep their lucrative businesses running. "There was a great rush of hotel keepers and 'restaurateurs' for cooks and waiters. They bid as high as three hundred dollars a month for my black cook, and . . . the poor wretch was fairly bewildered. She was beset on all sides, and came to me to know what she should do." Coffin selected for her a place with a New Englander, one of the few men in the town who had his family with him. "He agreed to give her one hundred dollars a month, with the promise of all his wife's cast-off clothing."

Like every other ship that reached San Francisco during the early months of the rush, the *Alhambra* was speedily emptied of both passengers and crew. All felt an overwhelming urge to go ashore at once and, having landed, to push on to the diggings. But despite their eagerness to set about the business of mining, some delay could not be avoided. The majority tarried in San Francisco at least a day or two, listening to stories of the comparative richness of the various camps, adding to their outfits or discarding whatever was useless or too bulky, studying routes and arranging transportation, and joining long queues before the post office in the plaza in the hope of letters from home.

Meantime they familiarized themselves with the bizarre settlement that had mushroomed over the shores of the cove. Almost to a man they found San Francisco dirty, overcrowded, noisy, and fantastically expensive, its streets filled night and day with crowds of men and vehicles, its gambling houses and grogshops operating around the clock, and with beds and meals to be had only by the expenditure of much time and money.

The first impressions of the newly landed were far from favorable. Enos Christman, just off the *Europe*, wrote in February 1850: "The town appeared to be nothing but a mud hole," with half the population living in tents and a third of the buildings given over to saloons and gambling-houses. He added:

"We visited a great number of the latter places where we saw all kinds of gaming going on. Gambling here is an occupation, day or night, Sunday or any other time. The grey-haired father and the beardless boy are to be seen side by side vying with each other who can win or lose the fastest, and even beautiful women engage in these games with the same earnestness as the sterner sex, betting their last ounce. I have even heard of preachers delivering a good sermon and going directly from the pulpit to the gaming table. . . ."

News from home was an urgent concern of all, and Christman tells of buying a copy of the *New York Tribune* "for which I willingly paid two bits and considered myself lucky, they having sold an hour previously for a dollar a copy." But his main interest was letters, and it was in quest of these that he set off as soon as his feet touched ground.

"I proceeded immediately to the post office, very anxious to hear something of the objects nearest my heart, and I was gratified to the fullest extent. Letter after letter and paper after paper were handed out until the postage amounted to six dollars out of my scanty purse of twenty-seven, but had they cost the whole sum . . . I should have willingly paid it. . . ."

The amount of money in circulation, both gold dust and coin, and the careless unconcern with which it passed from hand to hand aroused the wonder of those fresh from communities where frugality had long been a necessary virtue. Nelson Kingsley, newly arrived from Connecticut on the bark *Anna Reynolds*, found "heaps of gold and coin in every shop," and prices beyond all reason. Board cost twenty-five dollars a week, with everything else in proportion—"in fact a man wants a fortune to move here." Kingsley wrote that one of his companions was offered fifty dollars for the boots he was wearing, which he refused, whereupon the two "went up town and saw the Elephant, and it almost baffles description." He added that gambling seemed to be the only business that attracted the attention of all. "If I was in possession of one half the coin and dust I have seen tonight I could start for home immediately, but woe to the poor d—ls who are so foolish as to haunt those places." Another recent arrival wrote: "Money here goes like dirt; everything costs a dollar or dollars. What is considered a fortune at home is here mere pocket money. Today I purchased a single potato for 45 cents."

In the summer of 1849 Bayard Taylor found the economy of the town so bizarre that "in my communications to the *Tribune* I was almost afraid to write, with any hope of their obtaining credence." On landing, Taylor had found lodging, after a long search, in a garret room, which he shared with another at a cost of twenty-five dollars a week, paying an additional twenty dollars for board. But compensating for this was a profitable deal he himself managed to negotiate. Learning that a recent arrival had brought out fifteen hundred copies of New York newspapers and sold them all in two hours for a dollar each, Taylor recalled that he had about a dozen such journals, which he had used to "fill up crevices in packing my valise."

"There was a newspaper merchant at the corner of the City Hotel [he wrote] and to him I proposed the sale of them, asking him to name a price. 'I shall want to make a good profit on the retail price,' said he, 'and can't give you more than ten dollars for the lot.' I was satisfied with the wholesale price, which was a gain of just four thousand percent!"

4

How the Argonauts fared in the diggings is outside the scope of this narrative, but before taking final leave of them it might be interesting to summarize what befell them during their first weeks ashore.

A few tarried in San Francisco for long periods, attracted by the prevailing high wages and raising funds to finance an eventual foray into the foothills. By far the majority, however, headed direct for the gold fields, proceeding by river craft to Sacramento or Stockton, then pushing on afoot or by stage across the valley floor and into the labyrinth of mountain meadows and gulches and canyons. There for a few weeks they applied themselves to the enterprise they had come so far to undertake. The results were as various as the men themselves. Thousands, failing to strike pay dirt on their first attempts and lacking the physical strength for long continued work in the icy stream-beds, made their way back to the coast, their dreams of easy wealth blasted. Others were less easily discouraged. These, with more fortitude and tenacity, continued the quest, moving from place to place while they prospected one barren claim after another, gradually gaining experience in mining methods, and in the end—provided always that luck was with them—making a strike that handsomely repaid their large investment in time and effort.

But whatever the outcome of their stay in the diggings, the newcomers speedily learned that the realities of mining-camp life differed sharply from all their preconceived ideas. Plans that had been made during long, theoretical discussions at home or en route were found to be completely unworkable once they reached the gold fields. For mining in early California was an operation that did not lend itself to large groups working as a unit. It was an era of small placer claims that could be most efficiently worked by two or three men, or at most by half a dozen: one to dig the gravel, another to carry it, a third to operate the rocker or sluice box.

It was this practical defect in their planning that wrecked the scores of mining companies that descended on California during 1849 and 1850. For all such groups had been organized on a co-operative basis; all planned to march as a unit to the gold fields and there engage in a joint effort, depositing their gold dust in a common fund from which in the end each would receive his proportionate share. Once the obvious defects of such a program had become clear the disintegration of the companies followed swiftly. Some disbanded within a few hours after they landed at

San Francisco. Others held together a little longer, setting off in groups for the interior, only to fall apart by common consent long before they reached the mines. In Sacramento so many were dissolved during the fall of 1849 that the town became known as the "powder magazine." In general these partings were amicable, with the individual members glad to be free of the company rules under which they had lived so long. The end of one company was commemorated in a long mock-heroic ode, of which these are the first and last stanzas:

> *The San Francisco Company, of which I've often told,*
> *At Sacramento has arrived in search of glittering gold.*
> *The bark hauled in, the cargo out and that is not the*
> *   worst,*
> *The Company, like all the rest, has had a talk and burst.*
> *   For 'twas talk, talk, growl, growl, talk, talk away,*
> *   The devil a bit of comfort's here in Californi-a.*
>
> *Now whether it's for good or bad, since time alone can*
> *   show,*
> *The deed is done with our consent and that at least we*
> *   know,*
> *So let us all contented be and do the best we can,*
> *And may a fortune be in store for every honest man.*
> *   Chat, chat, sing, sing, chat, chat away,*
> *   And leave for home whene'er he likes from Cali-*
> *   forni-a.*

With the disbanding of these groups, the merchandise they brought out with them had, of course, to be converted into cash. The amounts realized from such sales varied widely, depending on whether or not the goods they had to

278

offer happened to be in demand. Shopkeepers in San
Francisco and in the supply towns of the interior lacked
storage facilities and so were interested only in what could
be promptly sold. Thus some companies realized almost
nothing on cargoes hopefully brought from home, while
others, catching the unstable market at one of its periodical
crests, reaped handsome profits. Examples of their luck—
both good and bad—are numerous. The captain of the brig
Tigress reported that "we find it extremely difficult to sell
even a small portion of the cargo at a rate that will pay
freight and charges," and members of the group that went
out in the *Metropolis* fared so badly that the forty men of the
company salvaged only fifty dollars each from their investment, part of which had to be taken in merchandise.
The *Attila* group divided three hundred dollars each; those
on the *Leonore* received about the same amount, and others
slightly more.

Some organizations owned not only the cargo but the
ships themselves, and the latter too were put on the market.
Few brought more than a small fraction of what they had
cost, being for the most part ancient craft, slow moving and
in bad repair. Thus the 150-ton *Tigress* was sold for $900;
and the *Edward Everett*, a fine new ship of 700 tons, brought
only $11,000, far less than her true value. "Vessels are
selling dog cheap," wrote a Sacramento trader in the fall
of 1849. "Fine large barks bring $3000 to $5000." On the
other hand, schooners small enough to operate on the
rivers were needed to handle the heavy traffic to and from
the mines, and these found a ready market at high prices.
In general, however, members of the organized groups
gained less than nothing by the trading ventures from which
they had hoped for so much.

Those who came out as individuals fared somewhat better; they had no proprietary interest in either ship or cargo and so escaped loss when both had to be sacrificed. But both groups were on an equality once they reached the gold fields. There all were free to make their own decisions, to mine where and when they liked, either singly or with companions of their own choosing. The degree of their success depended on many factors: industry, adaptability, judgment—most of all on luck. Some had the good fortune to locate claims that in a few days netted them tidy fortunes. Others, no less industrious, toiled for months without gathering enough dust to pay for their austere beans-and-salt-pork diet. How long the latter continued the search depended on their temperaments; a few stubbornly refused to admit defeat and, buoyed up by the miner's perennial hope, became permanently a part of the lode towns. Others drifted back to the coast or valley settlements, where they took such jobs as were offered, some to stay on the rest of their lives, others only until they had earned enough to pay their passage home.

It is said that of the tens of thousands who tried their luck in the diggings fewer than one in twenty returned to his starting-place in as sound a financial condition as he had been when he left. Certainly the California adventure was far from the sure and easy road to riches many had envisioned. Their diaries, begun in a spirit of unbridled optimism, usually end on a note of disillusion. Having failed in their primary objective, their dreams of wealth shattered, they gave way to melancholy, filling page after page with gloomy reflections on the hardness of their lot, emphasizing the privations of mining-camp life, its loneliness and violence, and contrasting it with the familiar, pleasant en-

THE SAN FRANCISCO WATERFRONT IN 1851

The San Francisco waterfront in 1851. This is a continuation of the view shown opposite page 273

ARRIVAL OF A MAIL STEAMER IN SAN FRANCISCO

From California Mercantile Journal

—The Bancroft Library

A PIONEER STEAMER LEAVING SAN FRANCISCO
FOR PANAMA IN THE EARLY 1850's

From The Annals of San Francisco

vironment they had left behind. Many who wrote in this vein complained too of bad health, and one surmises that their extreme pessimism often had a basis in physical weakness. For life was far from easy in the towns and camps of the mother lode, with long hours of exhausting labor each day, exposure to extremes of heat and cold, and nearly always with inadequate shelter and improper food, badly prepared.

It was a Spartan existence, for which not all were well fitted, and in this respect the emigrants who came by sea were under an added handicap. For while those who had followed the overland trails arrived with muscles hardened from months on the road, veterans of the sea journey were for the most part badly out of condition. The abrupt transition from their inactive life on shipboard to its exact opposite had a result that might be expected. Frequently the sea-borne emigrants reached the diggings exhausted from their unaccustomed exertions, and in their weakened condition fell easy victim to the diseases prevalent in the camps: fevers, dysentery, pneumonia, tuberculosis. Hundreds died; thousands found themselves physically unequal to the hard work of placer mining and drifted into other fields while they regained their health and strength.

But there was another side to the picture. Not all the Argonauts found only disappointment in California, and even those who gained nothing in a material way were seldom entirely unrewarded. For to have had a part in this world-wide movement was in itself a badge of distinction, one that profoundly influenced the future career of everyone who had shared it. It drew countless young men from obscure posts in quiet communities, sent them off to a distant frontier where they became part of a scramble for survival as fiercely competitive as any the nation had ever known. The life into which they were projected was a veritable forcing-ground in which their latent strengths and weaknesses stood revealed. The weak-willed or vicious fell easy victim to the abundant temptations of the wide-open towns and quickly went to ruin. On the other hand, men of industry and resourcefulness combined with sound judgment found in California opportunities far greater than those of the tradition-bound communities of home. Thousands of these, finding full scope for their newly realized talents, and disinclined to exchange the freedom of a frontier environment for the orthodox life they had left behind, elected to cast their lot permanently with the new land. Even among those who returned home there were many who found themselves unable to fit comfortably into their old niches and after a few restless months again turned their faces westward.

For the gold rush, despite its hardships and disappointments, had one profoundly significant result: it shook many thousands of quite ordinary young men out of the humdrum routine of their normal environments and awakened in them the spirit of adventure that at every age has been the hallmark of the pioneer.

ACKNOWLEDGMENTS & BIBLIOGRAPHY

THANKS are due the following libraries for making available their gold-rush diaries and journals, their files of early California newspapers and periodicals, and for permission to reproduce drawings or photographs from their collections: the Bancroft Library, Berkeley; the State Library, Sacramento; the Huntington Library, San Marino; and the Public Library, the California Historical Society, the Society of California Pioneers, and the Wells-Fargo History Room, all of San Francisco. Pertinent material or information was supplied, too, by certain individuals, and acknowledgment is made to the following: Dr. George D. Lyman, Edwin Grabhorn, Mrs. Edna Martin Parratt, Mrs. Helen S. Giffen, Edward N. Middleton, and Harry W. Abrahams, of San Francisco, John Haskell Kemble, of Pasadena, Edgar B. Jessup and Harold Holmes, of Oakland, Miss Caroline Wenzel and Carroll D. Hall, of Sacramento, Frank Brezee, of Berkeley, Mrs. Carol Mooney, of Larkspur, and Gates Hebbard, of New York City.

The purpose of this work is to present a general picture of how the Argonauts traveled by sea to California and what experiences they had en route, and it therefore would serve no useful purpose to give as detailed a listing of sources as would be expected in a formal history of the movement. For those, however, who wish to inquire further into the subject the following selected checklist has been compiled. Material in manuscript (of which there is a great abundance) has been excluded; this list is limited to fifty published works—chiefly books, but with a few articles in periodicals—each of which throws interesting light on some aspect of the migration.

AMENT, WILLIAM S.: *Oxcart to Airplane: By Sea to California.* Los Angeles: Powell Publishing Company; 1929.

ANON.: *The Adventures of a Captain's Wife.* San Francisco: A. Roman and Company; 1877.

Acknowledgments & Bibliography

BANCROFT, HUBERT H.: *California Inter Pocula.* San Francisco: The History Company; 1888.

BARRA, E. I.: *Tale of Two Oceans.* San Francisco: privately printed; 1893.

BATES, MRS. D. B.: *Incidents on Land and Water.* Boston, Mass.: James French and Company; 1857.

BENARD, ALBERT: *Last Adventure.* San Francisco: The Westgate Press; 1931.

BERTHOLD, VICTOR M.: *The Pioneer Steamer California.* Boston, Mass.: Houghton Mifflin Company; 1932.

BORTHWICK, J. D.: *Three Years in California.* Edinburgh: William Blackwood & Sons; 1857.

BUCK, FRANKLIN A.: *A Yankee Trader in the Gold Rush.* Boston, Mass.: Houghton Mifflin Company; 1930.

CAPRON, E. S.: *History of California.* Boston, Mass.: John P. Jewett & Company; 1854.

CHAVANNE, ANDRÉ: "The Burning of the Golden Gate in July 1862." (In the *California Historical Society Quarterly*, Vol. XIX, No. 1.) San Francisco: The California Historical Society; 1940.

CHAVER, EDWARD E.: "Through the Straits of Magellan in 1849." (In the *Quarterly of the Society of California Pioneers*, Vol. IV, No. 3.) San Francisco: The Society of California Pioneers; 1927.

CHRISTMAN, ENOS: *One Man's Gold.* New York: Whittlesey House; 1930.

COFFIN, GEORGE: *A Pioneer Voyage to California.* Chicago: privately printed; 1908.

CROSBY, ELISHA OSCAR: *Memoirs.* San Marino, Cal.: The Huntington Library; 1945.

CUSHING, JOHN M.: "From New York to San Francisco via the Isthmus of Panama." (In the *Quarterly of the Society of California Pioneers*, Vol. VI, No. 3.) San Francisco: The Society of California Pioneers; 1929.

DELANO, ALONZO: *Pen-Knife Sketches.* San Francisco: The Grabhorn Press; 1934.

Acknowledgments & Bibliography

DORE, BENJAMIN: "The Journal of Benjamin Dore." (In the *California Historical Society Quarterly*, Vol. II, No. 2.) San Francisco: The California Historical Society; 1923.

EVANS, ROBERT FRANK: *Notes on Land and Sea*. Boston, Mass.: Richard G. Badger; 1922.

GREGORY, JOSEPH W.: *Gregory's Guide for California Travellers via the Isthmus of Panama*. New York: Nafis & Cornish; 1850.

HALE, RICHARD L.: *The Log of a Forty-Niner*. Boston, Mass.: B. J. Brimmer Company; 1923.

HALL, JOHN LINVILLE: *Around the Horn in '49*. San Francisco: privately printed; 1849.

HASKINS, C. W.: *The Argonauts of California*. New York: Fords, Howard & Hulbert; 1890.

HELPER, HINTON R.: *The Land of Gold*. Baltimore: privately printed; 1855.

HOWE, OCTAVIUS T.: *Argonauts of '49*. Cambridge, Mass.: Harvard University Press; 1923.

JOHNSON, THEODORE T.: *Sights in the Gold Region*. New York: Baker & Scribner; 1849.

KEMBLE, JOHN HASKELL: *The Panama Route: 1848–1869*. Berkeley, Cal.: University of California Press; 1943.

KENDALL, JOSEPH: *A Landsman's Voyage to California*. San Francisco: privately printed; 1935.

KINGSLEY, NELSON: *Diary of a California Argonaut of 1849*. (*Publications of the Academy of Pacific Coast History*, Vol. III, No. 3.) Berkeley, Cal.: University of California; 1914.

LAMSON, J.: *Round Cape Horn*. Bangor, Me.: O. F. & W. H. Knowles; 1878.

LECOUVREUR, FRANK: *From East Prussia to the Golden Gate*. Los Angeles: Angelina Book Concern; 1906.

LETTS, J. M.: *California Illustrated*. New York: R. T. Young; 1853.

LOW, GARRETT: *Gold Rush by Sea*. Philadelphia: University of Pennsylvania Press; 1941.

LYMAN, ALBERT: *Journal of a Voyage to California*. Hartford: E. T. Pease; 1852.

MACK, GERSTLE: *The Land Divided: A History of the Panama Canal*. New York: Alfred A. Knopf; 1944.

MARRYAT, FRANK: *Mountains and Molehills*. New York: Harper & Brothers; 1855.

M'COLLUM, WILLIAM S.: *California As I Saw It*. Buffalo: H. Derby & Company; 1850.

OTIS, DR. F. N.: *Illustrated History of the Panama Railroad*. New York: Harper & Brothers; 1862.

PIERCE, HIRAM DWIGHT: *A Forty-Niner Speaks*. Oakland, Cal.: privately printed; 1930.

PIM, BEDFORD: *The Gate of the Pacific*. London: Lovell Reeve & Company; 1863.

PRATT, JULIUS H.: "To California by Panama in '49." (In the *Century Magazine*, Vol. XLI, No. 6.) New York, April 1891.

RYAN, WILLIAM REDMOND: *Personal Adventures in Upper and Lower California in 1848–9*. London: William Stroberl; 1850.

SCHAEFFER, L. M.: *Sketches of Travels*. New York: James Egbert; 1860.

SILL, EDWARD ROWLAND: *Around the Horn: A Journal*. New Haven: Yale University Press; 1944.

STILLMAN, J. D. B.: *Seeking the Golden Fleece*. San Francisco: A. Roman & Company; 1877.

TAYLOR, BAYARD: *Eldorado*. London: Richard Bentley; 1850.

TWAIN, MARK: *Travels with Mr. Brown*. New York: Alfred A. Knopf; 1940.

UPHAM, SAMUEL C.: *Notes of a Voyage to California*. Philadelphia: privately printed; 1878.

WARREN, T. ROBINSON: *Dust and Foam*. New York: Charles Scribner; 1859.

WILTSEE, ERNEST A.: *Gold Rush Steamers*. San Francisco: The Grabhorn Press; 1938.

INDEX

i

Index

Bryant, William Cullen, endorses Mrs. Farnham's enterprise, 39
Bulwer, Sir Henry Lytton, 209; Clayton-Bulwer Treaty, 209
Bunker Hill Company, 32
Bunker Hill Mining & Trading Company, 94

Cachalot, 108–10
California: first Pacific Mail steamer, 168, 225; round-the-Horn voyage to Panama, 169, 195–9 *passim*, 226; Panama to San Francisco, 226–9; livestock on deck, 226–7
California & New Haven Joint Stock Company, 24
Callao, 154, 155, 166, 195
Cantero, 60–1, 114, 117, 124, 125
Canton: fare, 33; horseplay, 57, 60; drinking, 57, 97; water supply, 78; round the Cape, 85; food, 107, 110–11, 112, 123, 158; livestock, 116; at Galapagos Islands, 157
Cape Horn, rounding, 80ff.
Capitol, 99, 110, 160
Capron, E. S., 174–5, 193
Cargoes, 24–9
Carrier Pigeon, 266
Chagres: semi-monthly sailings from New York to, 167; *Falcon* to, 168, 169; descriptions of, 170–1, 175; crossing to Panama City from, 173, 176ff.
Charlotte, 54
Chavanne, André, 255; description of *Golden Gate's* fire, 256, 257–8, and his escape, 258–60
Christiana, 106
Christman, Enos, 264, 269, 274–5
Civilian, 33
Clark, Dr., 90
Clark's Point, 28, 272
Clayton, John M., 209

Clayton-Bulwer Treaty, 209
Coffin, Capt. George, account of: refitting *Alhambra*, 17; Neptune's visit, 56; "Simon Spriggin's Trip to California," 90–2; Independence Day celebration, 96–7; catching shark, 118; description of Valparaiso, 148–9; on San Francisco's labor shortage, 273
Consuls, U.S.: authority, 100–1; care for passengers abandoned at Rio, 139, 141–2
Co-operative companies, *see* Joint-stock companies
Cortez, 240, 243
Crescent City, 110, 172, 175, 213, 226
Crosby, Elisha Oscar, quoted on: Panama crossing, 171; *California* trip to San Francisco, 227, 228
Cruces, 180, 181, 186
Crusoe, Robinson, 114, 151, 153–4
Cutter, Capt., 44

Dashing Wave, 266
De Massey, Ernest, 105–6
Departure, 3–45
Diaries, v–vii, 3–4; record expenses, 10–11; accounts of departure, 44–5; time-consuming, 72; complaints of food, 78, 101, 106, of fellow passengers, 102, 103; reports to consuls, 100; descriptions of South American ports, 126, 128, 132, 135, 144, 146, 147; disillusion, 280–1
Director, 215, 217
Disease, 241–4; in mining camps, 281
Dodd, Prof., 69–70
Doliff, John, 58–9
Dolphin, 52, 53
Dore, Benjamin, 61, 114, 117, 128

ii

Index

Le Maire, Strait of, 81, 106
León, 213
Leonore: cargo, 25; New England Mining & Trading Company owners, 28; passengers' interests, 51; Sacramento Minstrels, 73; at Talcahuano, 114, 144; cargo sold, 279
Letts, J. M., accounts of: landing at Chagres, 172; west-east trek, 213–15; *Niantic's* approach to Golden Gate, 263–4
Lewis, S.S., 254
Lima, 155–7
Liquor: rules against drinking, 95, 104; holiday toasts, 95–6; aguardiente, 129
Long Wharf, 26
Low Garrett W., account of *Washington Irving* voyage, 68–71, 159–60

Magellan, Strait of, 82–3; Port Famine, 82
Mail contracts: British subsidy, 166; U.S. government subsidy, 167, 183, 225; requirement of five steamers on Atlantic run and three on Pacific, 168
Manzanillo Island, 184
Marietta, 172
Marryat, Frank, accounts of: yellow fever, 191; epidemic on steamer for San Francisco, 241–3; arrival in San Francisco, 270
Mary, 205, 206
Mason, Col., report on conditions in California, 5–6
Metropolis, 116, 279
Mexican War: mentioned, 5, 166; annexation of California, 5
Monterey, *California* at, 228
Morale: low ebb in first days, 48; sermons to bolster, 94; rules of

Morale (*continued*)
conduct, 94ff., and methods of punishment, 95
Morehead, William G., 147
Morgan, Henry, 165
Mosquito Coast, 208
Mount Vernon, 27
Mount Vernon Mining Association, 27
Music, 72–6

Nelson, Horatio, 202; castle, 222
Neptune's visits, at equator, 55–7
New Granada, Republic of: 1846 treaty with U.S., 167; sovereignty guaranteed, 167; rights to French company for railroad, 183, canceled, 183; contract with American company, 183. *See also* Panama
New York, 42
New York Herald, 186, 226
New York Tribune: on effect of gold-rush exodus, 17–18; Mrs. Farnham's letter, 38, 39; salute to *Angelique,* 40; loss of *California,* 196–8; on San Francisco prices, 274
Newspapers, shipboard, 89–91; Hall's journal of *Henry Lee* voyage, 89; *Barometer,* 89; *Shark,* 89; *Emigrant,* 89–90
Niantic, 263
Nicaragua: length of crossing, 201–2; historical view, 202–3; Vanderbilt's plan, 203–4, 207–10; Gordon's California Association, 205–7; advantages over Panama, 215–16
Nonantum, 45
Noonday, 266
North America, 87, 250–1
North Star, 234

v

Index

A NOTE ON THE TYPE
IN WHICH THIS BOOK IS SET

This book is set in Monotype BASKERVILLE, *a facsimile cutting from type cast from the original matrices of a face designed by John Baskerville. The original face was the forerunner of the "modern" group of type faces.*

John Baskerville (1706–75), of Birmingham, England, a writing-master, with a special renown for cutting inscriptions in stone, began experimenting about 1750 with punch-cutting and making typographical material. It was not until 1757 that he published his first work, a Virgil in royal quarto, with great-primer letters. This was followed by his famous editions of Milton, the Bible, the Book of Common Prayer, and several Latin classic authors. His types, at first criticized as unnecessarily slender, delicate, and feminine, in time were recognized as both distinct and elegant, and his types as well as his printing were greatly admired. Four years after his death Baskerville's widow sold all his punches and matrices to the Société Littéraire-typographique, which used some of the types for the sumptuous Kehl edition of Voltaire's works in seventy volumes.

Composed, printed, and bound by Kingsport Press, Inc., Kingsport, Tennessee. Illustrations reproduced in Optak by Edward Stern and Company, Inc., Philadelphia, Pa. Binding adapted from designs by Warren Chappell.